A FAST AND
FRUGAL FINANCE

Perspectives in Behavioral
Economics and the Economics of
Behavior

A FAST AND
FRUGAL FINANCE

Bridging Contemporary
Behavioral Finance and
Ecological Rationality

WILLIAM P. FORBES

ALOYSIUS OBINNA IGBOEKWU

SHABNAM MOUSAVI

Series Editor

MORRIS ALTMAN

ACADEMIC PRESS
An imprint of Elsevier

Academic Press is an imprint of Elsevier
125 London Wall, London EC2Y 5AS, United Kingdom
525 B Street, Suite 1650, San Diego, CA 92101, United States
50 Hampshire Street, 5th Floor, Cambridge, MA 02139, United States
The Boulevard, Langford Lane, Kidlington, Oxford OX5 1GB, United Kingdom

Notices

Knowledge and best practice in this field are constantly changing. As new research and experience
broaden our understanding, changes in research methods, professional practices, or medical
treatment may become necessary.

Practitioners and researchers must always rely on their own experience and knowledge in
evaluating and using any information, methods, compounds, or experiments described herein. In
using such information or methods they should be mindful of their own safety and the safety of
others, including parties for whom they have a professional responsibility.

To the fullest extent of the law, neither the Publisher nor the authors, contributors, or editors,
assume any liability for any injury and/or damage to persons or property as a matter of products
liability, negligence or otherwise, or from any use or operation of any methods, products,
instructions, or ideas contained in the material herein.

Library of Congress Cataloging-in-Publication Data
A catalog record for this book is available from the Library of Congress

British Library Cataloguing-in-Publication Data
A catalogue record for this book is available from the British Library

ISBN: 978-0-12-812495-6

For information on all Academic Press publications
visit our website at https://www.elsevier.com/books-and-journals

Publisher: Candice Janco
Acquisition Editor: J. Scott Bentley
Editorial Project Manager: Susan Ikeda
Production Project Manager: Joy Christel Neumarin
Honest Thangiah
Designer: Mark Rogers

Typeset by VTeX

Working together
to grow libraries in
developing countries

www.elsevier.com • www.bookaid.org

Contents

Foreword

As far as we know, traders and investors have always used heuristics, including the pioneers of *technical analysis* and Benjamin Graham, whose book *The Intelligent Investor* was praised by Warren Buffet as being by far the best ever written on investing. Peter Lynch has suggested that lack of name recognition is grounds for eliminating a stock from consideration, which is a version of the *recognition heuristic* used more generally by humans and animals.

The science of heuristics was founded by the polymath Herbert A. Simon and is anchored in the distinction between situations of risk and uncertainty, commonly attributed to Frank Knight. Risk means that the future state space of all possible events and their consequences and probabilities is knowable, such as when buying a lottery ticket, or playing roulette. In situations of risk, probability theory provides the tools for calculating rational expectations. In situations of uncertainty, by contrast, this degree of certainty is not discernable, such as when entrepreneurs make investment decisions in high-stake and changing environments. Here the science of heuristics can provide tools for decision making.

Leonard Savage, John Maynard Keynes, and others made similar distinctions and restricted probability theory, and the theory of rational expectations, to well-defined situations of risk. Not so in modern finance theory, where the distinction between risk and uncertainty is rarely made. Following the portfolio allocation framework of Harry Markowitz and Robert Merton, it is generally assumed that all risks can be measured, priced, and hedged. The grand mathematical edifice created by finance theory is admirable; but in the uncertain world of financial markets a castle built on sand.

Five years after the distinguished macroeconomist Robert Lucas declared in his 2003 Presidential Address to the American Economic Association that the central problem of preventing depression had finally been solved, the greatest economic crisis since the Great Depression hit. George Soros noted in his *The Crash of 2008 and What It Means* that modern finance has totally misinterpreted how financial markets operate and that rational expectations theory is no longer taken seriously outside academic circles. One might think that by now the prevailing paradigm would have been replaced and the systematic study of how to deal with uncertainty would have begun.

With a few exceptions, such as the Bank of England's program "Taking uncertainty seriously" on developing simple heuristics for a safer financial world, the paradigm has unfortunately remained in place. Paradoxically, behavioural finance helps to retain it. Behavioural finance emerged with the goal of eliminating the psychological blind spot in modern finance; but largely ended up portraying psychology and heuristics as the source of irrationality.

Instead of systematically studying how successful investors make decisions, the mainstream of behavioural finance took Homo economicus as the benchmark for rational behaviour and attributed deviating behaviour to flaws in the human mind rather than in finance theory. Since the 1980s, the list of such "anomalies" and "cognitive biases" has rapidly expanded; Wikipedia currently list nearly 190 items. Using these makes it possible to blame the crisis of 2008 or the prevalence of obesity, or other societal problems, on people's shortcomings, without calling the theory into question.

Behavioural finance would have followed a different route had it followed the ideas of Herbert A. Simon. Simon's version of behavioural finance is based on two principles: taking uncertainty and heuristics to handle its effects seriously. In order to take heuristics seriously, one needs to replace terms such as availability with formal models of heuristics in order to test how well these actually perform.

The systematic study of the adaptive toolbox of heuristics began in the mid-1990s and revealed that under uncertainty, simple heuristics are often better at predicting than complex strategies. This surprising result is called the less-is-more effect and contradicts the assumption that ignoring part of the information always implies a cognitive bias in decision-making.

Harry Markowitz appears to have instinctively understood this effect for his own retirement investments, as he did not rely on his Nobel-prize winning mean-variance portfolio method but rather on the $\frac{1}{N}$ heuristic "Allocate the money equally across all N assets" to provide for his own family's needs. Subsequent studies showed that 1/N can outperform the mean-variance portfolio in terms of the Sharpe Ratio and other criteria. The key reason is that under uncertainty, fine-tuned optimisation models tend to be fragile and overfit noise, thereby creating illusions of certainty.

Demonstrating a less-is-more effect is, however, only the first step; the second is to prove the conditions under which it can be expected or not, a topic that is addressed by the study of the ecological rationality of heuristics. In this way, the study of heuristics is both descriptive for instance, it analyses how successful investors make decisions in the "real world" and prescriptive; that is, it answers the question of under what conditions a simple heuristic should be used in place of a complex strategy. *A Fast and Frugal Finance* is the first volume of its kind to undertake such an adventure. Each chapter provides a fresh look at the application and use of heuristics as useful, efficient, and successful tools for decision-making in different areas of finance. If we want to learn from the crisis and finally take uncertainty seriously, this is the time to rethink finance, and behavioural finance in particular.

Gerd Gigerenzer, Director
Harding Center for Risk Literacy,
Max Planck Institute for Human Development,
Berlin

Acknowledgements

Our book presages the development of a fast-and-frugal finance that is already under construction. But the fast-and-frugal reasoning that project springs forth from is the work of Gerd Gigerenzer and his, now disbanded, Adaptive Behaviour and Cognition (ABC) group within the Max Planck Institute for Human Development in Berlin. The fast-and-frugal approach has many brilliant forebears, Frank Knight, Herbert Simon, and Egon Brunswik; but Gigerenzer has fashioned a new school of thought out of these complimentary individual intellectual contributions. We are grateful to him for his scholarship and his personal encouragement and advice to us in our work on this book and related endeavours.

To write a book requires a lot of collaboration between the co-authors, but also those sharing their lives. Each of us thanks our partners and family, notably Sue, Tochukwu and Adoniram and Arielle and Naomi, Reza and Anoush. We are grateful to those who have influenced us in our own academic journey, including Florian Artinger, Deven Barthia, Alan Benson, Werner De Bondt, Robert Hudson, Gulnur Muradoglu, Cormac O'Keefe, Hersh Shefrin, Len Skerratt, Mona Soufian, Shyam Sunder, Mark Tippett, Rona Unrau, and Andrew Vivian. Shabnam Mousavi grately acknowledges the support provided through a long-term grant from the Think Forward Initiative in partnership with the ING Bank. This work would have not been possible without unfailing support from the excellent staff at Elsevier, our publisher, including, Susan Ikeda, Shella Josey, Graham Nisbet, Joy Chistel Neumarin, Honest Thangiah and all the wise guidance and encouragement from the Editor of this series, Morris Altman.

PART 1

A fast-and-frugal approach to finance

CHAPTER 1

Introduction

A fast-and-frugal finance might at last allow an understanding of how context and cognition shape the bewildering array of evidence we observe
regarding the operation and efficiency of financial markets and their funding of corporations. This has not been a great decade for Finance as an
academic subject or profession. Following the global financial crisis, the
ensuing Eurozone and LIBOR rigging crises finance academics are commonly portrayed as either knaves or fools. Shiller and Shiller (2011) ask if
finance as a subject is hindered by its excessive interest in the techniques
of optimising an individual's self-interest. One aspect of expanding finance
theory's focus is adopting a fast-and-frugal approach.

Fast-and-frugal reasoning offers a way out of this decline in finance
theory's influence and credibility. It does this by reducing one of the central planks of current finance theory, this is the expected utility model of
decision-making under uncertainty, or what Gigerenzer calls classical rationality (Gigerenzer and Goldstein (1996)), to a special case of a more general
theory of financial decision-making.

In the classical view the decision-maker's calculative powers are infinite
and costless. Information, if it is relevant, should always be used in making
a decision. Such heroic assumptions fit in with a broader modelling strategy
that we can model investors'/agents' behaviour "as if" they had unlimited
calculative powers, were aware of all possible outcomes, etc. The justification for such heroism being that what matters is a model's predictions not
its assumptions (Freidman (1953)).

But often researchers confuse statistical tests that *explain* data, used to
estimate the model well, and true *predictive* performance based on out–
of–sample performance Gigerenzer (2004). Indeed the very function of
statistical inference in establishing a maintained hypothesis is often hopelessly confused in social science, as argued below by Gigerenzer and Murray
(1987).

1.0.1 A fast-and-frugal alternative to behavioural finance

Fast-and-frugal reasoning, developed by Gerd Gigerenzer of the Max-
Planck Institute for Human Development in Berlin and his colleagues in

A Fast and Frugal Finance
https://doi.org/10.1016/B978-0-12-812495-6.00008-2

the Center for Adaptive Behavior and Cognition, reject the classical view of rational choice in favour of boundedly rational perspective.

Boundedly rational investors satisfice, rather than optimise, in their decision-making. Satisficing is a word of Northumbrian origin suggesting a choice algorithm which required limited information and calculative skill to achieve an acceptable, if not optimal, outcome. The focus is upon finding choices that yield an acceptable, rather than the best, outcome. This is in part because, following Herbert Simon, fast-and-frugal reasoning casts doubt on the notion of a global, or market-wide, best outcome.

Simon's concept of bounded rationality stresses the evolutionary adaption of our minds to the environment in which they operate. As Arrow (2004) has argued we have to be careful that such a definition does not become so broad as to be meaningless for

"there is no general criterion for determining which limit on rationality holds in any given context and the building of a complete theory of the economy is a project for the future."

For this reason our application of statistical reasoning must constrain itself to problems of limited domain, what Leonard Savage calls "small worlds" (Savage (1954)), within which we can adequately specify the bounds on reasonable behaviour that do apply.

Gigerenzer (2004) reminds us that the process of optimisation does not ensure an optimal, or best, outcome since in most applications it simply identifies the maxima/minima of some continuous, twice–differentiable, performance function. This is fine if the performance criteria studied can bear the weight of these assumptions; but simply "blackboard economics" if they cannot.

Gigerenzer and Selten (2001a) see the main characteristics of the adaptive-toolbox for decision-making as

"First it refers to a collection of rules or heuristics rather than a general purpose decision-making algorithm... Second these are fast, frugal and computationally cheap... Third, these heuristics are adapted to particular environments... This "ecological rationality... allows for the possibility that heuristics can be fast, frugal, and accurate all at the same time."

(Gigerenzer and Selten (2001a), p. 9)

Thus we can see Gerd Gigerenzer and the fast-and-frugal reasoning tradition as inheriting the baton of Simon's bounded rationality project. As such we agree with van der Sar (2004) (p. 442) that what is needed by finance scholars and practitioners is a credible alternative to the standard model, that embeds a coherent, credible, view of investor psychology. Professor Gigerenzer's fast-and-frugal reasoning may yet offer such an alternative.

1.1 Context and cognition

Many of us will recall being chastised by our parents for how calculators and spreadsheets have made us lazy in conducting the necessary mental arithmetic to do our shopping or budget for the month. In truth our minds have adapted to an environment in which we have access to a calculating machine in our pocket, mobile phone, or the cloud. In Simon's famous phrase

> *"Human rational behaviour is shaped by scissors whose two blades are the structure of the task environments and the computational capabilities of the actor."*
>
> *(Simon (1990), p. 7)*

While this may all seem rather banal and unworthy of comment it stands in marked opposition to the vast majority of finance theory we might think of. Simon (1959) points out nearly all economic models, including those in standard finance, assume agents are rational in the classical sense. Further these agents/investors inhabit a competitive world that swiftly culls the irrational from their midst. Thus

> *"the classical economic theory of markets with perfect competition and rational agents is a deductive theory that requires almost no contact with empirical data once its assumptions are accepted."*
>
> *(Simon (1959), p. 254.)*

Simon points out that there is a wide variety of problems where the assumptions of classical economics might seem a reasonable assumption, for example in heavily traded foreign exchange markets. But, importantly, there are many legitimate areas of inquiry in financial decision-making and investment practice where the assumptions of classical rationality seem honoured only in their breach.

Simon's early work, summarised in Simon (1959), focused upon areas where classical rationality seemed least likely to apply. Two of these were where perfect foresight regarding future outcomes was impossible and so the agent/investor was forced to predict outcomes and where decision-makers faced goal conflicts and perhaps uncertainty, rather than risk, regarding possible outcomes.

Both these deviations from classical rationality are likely to occur in financial markets. The relatively random evolution of asset prices is a central finding of empirical research in finance (Fama (1970)), while the multiple conflicting motives of investors are well documented Statman (2011).

Simon points out that while in experiments with toy gambles between known pay-offs expected utility theory/classical rationality appears to perform adequately as a description of decision-making under uncertainty problems emerge as soon as it is deployed into more realistic contexts of practical application. Simon (1959) points out that while economists took comfort in the affirmation of experimental results behavioural researchers felt inspired to look for alternatives to classical rationality.

Simon doubted whether classical rationality has much to offer in understanding everyday business decisions and investments.

> *"even with new powerful tools and machines, most real-life choices lie beyond the reach of maximising techniques–unless the situations are heroically simplified by drastic approximations. If man, according to this interpretation, makes decisions and choices that have some appearance of rationality, rationality in real life must involve something simpler than the maximisation of utility or profit."*

(Simon (1959), pp. 259–260)

It is from this quest for a simpler decision-making calculus that fast-and-frugal reasoning has emerged. A key concept inherited by fast-and-frugal reasoning researchers from Herbert Simon is the notion of satisficing and choices directed at reaching some "aspiration level" of wealth or well-being. These ideas have later been formalised by those collaborating within the fast-and-frugal tradition (Selten, 1998).

1.1.1 Context, cognition, and the "end of accounting"

The global financial reporting system constitutes a world-wide, largely invariant system of financial regulation. The International Accounting Standards Committee[1] (IASC) website proudly proclaims that 144 of 149, or 87%, accounting jurisdictions worldwide require the use of International Financial Reporting Standards, or 75% of G20 members (see https://www.ifrs.org/-/media/feature/around-the-world/adoption/use-of-ifrs-around-the-world-overview-sept-2018.pdf?la=en). The IASC clearly state the IASC's goal and the extent of support for it.

"The vision of a global set of accounting standards is supported by other organisations within the international regulatory framework, including the Basel Committee on Banking supervision, the Financial Stability Board, the G 20, the International Monetary Fund... and the World Bank"

It appears all good men support the adoption of a common accounting framework, regardless of national economic, social or legal setting. This mission has not gone mostly uncontested within the academic community in accounting (Ball (2016)).

Lev and Gu (2016) present a stark case that the fuel financial reports provide for the allocation of investment capital is contaminated and perhaps reaching the point of irrelevance. The primary source of financial reporting increasing irrelevance to a search for corporate value is its failure to transform itself in accordance with the changing dynamics of corporate value drivers

"uniformity deprives accounting of a major force for innovation and rejuvenation – the vital experimentation and evolution that come with diversity... the stagnation of the accounting system and the consequent loss of relevance... can in part be attributed to the absence of any experimentation with new information structures or modes of disclosure, which comes from diversity of reporting across countries or regions."

(Lev and Gu (2016), pp. xix–xx)

Some notion of the scale of the loss of relevance of reported accounting performance for measuring stock market performance is given in Chapter 3 of Lev and Gu's book. Correlating key accounting performance metrics

[1] As of April 2019.

with reported stock prices they find a rapid decline in reported earning's and book value's correlation with contemporaneous corporate market values from the 1950's until now. They note the decline became especially marked from the 1980's as elements of "intangible" value grew to dominate corporate balance sheets.

1.2 Less is more

Consider two criteria often seen as emblematic of classical rationality in decision-making.

1. more information, if costless, is better than less when deciding what to do,
2. the desirability of integrating all information into a single predictive value.

To oppose the first appears to make a virtue of ignorance and to oppose the second seems like simply a way of undermining the first principle. Despite this fast-and-frugal reasoning suggests "less is more" in the sense that, while ignorance may not be bliss, it may be a vital input into an accurate, robust, decision-making process. This Mies van der Rohe, Bauhaus, phrase has become a defining characteristic of the fast-and-frugal reasoning approach.

To see this consider a cue that depends on recognition of a company or its product. If you have heard of a brand of butter you may be more willing to use it believing it is of high quality, as a known brand. So if you know every conceivable brand of butter this knowledge is no longer useful in discriminating between brands on offer. It is better to simply know the leading, most popular, (best?) brands since this allows you to discriminate better between high and low quality offerings of butter products.

Engel and Gigerenzer (2006) describe the power of heuristic-driven reasoning thus

"The double grounding of a heuristic in the human brain and in the environment enables simple heuristics to be highly robust in an uncertain world, whereas complex strategies tend to overfit, that is, not generalize so well to new and changing situations. Less can be more."

Engel and Gigerenzer (2006), p. 4

This opportunity led Simon and his followers to try to design simple decision-making schemata for making near-optimal decisions using both limited information and little calculative effort. A world in which simplicity may prevent us from acting stupidly in a manner that over complicating things often can. Such decision-making schemata, or heuristic tools, must be evaluated according to the market terrain in which they are deployed, as opposed to some all-encompassing, a priori, notion of what is rational.

So "the rationality of heuristics is ecological not logical" as Gigerenzer and Brighton (2009) put it. So to study ecological rationality is to ask into which environment is a given heuristic best deployed. To understand this consider the standard decomposition of a forecast error.

$$\text{Forecast Error} = (\text{Bias})^2 + \text{Variance} + \text{Noise}$$

This decomposition is given in many statistical textbooks and stresses the trade-off between biased and volatile predictive methods (Geman et al. (1992)). Fast-and-frugal reasoning methods simply accept some bias in estimation if it offers a sufficiently compensating reducing in forecast variance. Such a bias heavy, but relatively invariant, prediction method gives rise to the claim that "less is more" for an appropriately constructed fast-and-frugal decision-making heuristic.

The model that explains the most recent data, on stock returns or mergers, may not be the best model to predict its evolution. Partly this is because of the danger of over-fitting. A model that is broad enough to encompass a wide variety of possible scenarios can also associate itself with a large amount of meaningless noise.

So, while avoiding bias, we want our models to be as flexible as possible, not constraining us to a tunnel vision perspective on the market. But to avoid wildly varying predictions we need to make our models as parsimonious as possible too.

The range of applicability of a fast-and-frugal model of financial decision-making

A distinct danger for the heuristics and bias program is that heuristics become applied so broadly they descend into an almost meaningless generality.

Fast-and-frugal models sit at the high bias/low forecast error variance end of the above mentioned forecast error decomposition. The question is when is this the right modelling strategy to adopt? Fast-and-frugal reasoning relies upon the selection, adoption, and abandonment of simple, tightly specified, decision-making heuristics within localised market conditions to which they are well suited.

We might expect minimising forecast error to be a serious problem in fast–moving environments where most data is not relevant to future events. These sorts of conditions seem to occur quite often in Finance, the fortunes of banks after the crash, or the value of the Euro post-Brexit. Often in financial markets it seems like we are entering a new world and past experience can do little to guide us. The financial future thus appears more uncertain than risky, defying a frequentist perspective on the construction of probabilities of possible outcomes. In such a world a fast-and-frugal finance has much to commend it (Mousavi and Gigerenzer, 2017).

Gigerenzer (2004) regards the program of ecological rationality to be to study of

1. the heuristics people really use in solving any given class of task,
2. the structure of the task environment,
3. what aspects of the task environment the selected heuristic can exploit.

Thus fast-and-frugal reasoning judges the merit of any decision-making tool against the environment into which it will be deployed. This defines a new *ecological* rationality which this book argues is more illuminating of financial market behaviour than the *classical* rationality guiding most current investment teaching and academic research.

1.3 There is more than one form of rationality

A striking, and perhaps initially alarming, part of fast-and-frugal reasoning is how it redefines what constitutes being rational. Vernon Smith (2008) distinguishes two types of rationality, the constructivist form prevailing in standard finance and an alternative ecological form which was the preferred version amongst classical political economy writers, such as Adam Smith and David Hume.

The constructivist form is defined at the individual investor/agent level and requires the application of rules of choice to select best outcomes from feasible alternatives. At an organisational level constructivist rationality sets out an "optimal design" to maximise the organisation's goals, maximise utility, etc. Ecological rationality by contrast emerges through social interaction, trading, and the evolution of social norms. Vernon Smith (2008, p. 2) defines it thus

"Ecological rationality refers to emergent order in the form of practices, norms, and evolving institutional rules governing action by individuals that are part

*of our cultural and biological heritage and are created by human interactions,
but not by conscious human design."*

In this Smith is clearly influenced, as he is in much of work, by Hayek's
notion of a "spontaneous order" (Hayek (1988)).

In economic modelling constructivist and ecological forms of rationality
are complements rather than substitutes. Often a constructivist perspective can use a game–theoretic model to determine the equilibrium given
"optimal" play by the investors/agents being studied, while an ecological
perspective helps us understand how investor/agents approximate the theoretical equilibrium in real markets/organisations. One example of this is
the series of studies of how the "tragedy of the commons" is resolved in
practice (Ostrom (1990)).

The complimentary nature of these differing forms of rationality is being exploited in the development of economic systems design, an emerging
new branch of study at the borders experimental and theoretical economics.

One application of this new mode of inquiry was sparked by the disas-
trous attempts at electricity market de-regulation in California in the late
90's. Regular power outrages, during the summer, when demand was highest (due to air-con usage), led to the Governor of the State being forced
to resign and vitriolic Congressional hearings. In attempting to determine
what caused the crisis experimental methods proved useful in exposing fault
lines in the system. This allowed at least some of the most glaring failings
in the system to be ironed out before electricity provision was once more
exposed to normal market competition in California.

1.3.1 A brief history of ecological rationality

Vernon Smith (2008, Chapter 2) points out that the tension between constructivist and ecological forms of rationality goes back at least to the work
of Adam Smith. Many have been concerned about the relationship, and
possible tensions, between Adam Smith's first major, but little read, work,
The Theory of Moral Sentiments (1759), and his more famous work The
Wealth of Nations (1776). While both books focus on our social interaction with others, the first concerns the domain of personal exchange with
family, friends, and those close to us, while the latter focuses upon market
exchange.

Vernon Smith (2008) points out that our mental formation is dominated
by unconscious learning, such as language development or social graces,
which may be almost impervious to conscious thought. Indeed the great

benefit of the operation of markets is that they operate largely through an "invisible hand" we can, for the most part, ignore. Thus both Adam Smith and David Hume stressed the importance of experience, as against reasoned thought, in the conduct of our everyday lives.

Thus classical political economy saw constructionist rationality as very useful in inducing variation, by suggesting new, possibly better, ways of doing things. But they very much relied on ecological rationality to select whether any new innovation in production, consumption or trade was worthwhile. One example of this emergent order is the co-operation observed in continuous double-auction experiments.

Both the Nobel Prizewinners Elinor Ostrom and Douglas North (North (1990)) build their reputation on understanding the emergence of social institutions no theory could adequately explain. As such solutions to the free-rider problem (Ostrom) and the abolition of slavery (North) can be seen as "natural experiments" in the evolution of a new institutional order.

Such evolved solutions seem hugely preferable to many when compared to consciously planned social and economic reform, of which China's Great Leap Forward[2] may be the most tragic in its results. Research, such as that by North and Olstrom, can help us understand how unseen factors operate to shape our shared history.

One weakness both econometric and historical studies share is the inability to capture the full scope of what did not happen. For this purpose experimental evidence is especially useful since the generation of counterfactual outcomes (at least for the world/markets we observe) can be explored quite easily.

Those in the fast-and-frugal reasoning tradition tend to be sceptical of claims that investors/agents are "irrational" simply because the do not conform in their actions to the predictions of some theoretical model. Fast-and-frugal reasoning makes us open to the possibility that our models themselves may fail to capture the full richness of the decision-making context the investor/agent faces.

Experiments can be good ways of capturing the possibilities in this regard. A practical example of such an emergent order, that went unpredicted by any economic theorist or commentator, was the emergence of a "hub-and-spoke" form of air travel in the US following deregulation in the early

[2] The Great Leap Forward initiated by Chairman Mao in the years 1958-62 to induce rapid industrialisation in China is conservatively estimated to have led to the deaths of 18 million Chinese.

1980's. Here experiments may have helped the aviation industry anticipate the likely effect of a regulatory change.

1.4 The goals and achievements of fast-and-frugal reasoning

Fast-and-frugal reasoning has three goals (Gigerenzer et al., 2011).

1. The development a typography of an *adaptive toolbox*, these are building blocks of decision-making routines. These include searching rules, rules for stopping search and, finally, decision-making formats themselves. Tracing the development of the adaptive toolbox requires an understanding of how each constituent heuristic proved its value in different market/competitive settings, so for any heuristic tool the question must be how did it serve/match attaining a specified goal (more profit, more volume) given the market setting into which it is deployed.

2. The emergence of a form of *ecological rationality* in which there exists a congruence between the heuristic tools deployed and the market setting into which they are deployed. A heuristic is ecologically rational not because of the beauty, or the consistency of its internal logic, but because its implied choices are best suited to the market setting, competitive environment, into which it is deployed. Since humanity creates its own environment this inevitably requires studying the co–evolution of environment and heuristic tools as history progresses

3. Applications of *intuitive design* to engineer new, revised, heuristic tools for improving specified financial outcomes, be that trading profit, market liquidity, access to financial capital, etc. Such heuristic design draws upon the known properties of investors, traders, their cognitive processes and the environment in which those processes are formed.

The term heuristic derives from the Greek meaning "serving to find out or discover" (Gigerenzer and Brighton (2009)). So while pure mathematicians regard heuristics as vital to uncovering a line of proof, they then proceed by the hard slog of line by line derivation to secure that proof's footing.

A central part of the value of heuristics in problem–solving by humans is in limiting the domain of search for possible solutions.

> *"an explanation of the observed behaviour of an organism is provided by a program of information–processing primitives that generates this behaviour."*
>
> *(Simon and Newell (1971, p. 147))*

So if we can design a computer program that faithfully replicates the decisions humans make we have gone at least some part of way to explaining human behaviour.

Of course such an explanation by programmed replication leaves out much of the human mind's intuition and supplety. The programs whose outputs broadly replicate human decisions only explain those decisions to the extent that the information processes they employ both can be and are used by humans themselves. One key element of human problem solving a replicating program can adopt is limited search though alternative solutions.

1.4.1 Heuristic reasoning in Chess

Chess Masters lacking the computational power to be able to envision the range of positions four of five moves hence develop a spatial awareness of what likely pathways look like and respond accordingly. Chase and Simon (1973) study the ability of Chess novices and Grand Masters to reconstruct from memory board positions after being exposed to them for just five seconds. They find when the pieces are randomly positioned the ability of Grand Masters and novices to reconstruct positions to which they are given a five second glimpse is roughly the same. But the ability of Grand Masters to reconstruct actual match positions from memory is much better than novices.

Clearly Grand Masters are better able to perceive structure in the match position that helps them to later reconstruct those match positions. In doing so they appear to use a limited number of cues they find useful.

Chase and Simon (1973, p. 80) describe this superiority of Grand Masters arising as follows

> *"[it] derives from the ability of those players to encode each position into larger perceptual chunks, each consisting of a larger configuration of pieces. Pieces within a single chunk are bound by relations of mutual defence, proximity, attack over small distances and colour and type."*
>
> **(Chase and Simon (1973), p. 80)**

Clearly the Grand Master's skill lies in reducing the board's configuration to a simple scheme familiar from their own past battles. In a board of randomly placed pieces such cues are missing and so their comparative advantage, over novices, in reconstructing the position is lost. In the construction of a fast-and-frugal finance the discernment of such decision-making cues is vital.

1.5 The value-added of a fast-and-frugal perspective upon finance

As alluded to before much of the first flourishing of the behavioural finance movement derived from the "heuristics-and-biases" program of Daniel Kahneman (Tversky and Kahneman, 1974). This program pointed to the presence of a range of "anomalies" in decision-making under conditions of uncertainty that seemed unreconcilable with expected utility/classical rationality (Kahnehman et al., 1991).

This approach viewed these deviations in decision-making from classical rationality as errors to be explained and incorporated into revised models of how decisions *are* made. At the same time it simply accepts that classical rationality captures how decisions *should* be made. This has led Reinhard Selten to view the heuristics and bias program of Kahneman and Tversky as a "repair program" (Selten (2001)) of a framework badly in need of replacement.

A major set of finding of the heuristics-and-biases program has been the breadth of the behaviour described as being anomalous with classical rationality. Often data is examined to expose evidence in favour/against behaviour described by a value label such as the "availability" or "representativeness" heuristic.

Fast-and-frugal finance has a different focus of proposing and verifying specific computational models for financial decisions, recalling the spirit of Simon's observation that[3]

> *"A running program is a moment of truth."*
>
> **Simon (1992)**

This is because the embedded logic of a computer program only encompasses a limited range of behaviour, allowing the refutability criterion of successful knowledge claims to be met. On the other hand, a label that is so broad almost no imaginable market behaviour refutes it is unlikely to serve as a useful guide to investment management or academic research.

While the reality that we are mere humans and have limited cognitive powers has long been recognised it has generally been thought that the use of heuristics is made acceptable by this human frailty. In his description of human cognition Daniel Kahneman distinguishes between system 1 and system 2 thinking.

---

[3] Cited in Gigerenzer and Brighton (2009).

System 1 is autopilot and lets me make my coffee while phoning ahead to work to sort out problems. System 2 lets me dwell at length on what $2 \times 17 \times 4$ is (Kahneman (2011)). Kahneman points out that system 1 works so effortlessly we have a tendency to overuse it, deploying it into contexts where it is unlikely to be appropriate. We might recognise this in the face of a driver overtaking us while on their mobile phone.

In such contexts errors arise because of a lack of the requisite effort the task demands. Thus a major theme of the "heuristics-and-biases" research program, established so brilliantly by Kahneman and his late co-author Amos Tversky, is the common cognitive errors induced in stylised settings precisely because we rely on heuristics to make decisions when they are not really appropriate.

Perhaps the most influential product of the heuristics-and-biases program of research is prospect theory in both its original and cumulative form (Kahneman and Tversky (1979), Tversky and Kahneman (1992)). This framework has underpinned a wide variety of applications in finance, for example Shefrin and Statman (1985), Barberis et al. (2001a), Coval and Shumway (2005)). The question thus arises when can a fast-and-frugal perspective on financial decision-making be more illuminating in explaining, predicting, financial choices? We focus on this issue in Chapter 5 of this book.

1.6 Reconciling classical and ecological rationality

Perhaps the most striking feature of fast-and-frugal reasoning is that it challenges the previously assumed superiority of classical rationality as a way of reasoning and specifically of making financial decisions. As Gigerenzer and Goldstein (1996, p. 666), state

> *"it is time to overcome the opposition between the rational and the psychological and unite the two... Models of inference do not have to forsake accuracy for simplicity. The mind can have it both ways."*

The heuristics-and-biases approach invoked psychology was simply invoked to explain why investors deviated from the presumptively (classically) correct form of decision-making. A fast-and-frugal finance, conversely, to show that simple, easy to deploy, heuristics can dominate decision-tools based on classical rationality and relying upon probability, bayesian inference and (constrained) optimisation.

In developing such an adaptive toolbox of preferred heuristic tools market psychology and the observed decision routines of market traders are central. In this new world of ecologically rational financial markets having limited calculative abilities and/or ignoring potentially relevant information can potentially enhance an investor's decision-making abilities.

In such a world simple models can beat their more complex counterparts in a fraught market/competitive setting. Indeed the specification of such simple heuristic tools is the primary purpose of the intuitive design of a superior adaptive toolbox.

Fast-and-frugal reasoning has, at least, two strengths over existing decision-making rules that rely on (utility or wealth) maximisation. Firstly they directly model investor choice and the inferences required to make that choice. Second they are parsimonious, simple, and robust (Gigerenzer (2004)).

1.7 From tools to heuristics

One central driver of the evolution of decision-making routines is the crafting and emergence of statistical decision-making tools which are then disseminated via University, especially Business School, teaching. The role of psychology in decision-making should go beyond explaining investors' failure to correctly apply the tenets of classical rationality. Indeed to fall into this trap is to focus on the wrong binary opposition

"I view the mind in relation to its environment rather than in opposition to the laws of logic or probability. In a complex and uncertain world psychology is indispensable to sound reasoning: it is rationality's fuel rather than its brake."

(Gigerenzer (2000), Preface)

When reflecting on the history of psychology Gigerenzer observes that

"In experimental psychology inferential statistics became almost synonymous with scientific method."

Would much change if the word "empirical finance" were substituted for "experimental psychology"? We think not. Indeed questionnaire, participative observation, or historical research is now rarely published in the leading

Finance journals, unless it by those who have already built a reputation in more traditional, statistically credible, research.[4]

1.8 A bird's-eye view

Fast-and-frugal reasoning is gaining increasing attention, if not popularity, with psychology and decision-making academics and practitioners. It has also been successfully applied in approaching engineering, medicine, and legal matters ((Katsikopolos et al., 2019), (Gigerenzer and Gray, 2011), (Engel and Gigerenzer, 2006)). But can it produce the goods for Finance professionals? Certainly the intense convulsions and resulting self–doubt induced by the 2008 financial crisis has created an audience for new ideas. Academics that were once considered hopelessly crackpot (Hyman Minsky?) are being re-read with a renewed humility. This book addresses this very possibility. Can we build a fast-and-frugal finance, not amongst the ruins of the old standard finance, but alongside those parts of standard finance which remain most illuminating.

Richard Thaler insightfully argues the end of the behavioural finance project will come when it is so woven into the fabric of finance that the term becomes redundant (Thaler (1999)). For this to happen fast-and-frugal reasoning must prove its worth in assessing central issues in finance, the origins of the recent financial crisis, asset pricing, investment appraisal, and capital structure.

1.8.1 A reader's guide to the book

This book aims to convert more of our colleagues and students to the possibilities of a fast-and-frugal finance that applies fast-and-frugal reasoning/modelling to common financial decision-making problems, asset pricing, financial analysis, and earnings management for example. The first five chapters try to introduce fast-and-frugal reasoning to finance scholars unfamiliar with that approach. We structure this discussion as follows:

2/Fast-and-Frugal heuristics, written by Shabnam Mousavi, which introduces the primary fruit of fast-and-frugal reasoning so far; insofar as this offers an "adaptive toolbox" of decision-making heuristics for making workable, if not optimal, choices,

---

[4] The joint work of John Graham and Campbell Harvey is noteworthy in this regard, see for example Graham et al. (2005).

3/Adaptive or Efficient Markets? exploring a credible contender to the efficient market hypothesis which has so much dominated standard finance modelling,

4/Financial regulations and heuristics, written by Shabnam Mousavi, which addresses the question of how a fast-and-frugal approach can inform the policy debate regarding financial reform in light of the 2007/8 global financial crisis.

5/When does fast-and-frugal work best? Which answers the "why bother with a fast-and-frugal approach to finance?" question. We indicate where such an approach might thrive, but argue there are few areas where it is not worth looking for its value-added. To some extent this is a recognition of the current parlous state of finance scholarship.

The subsequent four subsequent chapters give some illustrative applications of fast-and-frugal we are interested in, working on, ourselves. These applications are illustrative, not exhaustive. One of the exciting things about developing a fast-and-frugal finance is how many new research issues, methodological choices, it throws up for a future generation of scholars to address.

This book assesses the prospects for fast-and-frugal reasoning in contributing to these topics in its later chapters. Primary amongst these applications is asset pricing and portfolio theory, since these often seen as the jewels in the crown of the standard finance approach. The craft basis of financial accounting techniques, evolved over centuries without a centralised authority, suggests it is better understood from an ecological, rather than a classical, rationality perspective. To this end we study financial analysis and the process of earnings management in later chapters.

So the latter part of the book takes the form

6/Asset pricing, particularly the model popularised by Fama and French, pricing assets relative to 3/5 important risk factors,

7/Portfolio theory, exploring fast-and-frugal alternatives to the construction of a mean-variance portfolio,

8/Financial analysis, showing how analysts/fund managers construct simple, tractable, schemata for stock–picking which can be represented in the form of fast-and-frugal trees; a practical application of lexiographic choice, based on a structured set of answers to yes/no questions regarding a candidate stock's characteristics.

9/The law of small numbers, written by Aloysius Igboekwu, exploring how earnings sequences can be applied to explain/predict the stock market's response to earnings announcements; allowing a simple application of the tallying heuristic within financial markets.

Overall the book aims to survey and contribute to the building on a new fast-and-frugal finance. While no single text can complete such a project we may at least encourage others to join in the process of completing it. Where the author of the Chapter is not stated, the author is William Forbes.

CHAPTER 2

Fast-and-frugal heuristics*

This chapter introduces the vocabulary, definition, and concepts from the fast-and-frugal heuristics literature that will be used throughout this book. Behavioural finance has emerged from viewing financial decision making from the lens of cognitive psychology. Cognitive psychology is itself a vast field with different schools of thought. The mainstream behavioural economics and finance have borrowed much from the heuristics-and-biases approach to cognitive sciences. In this book, we focus on an alternative heuristic framework, namely, fast-and-frugal heuristics.

Investing in the financial markets is like gambling in Vegas! But the odds must be favourable for the rational investor to act. We all know that the house wins all the time, that is, the odds are unfavourable to gamblers. A typical course in financial investments teaches the ways in which these odds can be quantified and factored in investment decisions.

Asset pricing theories develop a framework and generate tools for finding the fair prices in the market and efficient portfolios are constructed based on diversification, which eliminates the diversifiable risk and accounts for premiums for the non-diversifiable risk. Risk is measured by a statistical scaler for the variability of the return. Thus, the optimal portfolio is created with a specified expected return and risk. The next step involves assessing investors' level of risk tolerance and customising portfolios that match this level by combining the efficient well-diversified portfolio with enough risk–free assets to adjust the risk.

In their beginning semester in a finance program, students raise their eyebrows when assumptions of efficiency and rationality are listed: But, this is not how we think. I don't make my decisions this way. Do financial managers really work like this?... The standard response to these human reactions, from professors, goes like this: Modelling and formalisation require simplification and abstraction in compliance with the grand theory from which the models are developed. Rational choice theory and the Efficient Market Hypothesis are the pillars of our discipline. As our students move onward, their initial doubts subside and early questions fade. We routinely send them out to the workplace with training rooted firmly in rationality

---

* This chapter is written by Shabnam Mousavi.

A Fast and Frugal Finance
https://doi.org/10.1016/B978-0-12-812495-6.00009-4

and efficiency, more recently flavoured with a taste of behavioural finance, which moves beyond those formal requirements and limits.

In Chapter 3, the Adaptive Market Hypothesis (Lo, 2004) will be introduced as an alternative new approach to investment behaviour informed by evolutionary theory and other behavioural insights. This chapter provides an introduction to an alternative approach to rational choice behaviour that puts heuristics in the front and centre of exploring decision-making processes.

2.1 What is a heuristic?

As an adjective, a heuristic refers to "enabling a person to discover or learn something for themselves" and as a noun, to "a heuristic process or method" (The Oxford Dictionary). The term heuristic has been extensively used across disciplines in relation to theories of rationality, knowledge, and action (Groner et al., 2009).

As noted in Chapter 1, mainstream behavioural economics and behavioural finance is built on the foundation of the heuristics-and-biases program pioneered by Tversky and Kahneman (1974), where heuristics are mental shortcuts that lead to biased behaviour and involve cognitive illusions (for a recent popular read, see Boatang and De Lara (2016)). In Kahnehman's words:

> "The difference in effort provides the most useful indications of whether a given mental process should be assigned to System 1 [fast thinking] or System 2 [slow thinking]. Because the overall capacity for mental effort is limited, effortful processes tend to disrupt each other, whereas effortless processes neither cause nor suffer much interference when combined with other tasks." (p. 1451)

Shifting the focus from trade-offs imposed by cognitive limitations to yielding efficient results ((Neth et al., 2014), (Mousavi and Gigerenzer, 2017), (Neth and Gigerenzer, 2015)), the fast-and-frugal heuristics program offers an alternative conceptualisation of heuristics.

Definition. Heuristics are adaptive tools that ignore information to make fast-and-frugal decisions that are accurate and robust under conditions of uncertainty. A heuristic is considered *ecologically rational* when it functionally matches the structure of environment.

This definition highlights two fundamental concepts for the study of fast-and-frugal heuristics, namely, the adaptive toolbox and ecological rationality. Exploring the contents of the mind's toolbox constitutes the descriptive branch (what heuristics are there and how do they work?) of these studies, whereas investigating ecological rationality concerns prescriptive aspects (where should a heuristic be used?).

In this framework, the mind is viewed as an adaptive *toolbox* that contains evolutionary capacities, learned abilities, and other elements that can be used as heuristic building blocks. We discuss ecological rationality in length later on in this chapter. Notably, the robustness of a heuristic emanates from its simplicity; it avoids fine-tuning of parameters that can cause large estimation error under uncertainty, and particularly under changing environmental conditions. As we shall see in what follows, heuristics stop the search for information before all available, or attainable, information is examined. As such, a heuristic process does not require full deliberation. However, heuristics can be brought to consciousness, formulated, and learned.

2.1.1 Describing a heuristic process

Heuristics can be decomposed into three building blocks: a search rule that directs the search in the information space, a stopping rule to stop search, and a decision rule for making the final choice. Each of these three rules itself can be a heuristic rule (Gigerenzer et al. 1999). The first formal model generated in the fast-and-frugal heuristics study program was take-the-best heuristic (Gigerenzer and Goldstein, 1996), which involves a sequence of binary comparisons in place of considering all information (cues) and weighing them at once. The take-the-best heuristic is composed of the following building blocks (Gigerenzer 2006, p. 125):

1. *Search rule*: Search through cues in order of their validity. Look up the cue value with the highest validity first.
2. *Stopping rule*: If one object has a positive cue value and the other does not (or is unknown), then stop search and proceed to Step 3. If no more cues are found, guess.
3. *Decision rule*: Predict that the object with the positive cue value has the higher value on the criterion.

The description of heuristic processes is not limited to a set of three building blocks and can be provided in other format, as in the examples presented in Tables 2.1, adapted from Todd et al. (2012).

All descriptions of heuristic processes in Tables 2.1 and 2.2 correspond to the definition of heuristics insofar as they include an element of ignoring some information, draw on evolutionary or learned capacities, and

Table 2.1 Twelve well-studied heuristics with evidence of use in the adaptive toolbox of humans (adopted with modifications from Table 1-1 in Todd et al. (2012)).

Heuristic	Description	Counterintuitive results
Recognition heuristic (Goldstein and Gigerenzer, 2002) Gigerenzer	If one of two alternatives is recognised, infer that it has the higher value on the criterion	Less-is-more-effect
Fluency heuristic (Schooler and Hertswig, 2005)	If both alternatives are recognised but one is recognised faster, infer that it has the higher value on the criterion	Less-is-more-effect
Tallying (Dawes, 1979)	To estimate a criterion, do not estimate weights but simply count the number of positive cues	Can predict as accurately as or better than multiple regression
Satisfying (Simon, 1955)	Search through alternatives and choose the first one that exceeds your aspiration level	Aspiration levels can lead to substantially better choices than by chance, even if they are arbitrary
One-bounce rule (Hey, 1982)	Continue searching (e.g. for prices) as long as options improve; at the first downturn, stop search and take previous best option	
Gaze heuristic	To catch a ball that is coming down (McBeath et al., 1995) from overhead, fix your gaze on it, start running, and adjust your running speed so that the angle of gaze remain constant	
$\frac{1}{N}$ rule (DeMiguel et al., 2009)	Allocate resources equally to each of N alternatives	Can outperform optimal asset allocation portfolios
Default heuristic (Johnson and Goldstein, 2003)	If there is a default, follow it	Explains why advertising has little effect on organ donor

continued on next page

Table 2.1 (*continued*)

Heuristic	Description	Counterintuitive results
Tit-for-tat (Axelrod, 1984)	Cooperate first and then imitate your partner's last behaviour	Can lead to a higher payoff than "rational" strategies (e.g. by backward induction)
Imitate the majority (Boyd and Richerson, 2005)	Determine the behaviour followed by the majority of people in your group and imitate it	A driving force in bonding, group identification, and moral behaviour
Imitate the successful (Boyd and Richerson, 2005)	Determine the most successful person and imitate his or her	A driving force in cultural evolution

are robust to ever–changing environments. Moreover, the last column of Table 2.1 presents another feature of heuristics, that of generating counter-intuitive results.

Recall from the first chapter that the most prevalent counterintuitive feature of heuristics is referred to as the less-is-more phenomenon. We will return to this phenomenon in other chapters, in particular when discussing financial regulations. The study of fast-and-frugal heuristics aims at building a science of heuristics and in doing so has moved beyond simply naming single heuristics to categorising them based on their structural properties, as the following section illustrates.

2.2 Classification and applications of heuristics

Heuristics can be classified with respect to a core processing property into four classes: recognition-based, satisficing, equal weights, and sequential consideration (Gigerenzer and Gaissaier, 2011). Table 2.2 provides examples of heuristics from each class, in Column 2, as well as references to some studies in business decision making in the last column. Notice that this classification is a work-in-progress and as such is neither complete nor unique.

The first class in Table 2.2 comprises recognition-based decision-making that process the information on alternative options according to recognition and assign a higher value to the recognised option. The recognition heuristic and fluency heuristic, defined below, belong to this class.

Table 2.2 A classification of models of heuristics and examples of economic applications.

Classes	Examples	Application
Recognition-based decision making: Evaluate options based on their being recognized	Recognition heuristic	Investment portfolio performance (Borges et al., 1999; Ortmann et al., 2008)
	Fluency heuristic	Performance of IPOs, and value estimates in the market (Alter and Oppenheimer, 2006, 2008)
Satisficing: Choose the first option that meets an aspiration level. (Information consideration does not follow a sequence ordering.)	Setting and adjusting aspiration levels	Aspiration adaptation theory (Selten, 1998) Investing in malls/high-rises (Berg, 2014) Pricing used cars (Artinger and Gigerenzer, 2016)
Equal weighing*: Assign simple— 0/1 or equal— weights. Forgo estimating weights to reduce estimation error.	Tallying	Emergency room decisions (Newman-Toker et al., 2009)
	1/N heuristic	Equal allocation of resources to investment options (DeMiguel et al., 2009)
Sequential consideration: Consider cues in a simple order such as lexicographical; stop consideration as soon as a decision can be made (Special case: base decision on a single cue)	One-clever-cue heuristics	Identifying active customers: the hiatus heuristic (Wübben and Wangenheim, 2008) Pricing by intuition (Rusetski, 2014) Crisis management: the credibility heuristic (MacGillivray, 2014)
	Priority heuristic	Logically implies the Allais paradox, certainty effect, and fourfold pattern of risk attitudes (Brandstätter et al., 2006)
	Take-the-best	Forming consideration sets for purchase (Hauser, 2014)

* Equal weighing can be perceived as a special case of a larger class of heuristics with rules that assign simple weights to cues. Future explorations can elaborate on this structure.

(Source: Mousavi et al., 2017a with modification.)

2.2.1 The recognition heuristic

If one of two alternatives is recognised and the other is not, then infer that the recognised alternative has the higher value with respect to the criterion. (Goldstein and Gigerenzer, 2002), see Table 2.1.

A simple and low-cost strategy based on the recognition heuristic trumped sophisticated analysis of financial markets: Portfolios of stocks recognised by laypeople in the USA and Germany outperformed the market index, whereas portfolios based on expert recognition did not ((Borges et al., 1999), (Ortmann et al., 2008)). Experts know too much and therefore are not able to benefit from the recognition heuristic in the same way that laypeople do.

Another heuristic in the recognition-based class is the fluency heuristic.

2.2.2 Fluency heuristic

If both alternatives are recognised but one is recognised faster, then infer that this alternative has the higher value with respect to the criterion (Schooler and Hertswig, 2005), see Table 2.1.

The fluency of recollecting the name of a stock correlates with its immediate performance in initial public offerings (Alter and Oppenheimer, 2008). Follow-up experimental studies revealed that the valuation process can be generally understood based on familiarity and fluency (Alter and Oppenheimer, 2008).

The second class in Table 2.2, satisficing, put forward by Simon (1955), is a heuristic-based behaviour and the initial inspiration for many studies in heuristic decision making. No specific order leads the search here. Once an aspiration level is met, or exceeded, the search stops and a "good enough" choice is made. During the search the initial aspiration level can be adjusted.

Satisficing: Set an aspiration level α and start the search in any order. Choose the first object with satisfying value $\alpha \neq = 0$. If no object is found after time, lower aspiration level by a set amount, say δ. Continue search with the updated aspiration level $\alpha - \delta$. Repeat the process until a choice can be made, see Table 2.2.

Defined as such, satisficing is viewed as a non-optimising process of aspiration adaptation ((Selten, 1998), (Nagel et al., 2017). This process describes the way in which people resolve ill–defined problems; such as choice of a lifetime partner or a job. Markets also manifest satisficing behaviour.

Berg (2014) interviewed entrepreneurs on the process of information search, setting an appropriate search threshold, α, that led them to the choice of location for building commercial high-rises. Interestingly, his data could not be described by a search cost model but instead by simple satisficing search and limited consideration of information in a process where "locations are frequently discovered by chance". These developers made high-impact decisions based on meeting a simple aspiration criterion, such as a fixed percentage return over a fixed period of time, and did not update their initial aspirations in the process of search. In another study, Artinger and Gigerenzer (2016) found that for second-hand cars, BMW dealers first set an initial aspiration level price, followed by gradual fixed percentage adjustments over fixed monthly intervals.

The third class of heuristics in Table 2.2 is *equal weighing*, which reduces the estimation error in comparison to multiple weights' estimation. Although simple unit weighting schemes are particularly efficient for small samples (Einhorn and Hogarth, 1975), they are rarely incorporated in econometrics. An example of equal weighing is a simple tallying heuristic that counts only the favoured cues by giving them a weight of one and ignores or gives zero weight to the rest. In emergency rooms, vital calls are made by tallying (Newman-Toker et al., 2009), and hikers use tallying to avoid avalanche accidents (McCammon and Hägeli, 2007). Another example for the equal weighing class is the 1/N heuristic, where resources are allocated equally among N options. Some behavioural economists have considered this equal allocation as an inferior strategy and, for instance, refer to the observed equal allocation of assets in retirement portfolios as naïve diversification (Benartzi and Thaler, 2001). A study by DeMiguel et al. (2009), however, empirically showed that $\frac{1}{N}$ outperforms Markowitz's mean-variance portfolio in 6 out of 7 tests and could not be consistently outperformed by any of another dozen sophisticated portfolio diversification algorithms—thereby shedding doubt on assuming this strategy to be naïve.

The fourth and last class in Table 2.2 contains sequential heuristics that consider pieces of information, or cues one at a time, until a decision can be made, with one-clever-cue heuristics as a subclass, where all but one cue is ignored. Hiatus heuristic is a case in point for this subclass, consisting of only one threshold value that Wübben and Wangenheim (2008) used for identifying active customers in three businesses: an airline industry, an online CD retailer, and an apparel vendor.

2.2.3 Hiatus heuristic

If a customer has not purchased within a certain number of months – the hiatus – the customer is classified as inactive; otherwise, the customer is classified as active.

The hiatus heuristic performs as good as or better than complex algorithms such as Pareto/NBD (negative binomial distribution). Another example is a survey of more than 100 brand managers showing that they made price decisions without using complex compensatory algorithms. Their simple pricing strategy considers only the competitors' price levels, followed by a consistent positioning above, equal to, or below that price (Rusetski, 2014). Yet another instance is a credibility heuristic used by managers, where detecting contaminated water sources is based simply on the perceived trustworthiness of the message conveyor.

The credibility heuristic is effective because situations in crisis management are subject to a high level of uncertainty and decisions need to be made without delay (MacGillivray, 2014). We will discuss these heuristics in more detail later on in this chapter.

Other examples in the last category are the priority heuristic and take-the-best. In the next section, we discuss the priority heuristic in detail. The take-the-best heuristic, whose building blocks were described earlier, orders cues unconditionally without taking their interdependencies into account. This heuristic process is used by consumers who are faced with many products and several attributes for each product, when they follow a consider-then-choose sequence. Hauser (2014) surveyed this phenomenon and named it the "consideration set" heuristic. He emphasises that understanding this process of choice is essential to successful managerial decisions on product development and marketing communication, where "consideration sets are key to business strategy" (p. 1688).

2.2.4 Priority heuristic: a non-EU model for choice between gambles

A vast volume of behavioural economics and finance originates from using insights generated from the swap of EUT for prospect theory. This has allowed discussions of "probability perceptions" associated with different values and ranges of possibilities. Also, different risk attitudes being demonstrated in the domain of loss vs. domain of gain. The hallmark of formalising risky behaviour remains throughout to be the analysis in form of lottery choices. Priority heuristic offers a method for analysing lottery choices which emanates from the psychology of choice in the fast-and-frugal approach.

Heuristics classes listed in Tables 2.2 can be used both for inference and preference. Inferential choice is usually studied with respect to an external metric. This avoids the difficulty of uniquely specifying a metric, as is required by preferential choice. The theory of revealed preferences ((Samuelson, 1938b), (Samuelson, 1938a), (Samuelson, 1948)), which remains to date the centrepiece of theoretical analysis and empirical testing of choice behaviour in the expected utility maximisation framework, postulates that people consider all options and have a stable order of preferences over options.

Any rational choice simply reflects such an order. Importantly, rationality implies an optimal trade-off in correspondence to the most preferred option involving weighting and adding of attributes of the available options. Similar to these trade-offs are gambles, which have been used to represent risky decision making since the origination of probability theory in the 17th century (Hacking, 2006).

Behavioural economics accumulates evidence on systematic violation of rationality axioms such as stable preference ordering, transitivity, and consistency. Cumulative prospect theory (CPT; Tversky and Kahneman (1992)) is the most influential formalism for capturing these systematic violations from Samuelsonian rationality. Here, prospect is another term for gambles. In this formalism, three parameters fit the shape of the value function and another two the shape of the probability weighting function. These flexible parameters of CPT increase its explanatory power in comparison to the expected utility theory, allowing it to account for the observed violations. As such, CPT does not model the process of decision making per se; but rather aims at fitting the data better as a result of using more parameters. This method might, however, lead to overfitting and even reduce the predictive power.

The priority heuristic, on the other hand, aims to model the process of information for the preferential choice between gambles. It was built to answer the following questions: What do people "actually" do when they make decisions? Do people use simple rules as the problem becomes more complex? If so, then a model without adjustable parameters can potentially capture such processes and could logically imply systematic deviations from expected utility theory.

Brandstätter et al. (2006) (BGH herein) constructed the priority heuristic model, which is a lexicographic model for preferential choice by taking the following steps (Mousavi and Meder, 2017).

1. Determine which heuristic form. From the set of all possible heuristics for two-alternative choice problems, the candidates were narrowed down to lexicographic rules and tallying (see Table 2.1 for definitions). Then tallying was ruled out because empirical evidence does not support equal treatment of reasons in choice between monetary gambles. Once the lexicographic form was chosen, reasons for consideration needed to be specified.

2. Start with nonnegative gambles, "gains", that contain three separate reasons:

    a maximum gain M;

    a minimum gain m; and

    the probabilities of each gain $p_M + p_m = 1$.

    Three numbers have 3! possible orderings, from which one order must be chosen by investigating the evidence on choice behaviour.

3. Choice experiments by Brandstätter and Küberger (2005) suggest that people consider the value of gains before their probabilities. This eliminates two order possibilities in which probabilities are the first reason, leaving four. Because people are evidenced to be risk averse in the gain domain, (Edwards, 1954), they consider m first in order to avoid the worst outcome. Which of the remaining two possible orders is actually followed needs to be further elicited.

4. To examine the remaining two orders of consideration, m-p-M versus m-M-p, BGH conducted an experiment in which m was kept constant to elicit the order for p and M. Their results agree with Slovic et al. (1990, Study 5) in that p preceded M in consideration order. Thus, the order of reasons was specified as m-p-M. However, heuristic search does not exhaust the space of information by examining all reasons; but rather stops when a good enough reason is found.

5. What is a good enough reason in the choice between simple gambles? This can be configured by finding empirically supported satisficing rules. For two simple gambles A and B, one starts by comparing their minimum gain values, $\Delta m = |m_A - m_b|$. Evidence suggests that whether Δm is considered large enough to stop the consideration of reasons depends on the maximum gain. That is, the aspiration level depends on M_A and M_B. Taking a simple metric that corresponds to our habitual decimal system, BGH postulated that people compare Δm

to one tenth of the larger maximum gain, denoted as $0.1\Delta M$, where $M=\max(M_A, M_B)$. Notice that 0.1 is an empirically informed fixed (not flexible) parameter.

6. Define the stopping rules.

$\Delta m > 0.1\Delta M$ then stop; otherwise consider the second reason (probabilities of minimum gains),

$\Delta p_m = (| p_{mA} - p_{mB} |) > 0.1$ then stop; otherwise consider the last reason (maximum gains).

7. Define the decision rule. For the choice between gambles BGH defined a decision rule based on "attractiveness". Once the search is stopped, the priority heuristic predicts that the gamble with the more attractive decisive feature, either gain or probability, will be chosen.

The priority heuristic model has the following three building blocks (BGH 2006, p. 413):

Priority Rule: Go through reasons in the order of minimum gain, probability of minimum gain, maximum gain.

Stopping Rule: Stop examination if the minimum gains differ by 1/10 (or more) of the maximum gain; otherwise stop examination if probabilities differ by 1/10 (or more) of the probability scale.

Decision Rule: Choose the gamble with the more attractive gain (probability).

In addition to simple positive gambles with two outcomes, this model accounts for both gambles with losses and gambles with more than two outcomes. How well does the priority heuristic predict violations of expected utility? Tested against three modifications of expected utility theory, including cumulative prospect theory, and ten previously studied heuristics, including tallying, across 260 problems, the priority heuristic ranked on top with a predictive accuracy of 87%. Cumulative prospect theory excelled in data fitting, i.e., explaining data already known, but predicted 77% of observed choice behaviour correctly. The reason is that CPT incurs variance error in parameter estimation, which is absent for the priority heuristic, which has no free parameters.

In the fast-and-frugal framework, the priority heuristic is part of a toolbox. What other "simple" strategies fare well in choice between lotteries? Different strategies can be viewed as adapted to either easy or difficult choices. The choice can be considered easy when the expected values of lottery options differ by a factor of 2 or more, and otherwise difficult. With respect to this criterion, the priority heuristic predicted best for difficult choices.

Cumulative prospect theory was better at predicting easy choices, but the best predictor of easy choices was simple expected value. In sum, two simple strategies with zero adjustable parameters, the priority heuristic, and expected value (not expected utility), were most effective in predicting the data for difficult and simple choice problems, respectively. This result speaks volumes for rethinking the prevalent method of modelling risky choice behaviour with Bernoulli functions, which are notoriously unreliable in out–of–sample prediction ((Freidman et al., 2014), (Stewart et al., 2015)).

2.3 Overconfidence: the most studied behavioural phenomenon in finance

In the study of behavioural biases associated with the financial choice behaviour of both investors and managers, overconfidence and excessive optimism stand out. "The most robust effect of overconfidence" (Odean, 1998) can be viewed in consideration of at least two aspects of knowledge or ability. When the facts are ignored or altered (think about "alternative facts" as an extreme case!), overconfidence in knowledge is manifested, whereas presuming the capability to deliver beyond an objectively verifiable basis demonstrates overconfidence in ability. The latter can be viewed routinely when high-level executives describe their vision of mobilising synergies for their planned mergers and acquisitions.

Mousavi and Gigerenzer (2011) developed the following typology of overconfidence, wherein the reported bias in each case is juxtaposed with related evaluative studies and categorised into types one to four. Type five, functional overconfidence, takes a different approach to overconfidence by focusing on its functionality; as opposed to characterising it as a biased behaviour. This is another instance of shifting the focus from investors' dispositions to making errors, rooted in the use of simple heuristics, to scrutinising observed behaviours in order to tease out their beneficial functions.

2.3.1 Better-than-average

The tendency to deem oneself better than average is referred to as an optimism bias. This effect was documented, among others, in studies where a clear majority of subjects viewed themselves as better than average drivers with respect to criteria such as likelihood of incurring injury in driving accidents ((Johansson and Rumar, 1968), (Svenson, 1981), (Svenson et al., 1985). Svenson et al. (1985) commented on these observations: "[but] It is no more possible for most people to be safer [drivers] than average than it is for most to have above average intelligence" (p. 119). Is this comparison correct? It is if both safe driving and intelligence have symmetric (not skewed) distributions. IQ distributions are standardised to be normally distributed and symmetric so that the median and mean coincide. The distribution of car accidents, however, is asymmetric (skewed), indicating that more than 50% of drivers have fewer accidents than the mean. Analysing the data on approximately 7800 drivers in the USA (Finklestein and Levin, 2001) shows that 80% of American drivers had fewer than the average number of accidents.

Many studies avoid this oversight of the difference between symmetric and asymmetric distributions and correctly account for the skewness in their analysis. There remains another pitfall, that of asking questions without clear correct answers. The question of whether someone is above average without specifying the referent of "average" leaves the statement interpretable by different subjects in individual ways. If subjects simply view themselves as being better than others at what they believe should be done, the ambiguous question will produce what looks like overconfidence. For example, a good driver could be viewed as one who can drive faster than others, one who can hold a mobile phone and a cigarette while driving, or one who obeys the law and drives cautiously.

Yet a third cautionary point remains regarding quick judgements about what is right and wrong. Consider the question "Is your IQ above or below the mean of 100?" that avoids the two above mentioned problems arising from asymmetry and ambiguity because it is fairly precise (aside from the fact that different IQ tests can lead to significantly different scores for the same person). Remarkably, the very statement that "50% of all people have an IQ over 100" is not always correct. This is because of the so called "Flynn effect", which indicates an average annual increase of about 0.3 points in IQ measurements, which implies the need for re-standardising the test. The more years that pass (since the last standardisation), the more people will have above-average IQs. The statement that "more than 50% of people are better than average" becomes a fact about the world rather than a judgement error, as some researchers too quickly assume.

2.3.2 (Too) narrow confidence intervals

Overconfidence is documented in a variety of ways in the lab, one of which is when individuals tend to indicate too narrow confidence intervals. One of the studies in Juslin et al. (2007) survey reports on subjects who were asked to guess a credible interval in which next year's interest rate would fall, that included the true value with a probability of 0.90. Only 0.40 to 0.50 of the intervals suggested by respondents included the true value. Note that this is not the same phenomenon as better-than-average (Section 3.2.1); these two phenomena do not formally imply one another in either direction, nor do we know of a study demonstrating that people who show the first phenomenon also show the second.

Once again, we ask whether this observation necessarily indicates overconfidence? The answer is negative, as demonstrated in the Naive Sampling Model (NSM) developed by Juslin et al. (2007), which offers a causal explanation for the observed phenomena. According to NSM, although the estimation of means is unbiased, when everyday experiences (random samples) are transferred directly to a population, a systematic error will appear in estimating the variance and therefore in producing confidence intervals. Thus, when the experimenter provides a probability (an average) and asks about an interval for this probability, the reported phenomenon of "overconfidence" appears. Alternatively, if an interval is provided and subjects are asked to produce "the probability that the true value lies in the interval" the very same phenomenon disappears. That is, depending on the setup of the experiment, the phenomenon can be elicited, or eliminated, even from the same subject in an experiment. This result suggests that this form of overconfidence cannot be interpreted as a stable personality trait.

2.3.3 Mean confidence > percentage correct

Since the 1970's a type of overconfidence emerged from posing two-step questions such as "Which city lies further south, Rome or New York? How certain are you that your answer is correct?" A decisive majority of subjects in such studies have demonstrated a level of confidence in their own judgement that stands well above the percentage of correct answers. In one case, Griffin and Tversky (1992) proclaim: "The significance of overconfidence to the conduct of human affairs can hardly be overstated."

Is this a robust phenomenon? The Probabilistic Mental Models theory of Gigerenzer et al. (1991) predicted that such results interpreted as overconfidence can appear when the experimenter systematically selects the tasks but will disappear when tasks are chosen randomly. The explanation is to be found in how human judgement is adapted to the real world, which can lead to errors when artificially faced with selected and therefore non-representative tasks. In the case of temperature, which is generally a good indicator of the geographic location for the majority of cities, subjects would err if faced with an unusual case. That is, overconfidence appears when judging whether Rome or New York lies further south because the general relationship does not hold: Rome lies on a higher latitude than New York. Juslin et al. (2000) analysed 130 studies in which this form of overconfidence appeared only if tasks were selected systematically, rather than randomly, confirming the prediction of the Probabilistic Mental Models theory.

The fact that this type of overconfidence can be absent, or elicited from even the same subject, depending on whether questions are sampled in a representative or selective manner suggests that this phenomenon cannot be a general trait or disposition.

2.3.4 Overconfidence equals miscalibration

A fourth demonstration of overconfidence that appears in miscalibrations has been found in another analysis of data from the same questions as in the previous case (Section 2.3.3): "Which city lies further south, Rome or New York? How certain are you that your answer is correct?" Here, instead of assessing the difference between average confidence and the proportion correct, the total calibration curve is assessed by recording values for percentage sure versus percentage correct – say, 100% sure that the answer was correct versus 80% proportion correct, 90% confident versus 70% proportion correct, and so on. Overconfidence in this situation is attributed to a mismatch between confidence categories and the proportion correct, which is referred to as miscalibration – a distinct phenomenon, that can appear independently from the overconfidence discussed in the previous section. Notably, the difference between mean correct and percentage correct (overconfidence in Section 2.3.3) can be zero, where miscalibration is nevertheless substantial, e.g., when the curve for the proportion correct crosses the calibration line at 50%, as in a regression curve.

Does this difference correspond to a mental bias? In 1994 Erev et al. (1994) showed independently that a regression to the mean is at work. For noisy data such as confidence judgements data, conditional variance is nonzero, which in itself is equivalent to imperfect correlation between confidence and proportion correct. An imperfect correlation implies that when the reported confidence ratings are high, the corresponding proportions correct will be smaller — which resembles the miscalibration that was attributed to overconfidence. The regression line for general knowledge questions that sampled randomly from a large domain, is typically symmetrical around the midpoint of the reported confidence scale, e.g., 50% when the confidence scale is from 0 to 100% and 75% when the confidence scale is from 50 to 100% (Juslin et al., 2000). Francis Galton's famous example that sons of tall fathers are likely to be smaller in height, and sons of small fathers are likely to be taller is a case in point for this type of conditional variance in the absence of any bias in the data (Stigler, 2002). Thus, the observed phenomenon here is a normal consequence of regression, and not a cognitive bias.

Interestingly, a mirror phenomenon – that can be interpreted as an underconfidence bias – can be derived by reversing the process, i.e., by estimating the confidence judgements from the proportion answered correct rather than vice versa. If for all items that the subjects assessed 100% correctly, the average confidence is lower, say 80%, this seems to indicate underconfidence. Conversely, one can report finding overconfidence if all items for which participants were 100% confident but had a lower average proportion correct, say 80%. In an analysis of three empirical data sets by Erev et al. (1994) regression towards the mean accounted for all the effects that would otherwise have been interpreted as overconfidence or underconfidence, depending on how the data were plotted. Another study by Dawes and Mulford (1996) revealed the same phenomenon for a different empirical data set. To extract under- or overconfidence beyond regression to the mean, one needs to plot the data both ways and look for consistent results.

2.3.5 Functional overconfidence

The last type we consider here is yet another phenomenon that involves a functional and often profitable mechanism – hence the name functional overconfidence. Many professional tasks, such as predicting the stock market, are too difficult to consistently generate performances higher than those of laypeople. Moreover, sophisticated statistical strategies are not consistently better than intuition.

DeMiguel et al. (2009) ran a horserace between a dozen optimisation methods and the simple $\frac{1}{N}$ heuristic (equal allocation of money to all options) for investment allocation decisions. The result was surprising as 1/N won over in most cases. Needless to say, these results did not change the general practice of hiring financial analysts. Many investors prefer to believe that experts know the best strategy, and delegate the responsibility for selecting strategies to them.

An expert's "role is mainly to convey security and confidence" it seems, even if that is ill-founded. The same applies to fortune tellers and, in some cases, physicians. Without unrealistic self-confidence, option advisers and astrologers would lose their customers — and many physicians their patients. Professional overconfidence is essential to sustaining the functionality of institutions through providing emotional security. This phenomenon – which shares little in common with the four other types of overconfidence discussed in this section – is a fertile ground for examining the illusion of certainty and its role in determining human behaviour (Goldstein and Gigerenzer, 2002).

2.3.6 Is overconfidence bias an error?

To date, overconfidence research remains a pillar of behavioural finance. Despite extensive arguments to the contrary, some of which are cited in this section, many researchers hold that there is clear evidence for a human tendency toward overconfidence. What does appear clear is one instantiation of this bias: the overconfidence of many researchers in a phenomenon called overconfidence!

As discussed in this section, a good number of studies that reported finding evidence of overconfidence bias can be revised in light of careful statistical analysis of their data. Also, the very phenomenon of overconfidence can be functionally beneficial, as opposed to an error that requires correction.

All five phenomena referred to as overconfidence better-than-average, too-narrow confidence interval, mean confidence vs. percentage correct, and miscalibration thus can be explained by understanding their different natures. One key element is to tease out adaptive processes before precipitously labelling an observed behaviour as a cognitive bias and motivational deficit. Another important issue arises from the mainstream treatment of some such phenomena as stable personality traits.

This stance does not hold when a behaviour (overconfidence) and its opposite (underconfidence) can be elicited as a result of different experimental setups. In sum, incentives and goals other than logical truth or factual correctness direct human decisions.

One of the dangers of focusing on toy problems such as many overconfidence tasks is that these abandon the systematic study of real-world situations where people make real errors outside the laboratory. The next section introduces the framework of ecological rationality and discusses how an ecological, rather than a logical, approach to cognition can reveal criteria for success emanating from the use of simple but robust heuristics.

2.4 When do heuristics work?

A heuristic is ecologically rational if it matches the task environment. Situations where simple strategies can outperform complex ones are instances of the less-is-more effect. The study of the ecological rationality of heuristics explains when and why less can be more. It specifies the conditions under which a given heuristic can be effective. That is, it does not claim that simplicity is simply better but explores the environmental structures in which simple heuristics would fare well. For example, the recognition heuristic works for a person with partial recognition-based knowledge that correlates with the task environment. It does not work for a person who completely lacks knowledge or is fully knowledgeable. Another form of simplicity is naivety. The naïve portfolio selection strategy $\frac{1}{N}$ can be ecologically rational under the following conditions: N is large, sample size is small, and predictive uncertainty is high. A testable heuristic model can provide normative recommendations for successful action, such as to use $\frac{1}{N}$ when the success criteria hold.

2.4.1 Ecological rationality in economics and psychology

In experimental labs, behavioural scientists have documented many systematic deviations (biases) from a statistically or logically defined "correct" choice. The reason for people demonstrating this behaviour has been largely attributed to their following rules of thumb or simple heuristics. The study of fast-and-frugal heuristics, on the other hand, has focused on the functionality and adaptive features of simple heuristics.

At the centre of ecological rationality is adaptive behaviour and the way in which adaptive individuals, or institutions, make a choice in a given environment. The resulting methodology provides a practical normative stance on value judgement, a positive framework of factual and testable models, and a descriptive framework for the study of human choice behaviour with respect to the mind as an adaptive toolbox. The path to understanding how human minds process information, and to eventually develop decision-making aids goes through discovering the mechanisms of successful heuristics at work. This in turn calls for unearthing relevant norms.

Ecological rationality provides an empirically based framework for evaluating both logically rational behaviour and cases in which it is not rational to be logically rational. It is from this perspective that the two prominent scholars from both sides of the aisle can meet and concur on one definition: "A heuristic is ecologically rational to the degree that it is adapted to the structure of an environment" ((Gigerenzer and Todd, 1999), (Smith, 2008)).

Behavioural economics and finance are defined as perspectives that arise from merging the rigour of economic theory with the insights from psychology. As such, a conceptualisation of the ecological rationality of heuristics by an economist juxtaposed with that of a psychologist is of interest to behavioural scientists.

Gigerenzer views ecological rationality as the normative element of a science of heuristics, and Smith depicts the scientific pursuits of economics as an ongoing investigation that considers two forms of rationality. In Smith's view, rationality norms, in their constructivist form, provide possible reasons, whereas ecological rationality picks the choice. Highlights from Smith's and Gigerenzer's views on this subject are tabulated below. The last column in Table 2.3 outlines the overlap between the two views on each topic.

2.5 Teasing out elements of success based on ecological rationality

Fast-and-frugal heuristics can be successful when they are ecologically rational. Gigerenzer and I collated a number of studies on the successful use of heuristics in business decision making, which constituted a special section in the August 2014 issue of the *Journal of Business Research*. This section provides an overview of the contents of this collection in addition to some related work outside the collection. Each item can be viewed as an illustration of how ecological rationality can help us understand the criteria for successful decision making. Mousavi (2017) classified these articles and their findings in the following four categories depending on the domain of business in which the process of decision making is studied. A common method in all these studies is providing a configuration of the observed strategies in the field, or the lab, in terms of fast-and-frugal heuristics. The reader can trace back every one of the heuristics in this Section to the classification provided in Table 2.3.

2.5.1 Heuristics in the financial sector

Banks issue credit cards, which allow consumers to spend their future income. This concerns the regulator because repayment of credit card debt turns out to be a much more difficult task than perceived by credit card

Table 2.3 Ecological rationality in economics and psychology.

Subject	Economic view à la Gigerenzer	Psychological view à la Gigerenzer	Overlap
Definition of ecological rationality	A heuristic is ecologically concerned with adaptions that occur within institutions, markets, management, and social and other associations governed by informal or formal rule systems	A heuristic is ecological rational to the degree is adapted to the structure of environment. Humans have to adapt to a social and physical world syntax, such as logic	Smith uses the same definition of ecological rationality as Gigerenzer wherein heuristics can be replaced by markets, management, or other rule systems
The normative aspect of constructionism and unbounded rationality	Constructivism or reason provides a variety of ideas to try out but often no relevant selection criteria, whereas the ecological process selects the norms and institutions that serve the stability of societies	Unbounded rationality can generate optimal solutions for simple situations, e.g., tic tac toe; omniscience and omnipotence can also be used for theoretical examination of human behaviour, but applying as a universal standard of rationality is a scientific error	Norms produced by unbounded or constructivist rationality are not useful as selection criteria in complex situations; the ultimate evaluation comes from the real world, not from theoretical sophistication
Observation and experiments	Observing how people actually behave reveals unanticipated system rules, e.g., the unexpected emergence of hubs (like an equilibrium) when airlines were deregulated	Experimental games are bound to study social behaviour as rule–obeying behaviour and not as rule– negotiating or rule–changing behaviour	Rules are to be discovered as they emerge from social behaviour. Formal models can be used to provide a possible description of what was observed
Heuristic rules	Heuristics are a kind of cognitive capacity that we can access without being entirely aware of doing so	Fast-and-frugal heuristics are strategies triggered by environmental situations and enabled evolved or learned capacities	The choice of heuristic strategy is often not fully deliberate. This does not exclude the possibility of training altering the trigger conditions

Note: Source: Mousavi et al. (2017b). Based on interviews in Mousavi and Kheirandish (2014).

holders or rational choice theory. Cardholders often collect a considerable amount of debt on which they pay high amounts of interest for extensive periods of time. Federal reserve board reports indicate that on average American households spent above 15% of their income on financial obligation payments (http://www.federalreserve.gov/releases/housedebt/). The situation is particularly crucial for low- and middle-class Americans, for whom this ratio reaches half of their disposable income. To protect consumers, American lawmakers passed the Credit Card Accountability, Responsibility, and Disclosure Act (CARD, 2019). This led to many banks hiring consultants to implement their obligations.

Shefrin and Nichols (2014) report on their consulting work that contributed to the Chase Blueprint Program for helping cardholders better manage their spending and borrowing behaviour. They note that "by nature, household decision making is a heuristic enterprise, as most household decision tasks are far too complex to be fully specified, let alone solved through optimisation." Even if an optimisation solution is applicable, it may not be practical because rational preference ordering is primarily concerned with the consistency criterion, with precious little attention to the quality of the decisions.

In addition to being faced with complex household decisions and constrained by limitations of technical (rational choice theory) measurement tools, they found that customers' mathematical abilities were too low. Only half of those who self-assessed their mathematical skills as "high-level" were able to correctly calculate interest rate and inflation. How did they tackle this situation? Shefrin and Nichols (2014) developed a fast-and-frugal decision tool for the cardholders to find their personal financial styles. Cardholders' financial styles are matched with appropriate financial advice from a menu.

After responding to a short series of binary questions, consumers are classified into one of the four categories: low control, minimum payer; high control, minimum payer; full balance paying, multiple cardholder; and full balance paying, single cardholder. This categorisation task has four options and three cues, lending itself to an elimination heuristic process. Shefrin and Nichols (2014) report that this financial style categorisation heuristic is more accessible to bank customers (especially the 25% with self-ranked low confidence in their online skills) and also technically advantageous over cluster analysis.

The use of heuristics is not limited to bank customers, bankers use heuristics too. Banks have access to detailed longitudinal data on their consumer base, so it would be natural to assume that the banks use optimisation and exact analysis, say, when it comes to consumer relationship management (CRM). Well, they don't. An examination of CRM processes at nine of the largest retail Nordic banks by Azar (2014), Persson and Ryals (2014) revealed that although CLV calculations were performed in these banks, their decisions were made based on a handful of simple heuristics. Not only these heuristics deliberately ignore a large set of technically relevant results available from data analysis, but customers prefer these banks over those that applied the CLV method results directly to their consumer relations. For example, the active status of a bank customer is assessed based on a threshold value in a manner resembling the hiatus heuristic of Wübben and Wangenheim (2008) introduced in Table 2.2.

Heuristics appear once again, when it comes to the choice of financial consultants. At an Italian corporate bank Monti et al. (2014) interviewed 20 financial advisors and 99 retailers who were active bank customers. What retailers valued in their advisors, more than past performance record, were trustworthiness, clarity, and attention. Interestingly, these retailers held little trust in the financial system as a whole. Monti et al.'s model of trust formation resonates with the honest signals defined by Pelligra (2010) as "behaviours that are so expressive or so directly connected to our underlying biology that they become generally reliable indicators used by people to guide their own internal psychological production of trust." Advice taking can thus be viewed as an adaptive behaviour, and trust as a simple heuristic, whereby investors' perceptions of the investor-advisor relationship reflected portfolio decisions better than the risk-return trade-off.

A final remark concerns the artifactual trade role of those agents who are referred to as noise trades, as a technical tool to overcome the no-trade situation in informationally efficient markets ((Black, 1986), (Shleifer and Summers, 1990), (De Long et al., 1990), (De Long et al., 1991)). This topic remains outside the scope of the current discussion. Moreover, following that form of operationalisation coincides with the distinction between rational and irrational agents, which too falls outside the heuristic-based framework of viewing market activities which is one we attempt to build here. Nor are "noise traders" necessarily irrational. They may be liquidity traders who trade for information unrelated to asset value, but the fact remains that they may need elective surgery or to top up their kid's education fund. There is nothing irrational about this. It is simply not justified by information in financial markets, just by information about other sources of utility.

2.5.2 Heuristics in strategic corporate decision making

Managers make a variety of decisions based on heuristics. The range includes innovation adoption, entrepreneurial decisions, as well as routine choices such as setting corporate strategic policies. For instance, Azar (2014) explains that firms follow a default heuristic when the cost of obtaining information is high and/or the variation in possible outcomes is low. All in all, whether these decisions involve. A complex strategic process such as innovation adoption can also be understood in terms of simple heuristics.

Using a cognitive lens to observe this phenomenon, Nikolaeva (2014) finds that managers regularly copy predecessors for improving upon the status quo, i.e., they use imitate the successful and imitate the majority heuristics. Moreover, the interaction between the framing dictated by the status quo and the pattern/sequence of imitative strategies determines the speed of innovation adoption.

Finally, Berg (2014) interviews with commercial high-rise builder reveal that successful entrepreneurs form small consideration sets based on satisficing and imitation. For the choice of location, they set a simple aspiration, such as aiming for x% return after y years (satisficing), and consider similar locations chosen by their peers (imitation) for the choice of location for building high-rises.

2.5.3 Heuristics in human resource and hiring decisions

Human resource managers use simple heuristics for hiring and delegation. Hu and Wang (2014) consider trust as a risky choice that is frequently used by these managers. They investigated the use of four strategies by 120 HR managers: take-the-best, the minimum requirement heuristic, likelihood expectancy, and the Franklin rule. Then they teased out the conditions under which each one of these strategies performs best. When the alternative options can be differentiated by the most valid cue, take-the-best is most effective.

The minimum requirement heuristic is a form of tallying that chooses the option that meets the highest number of minimum requirements. It performs best when a limited number of cues are used as a minimum requirement for differentiating between options. A likelihood expectancy heuristic, on the other hand, examines the space of cues exhaustively and chooses the option with the highest sum of cue-values. Finally, the Franklin rule calculates a weighted sum of cue values and selects the one with the highest score.

Hu and Wang (2014) analysis shows that the simple heuristics minimum requirement and take-the-best have a better predictive accuracy than the complex likelihood expectancy and Franklin rule. Overall, because cues often have a similar validity in this environment, minimum requirement outperforms take-the-best.

In another study, Fific and Gigerenzer (2014) asked whether more interviewers increase the quality of hired employees. Surprisingly, the answer was no! Analysing data from the recruitment procedures of several corporations they found that the chances of choosing higher-quality interviewees from a pool of applicants by a single interviewer (hit rate) is higher than when more than one interviewer is involved. Moreover, adding more interviewers will not increase the expected collective hit, manifesting a less-is-more instance.

2.5.4 Heuristics in pricing, marketing, and crisis management

A majority of managers (69%), according to Rusetski (2014), rely on an identifiable heuristic when making their pricing decisions under limited information. A cluster analysis revealed that intuitive decision-making algorithms use brand strength as a dominant factor in pricing, leaving a minor role for product quality. Managers price their products above, equal to, or below those of their competitors rather than adjusting according to attributes such as quality. These simple pricing heuristics are ecologically rational in drawing on past experience and best practices for a given environment. Pricing decisions have to satisfy multiple criteria in complex environments and are made under time pressure. Fast-and-frugal intuitive pricing, Rusetski finds, is often more effective than pricing based on a complicated analysis that takes account of all involving variables.

Hauser (2014) surveys consumers who face many complex product categories with large numbers of product features and feature levels, e.g., cellphones. He models the decision processes of consumers as sequences of consider-then-choose or consideration-set heuristics. Hauser notes that successful marketing management, product development, and marketing communication decisions depend on effective identification of such heuristics.

Are heuristics only intuitive? No, they can be deliberate. MacGillivray (2014) studies the heuristics used in crisis management that have explicit structure and involve deliberate execution. In the water supply sector "the relations between rule-based reasoning and social, political, and organisational structures" are evident in his field studies. His three heuristic

Table 2.4 Crisis management heuristics.

Heuristic	Rule form
Credibility heuristic	If the *conveyor* of the warning message passes a threshold of perceived credibility, then threat the message as being a signal from the target; if not, treat the message as being noise from a distracter.
Precedent heuristic	Search for precedent(s) for the unfolding event (i.e. historical analogue(s)), and if identified, then treat the current event in the same fashion as its precedent was treated.
Facts-trump-speculation	When faced with conflicting lines of evidence relating to a phenomenon, order them according to a predefined (but possibly implicit) hierarchy of evidence (cue validities), and treat the highest ranked line of evidence as true.

Source: MacGillivray (2014).

formulations of observed fast-and-frugal crisis management are credibility, precedent, and facts-trump-speculation as described in Table 2.4 credibility discriminates between signal and noise, the precedent heuristic uses analogy, and facts-trump-speculation is a non-compensatory process.

In sum, shifting the focus from the underlying biases associated with heuristics to exploring heuristic decision making as a legitimate approach to the study of choice under uncertainty adds a third scientific method to the two more familiar approaches based on probability theory and logic (Gigerenzer, 2008). This comprises the essence of the study of the ecological rationality of fast-and-frugal heuristics. A heuristic works when it meets the conditions of ecological rationality, otherwise it fails. A heuristic is neither good nor bad per se, its value remains to be assessed in the context.

2.6 Summary

Heuristics are effective decision tools when the success criteria are met, i.e., under conditions specified by ecological rationality. Their effectiveness is rooted in fast execution and selective frugal use of information. This chapter provided definitions of several fast-and-frugal heuristics as well as a classification of heuristic models. The priority heuristic was explained in details as an example of a heuristic model that applies to the central problem format of choice between lotteries. It is a non-expected utility model with only fixed parameters that has high predictive power and can account for a good number of so called anomalies.

In Section 2.3, we provided a typology for a few observed behaviours known in the literature as overconfidence. For some types, a closer statistical analysis simply eliminated the bias; for others, we shed doubt on overconfidence counting as a personality trait. The functional role of overconfidence in experts was also elaborated on.

Finally, ecological rationality was defined and examined as a central concept in both economics and the psychology of human behaviour. Several studies were reviewed in which ecological rationality constitutes a framework for studying business strategies and teasing out their elements of success.

CHAPTER 3

Adaptive or efficient financial markets?

A standard criticism of the behavioural approach is that, despite all its allure, "it takes a theory to beat a theory" and no coherent behavioural theory of asset pricing, or corporate acquisitions, has yet emerged. Even when, as in the case of the overreaction/under–reaction to earnings–announcements, such fully specified models exist (Barberis et al. (1998), Daniel et al. (1998), Hong and Stein (1999)) they are so varied, and even contradictory, as to make them almost useless as a foil to standard theory. Furthermore none of these behavioural models really address why a misvaluation of stocks with particular characteristics, say high earnings, or extreme earnings forecasts, are not arbitraged out within the aggregate market portfolio. That is to say these particular forms of partial equilibrium models of mispricing do not indicate how a general equilibrium model of asset pricing might embed their insights in constructing the market portfolio a fully diversified investor will hold ((van der Sar, 2004), p. 436).

Professor Andrew Lo, of MIT, has attempted the development of a single, coherent, theory that might yet emerge as a knock-out challenger to prevailing finance theory. This is the Adaptive Markets Hypothesis (AMH), first advanced by Professor Lo over a decade ago now (Lo (2004)) and recently more fully stated in his book *Adaptive Markets* (Lo (2017)) upon which we draw heavily in this Chapter.

This alternative to the standard Efficient Market Hypothesis (EMH) stresses the matching of our decision-making process to the environment into which it is deployed. Often we are using cognitive processes, evolved amongst hunter-gatherer communities before we entered our modern "great society" and commenced trading in modern financial markets. For Lo context is all and

> *"Financial behaviour that may be seen as irrational now is really behaviour that hasn't had time to adapt in modern contexts."*

(Lo (2017), p. 9)

When this happens the EMH's wisdom of crowds can get lost in the folly of mobs. Lo points out on the last page of this book the balance between

A Fast and Frugal Finance
https://doi.org/10.1016/B978-0-12-812495-6.00010-0

the wisdom and folly of markets is man's own choice; insofar as we can consciously shape the environment in which trading occurs. This is a talent unique to humanity.

Lo uses evidence uncovered by neuroscience to describe how primal/visceral emotions; such as greed, fear, hope, and regret impinge upon the "rational" calculus embedded so well into the EMH. Lo argues man is better seen as a "rationalising" animal; not a "rational" one as such.

He points out much of our mental effort goes into arranging our own and others' lives into credible, and importantly, predictive, narratives. If politics is the "art of the possible", as Bismark claimed, Finance is "the facilitator of the possible" (Lo, 2017, p. 417) and the AMH might give us a bigger vision of what the possibilities for our lives can be.

3.1 A bigger, better, story

So good intelligent minds create predictive, reliable, narratives confirming Danny Kahneman's belief in the centrality of "coherence" in any framework adopted for action/understanding (Kahneman (2011)). One way of viewing Lo's ambition is to supplant a story of financial markets, based in Physics and optimisation, with one based on Biology and the evolution of our humanity.

Few can doubt, and much evidence attests, to the power of narrative, those shared stories in our lives, the greedy Banker, the absent minded Professor, the angelic Nurse (Tuckett (2012), Tuckett and Nikolic (2017)). Lo (p. 312) argues we can regard such stories "as an advanced form of simulation, using a very high degree of abstraction to describe phenomena". One such strongly predictive story/theory is Darwin's theory of evolution, induced by careful observation, and published in 1859, long before the description of DNA sequences in 1953 made our inheritance visible.

Lo (pp. 135–136) describes how a trip to the Washington National Zoo first triggered his conception of the AMH. He noticed how his own behaviour seemed close in some ways to that of an orangutan, yet, as he stood there with his kids, their lives were so different. While Lo, and the rest of us, share 97% of our DNA with orangutans the 3% difference seems to have huge consequences for our lives. Lo wondered if there was something in this difference that might illuminate the nature of financial markets. He points out while we often speak of "survival of the fittest" it is most probably more accurate to speak of the survival of those most fit for their environment.

This itself implies there is a natural limit of the degree of beneficial adaption to our environment. If beneficial adaptions do not proceed far enough our genetic make-up remains out of kilter with the environment. But if we become too adapted to our environment an environmental change might threaten our very existence as a species.

Here (some) diversity is literally our strength; because it means there is a sufficiently broad gene pool to make us robust against environmental changes, such as global warming, or in the very long-run needing to take refuge on other planets. A striking physical feature of our evolution from the Homo genus about 2 million years ago to Homo sapiens about 200,000 years ago is the growth in the size of our brains, from about 400 cubic centimetres then to roughly 1200 cubic centimetres today, with a wide dispersion around that mean. Nor have our brain parts developed at equal rates, with greater proportional growth occurring in the pre-frontal cortex which is associated with abstract thought/planning (Lo, p. 152), etc.

While the proximate spur for this growth in our brains is unclear its effects are all around us. In an example of evolutionary *exaptation* our cognitive processes expanded to match our enlarged mental capacity. Lo describes the process thus

"A 'virtuous circle' described by our behaviour, our neurologically plastic brain, and natural selection led to a rapid evolution of a brain that was much more capable of forward looking behaviour, planning and abstract thought."

(Lo, 2017, p. 155)

Evolution at the speed of thought

A vital application of natural selection is the process of scientific discovery itself. Here in our academic exchanges we adopt, adapt and reject failed ideas every day in an attempt to refine our own ideas and advance our own careers. Lo points out this unshackles evolution from the frailty of our bodies allowing for "evolution at the speed of thought" (Lo, 2017, p. 164). Indeed it is this powerhouse of intellectual discovery that has perhaps been our primary distinction in separating us out from our non-human primate forebears.

One important set of tools that develop at the speed of thought are the decision-making tools we use to stylise/simplify every–day choices. Here the rapid evolutionary process has had dramatic consequences for our lives.

"our heuristics develop at the speed of thought. ... We don't require millions of years to develop a better mousetrap—we can develop new variations .. every day."

Lo (2017), p. 183.

Such evolution at the speed of thought greatly intensifies the evolutionary process, condensing the work of generations into months, if not days, in swiftly moving financial markets. Here behaviour that strikes us as wildly "irrational" may simply be *maladaptive*; applying the conquering tactics of the last war to our current battles.

So the estate agents, property dealers trained upon the excesses of the 1980/90's property boom were badly placed to survive in the 2007/8 financial crisis. This process of maladaptation may have been greatly intensified by bonuses, triggered by quarterly sales figures, with no clawbacks in response to subsequent market declines included. That such maladaptation can occur should not surprise us given the disjuncture between classically rational benchmarks and ecologically rational behaviours.

A major theme of Lo's book is that Finance/Economics has simply modelled its theoretical discussion on the wrong branch of the physical sciences. No doubt dazzled by the brilliance of Paul Samuelson, himself a product of the influence of a Harvard Physicist, much of the development of neoclassical economics lifted theoretical methods wholesale from Physics. But in doing so economists ignored the even closer analogies between discussions in Biology of resource allocation and competition between species.

Much of Lo's (2017) book aims to redress this imbalance and advances the AMH as a credible replacement for the EMH. Lo states (2017, p. 29)

"the financial system isn't a physical or mechanical system, but an ecosystem.... a collection of interdependent species all struggling for survival and reproductive excess in an ever-changing environment".

3.1.1 What evidence is there markets adapt?

The Adaptive Market Hypothesis certainly has an intuitive appeal. But we might wonder whether evidence from stock markets themselves will play along with this persuasive story. Evidence supportive of the AMH, relative to the EMH, comes from studies by Urquhart and Hudson (2013), Urquhart et al. (2015), Urquhart and McGoarty (2016). While evidence is mixed, depending on the nation examined and the time–period over which that nation's market is studied, that evidence we have is supportive on balance of the AMH over the EMH.

Urquhart and Hudson (2013) examine daily stock returns, drawn from the US, UK, and Japan, over a very long period from 1897. This approach can only be used for the market indices of very successful stock markets,[1] perhaps allowing some "survival" bias to creep in (see Brown et al. (1995)). But it has the great strength of allowing us to see how stock markets have evolved, in different institutional settings, over the very long run, when we might expect huge shifts in the social, economic, and political settlement even within one country.

Urquhart and Hudson (2013) look at various regression based tests as well as tests that allow for non-linear time–series dependencies in the data, drawn from sequential five year time periods from 1897 onwards, ending with the period 2005–2009. Their linear tests give strong evidence of fluctuating daily time–series dependencies in the data. Figs. 3.1 and 3.2 present results from two of their linear tests of how time–series dependencies vary over the long period of years they study.

First order daily autocorrelations, capturing the correlation between today's price and that on the previous trading day, shown in Fig. 3.1, vary dramatically over the long sample period the authors' study; even turning up in the most recent decade.

Nor is this a statistical artefact induced by non-normality, or outliers in the data, as the results of a non-parametric "runs" test shows, see Fig. 3.2. Whether measured by standard parametric time–series tests or, more robust, but less powerful, non-parametric tests, the degree, and even direction of, time–series dependence varies markedly over the length of the sample period studied.

Can simple trading rules consistently make investors money?

Weak–form stock market efficiency requires that there be no pattern/dependency of current price on past prices. But a long, heretical, tradition of technical analysis/Chartism, especially amongst professionals rather than academic scholars, has kept the belief that such patterns in stock prices exist alive (Lo and Hasanhodzic (2010)).

One commonly examined pattern of dependence is that a stock's/stock index's current price, P, is driven by the correspondence between a stock's/stock index's short–term and long–term moving average value.

[1] That have endured over a hundred years of continuous trading.

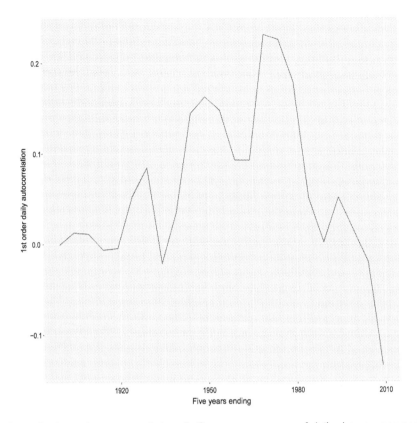

Figure 3.1 1st order autocorrelations in five-year sequences of daily data as reported by Urquhart and Hudson (2013). *Note*: Figure on Figure 2 on p. 135 of (Urquhart and Hudson, 2013), taken from third column of table.

Under the moving average rule investors should buy the stock, or index, when it's short–term moving average exceeds it's long–term moving average by a given band/% of value and sell if the reverse. So the moving average rule of trading dictates

If short–term moving average>long–term moving average by x% ⇒ Buy
If short–term moving average<long–term moving average by x% ⇒ Sell

Or more formally:

$$\left(\sum_{\lambda=1}^{S} \frac{P_{t-(\lambda-1)}}{S} \right) > \left(\sum_{\lambda=1}^{L} \frac{P_{t-(\lambda-1)}}{L} \right) + band \Rightarrow \text{Buy at time t}$$

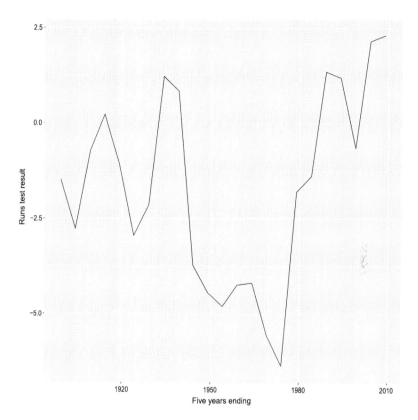

Figure 3.2 Runs test value five-year sequences of daily data as reported by Urquhart and Hudson (2013). *Note*: Figure on Figure 2 on p. 135 of (Urquhart and Hudson, 2013), taken from sixth column of table.

$$\left(\sum_{\lambda=1}^{S} \frac{P_{t-(\lambda-1)}}{S} \right) < \left(\sum_{\lambda=1}^{L} \frac{P_{t-(\lambda-1)}}{L} \right) + band \Rightarrow \text{Sell at time t} \qquad (3.1)$$

where L is the measurement window for calculating the long–term moving average, and S, is the measurement window for calculating the short–term moving average, where $L > S$, λ is the leg length used in the implementation of the test, and finally, a band of 1% is often used in statistical tests of the rule. So if the short–term moving average exceeds the long–term moving average by 1% or more the investor is directed to buy, and if the reverse holds, sell.

This moving–average rule had already been shown to be consistently profitable over ninety years of trading of the Dow Jones Industrial Index by Brock et al. (1992) in contradiction of the EMH. Urquhart et al. (2015) document secular variations in the profitability of the moving-average trading rule; a finding which is more consistent with the AMH than the EMH.

Specifically Urquhart et al. (2015) report a substantial deterioration in the profitability of the moving–average trading rule after the years examined by Brock et al. (1992). Brock et al. (1992) examine the years 1897–1986, so Urquhart et al. (2015) examine the subsequent period 1987 to 2013 as a sort of "hold-out" sample to determine the predictive value of Brock et al.'s results.

A finding that simple technical trading rules exhibit sporadic profitability supports the AMH over the EMH by implying the profitability of a given trading rule varies with the trading environment into which it is deployed. Here an efficient market, which holds here when the long and short–term averages lies within 1% point of one another, is just a special case which is certainly not the norm.

Urquhart et al. (2015) find that the moving–average trading rule is no longer profitable for the U.S.'s Dow Jones Industrial Index or the U.K.'s FT 30 Index.

But interestingly they also find that a simple reformulation (adaption?) of the original Brock et al. (1992) trading rule, given in Eq. (3.1), to allow for one day's anticipation of the moving–average rule signal to buy-sell, restores the trading rule to profitability. This suggests trader's relying on the rule may have learnt to adapt its use to the more forward–looking environment into which its being deployed after 1986; consistent with the AMH's description of how market strategies and the environments into which they are deployed co-evolve.

3.2 Biology repays the compliment: evolutionary game–theory in genetics

An interesting part of development of evolutionary game–theory is how it constitutes a rare example of a natural and social science program working co-operatively, rather than awkwardly staring at each other in disbelief. Lo and Mueller (2010) warn of the dangers of economists/finance academics simply lifting modelling techniques developed in Physics wholesale, but the cross-fertilisation between game–theorists working in Biology and Economics has been far more fruitful (Hammerstein, 2012).

The influence of Thomas Malthus's *Essays on the Principles of Population* (1798) on Darwin's *Origin of Species* (1859) is well known. Malthus warned of the dangers of competition for resources and Darwin pointed out a mechanism by which that competition occurred. An important distinction this interaction has produced, that might be usefully applied in a finance context, is the difference between an organism's genotype and phenotype. While the former is determined by the organism's genetic profile alone the latter is determined by the interaction of the organism's genotype and the environment into which it is deployed.

Frank (2011) points out an important point in favour of adapting a biological/Darwinian perspective is the importance of the *relative* strength of a trader's strategy in survival. Tests of the EMH usually look for evidence of significant, positive, returns to a strategy, being that contrarian, momentum, high-frequency, etc. But to win new adherents in a market a strategy does not have to be *absolutely* profitable, just *relatively* so.

Frank (2011) considers a number of examples where competition takes a relative form with socially damaging consequence. A sad example of this is the quest for military prowess. Often a country simply wants new weaponry to match, or trump, that of its rival. They seek "mutual assured destruction"; even while fully understanding the insanity of such an objective.

> *"losses from collective action problems are more difficult to remedy than those by individuals, they are also vastly larger than the losses caused by cognitive errors... economists a hundred years from now will be more likely to name Charles Darwin than Adam Smith as the intellectual founder of their discipline."*
>
> ***Frank (2011), p. xii***

Frank (2011) points out Darwin's work uncovers a tension between the interests of the individual animal/human and that of the species/humanity as a whole. He quotes Smith's *Wealth of Nations* (1776), (p. 213) as follows in describing the activity of traders as

> *"an order of men, whose interest is never exactly the same with that of the public, who generally have an interest to deceive and even oppress the public."*

One way in which can be done is via "manufactured needs"; such as the need to own the latest mobile phone, or training shoes. This divergence of our personal and private interest induces an excess of, or misplaced, competitive spirit.

Frank (2011) focuses on two weaknesses in the Smithian view of competition. These are that we are often

not attentive to costs, especially if they are small or are not immediately incurred, and,

more concerned with relative income status, compared to our peer group, and not the *absolute* income that Adam Smith was originally concerned with.

Everything's relative

In Nature we observe natural selection by means of comparative advantage. So bull elks with bigger antlers do better in fights for territory/female elks than their smaller horned peers. Unfortunately, beyond some point, having bigger antlers slows a bull elk's speed is escaping lions and other predators. So within species bigger antlers are better, but in cross-specie rivalry smaller antlers can be betters ones. So here reproductive fitness is a relative concept; the elk with the biggest antlers gets the female. But as a species elks might be better served by small, if not simply no, antlers. This reminds us not all evolutionary adaptions are positive, life-enhancing, or even useful to the Species that makes them (Popper, 1978).

This edge between the personal and social interest drives much of the alleged market failures we hear about. Frank points out, for example that the failure of labour managed firm to attract funding is unlikely to reflect a prejudice of capitalist bankers to fund labour–managed, proto communist, concerns.

Frank points out such conspiracy theory makes little sense; because if a firm offers a higher risk-adjusted return in response the offer of a loan an individual bank would be stupid to turn refuse to borrow to them. Even if the collapse of capitalism rested upon maintaining a social sanction against lending to worker–managed firms it is still in the bank's own interest to offer a loan at a higher interest rate than is justified by an objective assessment of the risk of recovering the loan from the labour–managed firm.

A crude version of classical economics puts selfishness and seeking to better your own interest in a central place. But we know a successful life requires us to co-operate, befriend, and build trust with others. This is especially true in family life. So while the Darwinian visions allow for a variety of mixed motivations, each representing a different aspect of a fertile life, economists, and especially financial economists, simply focus on one. Discussions of work–life balance, reflect the fact that a wealthy, but lonely, perhaps childless, life can seem an unattractive life to many of us.

Thus a Darwinian perspective on competition allows us to at least discuss a decision-maker's motives in a way standard finance precludes by its wealth–maximisation. Frank (2011, p. 41) states the division as follows

"Darwin clearly recognised, many of the most important domains of life are graded on a curve. It's relative, not absolute, income that predicts who will be able to buy a house in a good school district, or one with a breathtaking view. And when relative income is important, the invisible hand breaks down. There's no longer any clear reason to believe that individual incentives guide resources to their most valuable uses."

Hence intensely competitive markets are not, allocatively, efficient markets in a "Darwinian economy"; where competition is based on rank rather than absolute well-being.

The evolution of market equilibrium

So successive generations of off-spring reflect the interplay between nature and nurture. But what determines which genotype/environment combinations are most productive and swell in proportion to their competitors in future generations?

The traditional Nash equilibrium tells us what is the best strategy, given every other player in the game deploys their best strategy. But here the best strategy choices are known, to each player and to their competitors, under an assumption of "common knowledge" routinely applied in game–theory.

To answer the more dynamic question of what sort of genotype/environment combinations are the *fittest*, most successful in passing on their genes to later generations, evolutionary game–theory has refined the Nash equilibrium to describe an *Evolutionary Stable Equilibrium*, (ESE) which defines behaviour which will ultimately come to characterise, predominate in, the future population. The conception of an ESE is to some degree a useful refinement of a standard mixed-strategy Nash Equilibrium which is now widely used to discuss the evolution of social/economic/financial practice.

But an evolutionary game–theory approach also neatly circumvents one of the major drawbacks of regarding observed economic/social behaviour as the outcome of a Nash equilibrium in best strategies. This is the huge, computational demands such a feat requires of those playing such a game; which even in our digital age seem quite impractical.

We interact with others like ourselves and not all-seeing "Laplacian Demons".[2] In the evolutionary equilibrium, the best, fittest, strategies are selected by trial and error in successive generations of the players' chosen strategies. A pointless mutation in one generation might become a life-saving characteristic in the next.

A simple evolutionary game

A classic toy game, featuring in many game–theory textbooks, used to indicate the relative value of co-operative versus confrontational strategies is the Hawk-Dove game, illustrated in Fig. 3.3. In this game Hawks always fight for food if they encounter other birds in foraging. Doves, by contrast, always share with the other bird they meet while foraging. So if a Hawk meets a Dove its tough luck for the Dove, because they will simply have to surrender the food, of value equal to V.

But fighting itself is costly as it results in one of the two hawks being wounded at a cost to them of W. Here we assume $W > V$, so when two Hawks meet they can expect the resulting fight to hurt them on average (although sometimes they will be lucky of course), despite the value of the food they may win by fighting. Here we assume all hawks have an equal chance of winning a fight. Doves never fight.

In this game it is ratio $\frac{V}{W}$ which determines the relative *fitness* of the Hawk/Dove strategies, with increases in W, the cost of fighting, reducing the attractions of the Hawk strategy. Where fitness here is defined as the ability to attract converts to the strategy based on its relatively higher expected pay-off.

In the Hawk-Dove game there are three strict equilibria, two in pure strategies, one in mixed. These are

1st pure Hawk, Dove.

2nd pure Dove, Hawk.

mixed A mixed strategy equilibrium in which both strategies are played with some probability.

While the pure-strategy equilibrium strategy is clear, one wonders in what proportion the Hawk/Dove strategies can be mixed to yield

[2] "An intellect which at a certain moment would know all forces that set nature in motion, and all positions of all items of which nature is composed, if this intellect were also vast enough to submit these data to analysis, it would embrace in a single formula the movements of the greatest bodies of the universe and those of the tiniest atom; for such an intellect nothing would be uncertain and the future, just like the past, would be present before its eyes.", p. 4, Laplace (1951).

Strategies	Hawk	Dove
Hawk	$\frac{1}{2}(V-W)$ $\frac{1}{2}(V-W)$	V 0
Dove	0 V	$\frac{1}{2}V$ $\frac{1}{2}V$

Figure 3.3 The Hawk-Dove game. *Note*: See Section 3, pp. 937–942 of Hammerstein and Selten (1994) and Chapter 6 of Carmichael (2005).

Strategies	Hawk	Dove
Hawk	$\frac{1}{2} \times (V - W) = \frac{1}{2} \times (5 - 10) = -2.5$ $\frac{1}{2} \times (V - W) = \frac{1}{2} \times (5 - 10) = -2.5$	$V = 5$ 0
Dove	0 $V = 5$	$\frac{1}{2}V = \frac{1}{2} \times 5 = 2.5$ $\frac{1}{2}V = \frac{1}{2} \times 5 = 2.5$

Figure 3.4 Illustrative Hawk-Dove game. *Note*: See Section 3, pp. 937–942 of Hammerstein and Selten (1994) and Chapter 6 of Carmichael (2005).

an equilibrium? In any equilibrium we might expect the Hawk/Dove strategies to be mixed until their expected pay-offs (EPO_H, EPO_D) are equalised.

A numerical example of playing Hawk-Dove game

To see this let us put some illustrative numbers into the Hawk/Dove game of Fig. 3.3 in Fig. 3.4, where we assume the value of the food resource the birds fight over is 5, V=5, and cost of being wounded in a fight over that food is 10, W=10.

Here the expected pay-off to the two strategies, assuming they are played in equal proportion, is calculated as follows:

Expected pay-off to deploying Hawk strategy $= EPO_H = \frac{1}{2} \times -2.5 + \frac{1}{2} \times 5 = 1.25$

Expected pay-off to deploying Hawk strategy $= EPO_D = \frac{1}{2} \times 2.5 + \frac{1}{2} \times 0 = 1.25$

It appears that when the Hawk and Dove strategies are played equally often the pay-offs they can be expected to yield are equalised. But this outcome is sensitive to the ratio $\frac{V}{W}$.

If one of the strategies has a higher expected pay-off we might expect it to get new adherents, while the relatively unattractive strategy wanes. Hammerstein and Selten (1994) show how the trajectory of the evolutionary stable equilibrium can be traced across successive generation of birds (1994, p. 938).

When history matters: conditions for dynamic conditions for an evolutionary stable state

To do this consider a large population of players/birds, living in discrete, non over-lapping generations. A strong convention to support a particular strategy has arisen (say a Hawk or Dove strategy, be mean or be nice). Assume the conventional strategy is played with some, high, probability, p.

One bright morning over the horizon appears a stranger who brings a new strategy to the game, r, which enters into the game with some frequency x_t. Then the average strategy of that generation's population, q_t is given by the equation

$$q_t = (1 - x_t)p + x_t r \qquad (3.2)$$

The total fitness of the generation in the new generation is the sum of its pre-existing fitness, F, plus the pay-off to the evolutionary game of that generation, including the strategies deployed by the new, stranger, players/birds with their mutant strategy, r.

So the relative fitness in the new generation of stranger/mutant strategy players versus the majority population into which they are entering, who play strategy p, are given by the equations

$$F + E(r, q_t)$$
$$F + E(p, q_t) \qquad (3.3)$$

where F is the established fitness of the previous generation, averaged over the mutant strategy entrants of the prior generation and their majority, p playing, hosts. $E(r, q_t)$ and $E(p, q_t)$ are the expected pay-offs to the newly arrived stranger, playing the mutant strategy, r, and its more established competitor, p, respectively.

The relative *fitness* of the two strategies, p and r, is demonstrated by the ability of the mutant strategy playing strangers in successive generations to add to their own number, i.e. $\frac{x_{t+1}}{x_t}$. Where the trajectory of mutant's fitness is traced by the difference equation

$$x_{t+1} = \frac{F + E(r, q_t)}{F + E(q_t, q_t)} x_t \qquad \forall t = 0, 1, 2, \ldots \qquad (3.4)$$

For an evolutionary stable equilibrium we require the proportion of mutants in the overall population to converge on zero in the long run, so $x_t \to 0$ as $t \to \infty$.

To evaluate this limiting condition we examine the difference in relative frequency of mutant/strangers, playing r, in successive generations

$$x_t - x_{t+1} = \frac{E(q_t, q_t) - E(r, q_t)}{F + E(q_t, q_t)} x_t \qquad (3.5)$$

Clearly for x_t to be declining the expected pay-off to the currently most popular strategy, p, must be superior to the incoming mutant strategy, r, so the numerator of Eq. (3.5) must be positive. It is thus a condition of an evolutionary stationary equilibrium that the right–hand–side of Eq. (3.4) converges to 0 over time.

But note for the trajectory of mutant strategies both past fitness, F, and current relative pay-offs, to playing either p or r, matter in determining which strategy finally dominates. So the past matters for current conditions in a way that neo-classical economics has generally preferred to ignore.

3.2.1 Social heuristics, conformity, ostentation and self-deprecation

A primary insight of evolutionary theory is that we are a product of both nature and nurture. Each of us are a mixture of where we come from and how we have lived, what we are given and what we have made. Part of what makes us is our social circle, of family, friends, colleagues and it should not surprise us that our social circle hugely informs both our beliefs and the choices we make based on those believes.

Pachur et al. (2004) point out the importance and predictive power of limited search amongst those we know best, to resolve simple questions of frequency, for example, which name is more common, Martin or Simon? Or which cancer is more common bladder or renal cancer? One easy way to resolve these questions is to look at our own name or health. If we are called neither name, or had neither cancerous condition, we might look to our family, for Martins or Simons or bladder/renal cancer victims. If our family proves uninformative we might look to a broader, social circle of friends and colleagues.

Such inference based on successively larger, but still small, samples always runs the risk of errors such over inference can bring. Galesic et al. (2012) (p. 1) summarise the evidence thus

"Across cultures, people appear to suffer from self–enhancement biases, such as better-than-average and optimism biases, which lead them to believe they have better traits (e.g., friendliness and intelligence), and future prospects than others do... Why would people be consistently biased in representing their social environment? The dominant explanation is motivational bias: People distort reality to improve their sense of self–esteem and well-being."

This is the very social posturing, ostentation and misplaced pride that we find amusing in colleagues and friends; yet seem impervious to in ourselves. But as Pachur et al. (2013a) point out the reason why such (over) inference, from small sample, social circle, heuristics, endure is precisely because they work so well. It appears that our minds' work as an "intuitive pollster" (Pachur et al., 2013b) precisely because the social circle, limited search, heuristic competes so well with full–information strategies, especially in environments with a skewed distribution of outcomes. The presence of right–hand skew in asset prices has already launched a vibrant literature in the standard behavioural finance literature (Barberis and Huang, 2008). An understanding of the social circle heuristic may yet help resolve these apparent anomalies.

3.3 History matters

The separation of economics, history, and sociology is now embedded in Graduate School training and University Library shelves. But this was not always the case. The demise of political economy and the emergence of Economics as a separate "scientific" discipline left behind a rich tradition which allowed history to have a more explicit role in the development of theory.

Hodgson (2001) has traced the influence and insights of the German Historical School and their descendants the American Institutionalists. Hodgson (2001, p. xvi) laments the delegation of duties the triumph of neo-classical economics required, stating:

"In abandoning its former historical orientation economics as a whole was radically transformed. It lost its emphasis on the study of real, socio-economic systems, instead to become a deductivist exploration of "individual choice". The task of the choosing agent was consigned to psychology."

In this drive for an ever more general theory neo–classical economists were emulating the greatest achievements of Science, Isaac Newton and his laws of motion, Faraday and his theory of electro magnetic radiation. But the outsourcing of psychology by economists has come at a high price.

John Clark, recognised the problem a century ago warning[3]

"The Economist may ignore Psychology, but it is sheer impossibility to ignore human nature…. If the economist borrows his conception of man from the Psychologist, his constructive work may have some chance of remaining purely economic in character. But if he does not, he will not thereby avoid psychology. Rather he will force himself to make his own, and it will be bad psychology."

(Clark (1918), p. 4)

So the appeal to homo economicus, the economic man, is almost certainly a bridge too far in our ambition. But any knowledge claim based on pure empiricism is not so much "mindless" as futile.

Almost any empirical claim requires classification, measurement and some broad notion of causation, which invoke some implicit (and thus perhaps doubtful) theoretical distinctions. Any sane theorisation thus involves a theory of broad, but not universal, application.

3.3.1 Heuristic tools as guides to economic models

Here Gerd Gigerenzer's development of the "heuristic toolbox" (Gigerenzer and Selten (2002)) can be illuminating in determining which economic/social practice will emerge in the new evolutionary stable state. The biologists Levins and Lewontin (1985) point out "Things are similar: this makes science possible. Things are different: this makes science necessary".

A productive research method recognises the value of generalising, without engaging in overreach. Even without this recognition, the limits of computational power often necessitates some imposition of simplifying assumptions. When we consider a network within which there are n distinct nodes then $\frac{n \times (n-1)}{2}$ linkages are possible. When n is 1000 the number of possible connections in the system is about half a million.

If one wished to record whether such a connection was present in the network of nodes by a binary 0/1 code then the number of possible connections in the system is given by $2^{\frac{n \times (n-1)}{2}}$. When n=1000 this expres-

---

[3] I found this quotation in Professor Werner De Bondt's excellent teaching materials.

sion becomes $10^{150,000}$, a number even the most powerful computer might blanche at.

Such purely calculative tasks require limits, which most likely comes from our everyday knowledge of the structure of the task/environment into which the calculative method is being deployed. One example of this is the empirical vacuity of general equilibrium theory, despite its pristine elegance as a mathematical construct (see Radner (1968)).

General equilibrium theory posits markets in many good and services, at many dates, under many states of the world. Once again the computational demands implied can soon explode and some restriction on the range of goods traded, or possible states of nature arising, will be imposed. Hence general theories are almost useless for prediction/explanation and theories with empirical content are very far from general.

Out of the wreckage of the dreams of a truly general (equilibrium) theory in economics has emerged the idea of "exemplary" theory of common economic transactions, the labour contract, the initial public offering, the acquisition of another company, often by means of highly stylised games. Game Theory's ascendance began during early cold war and its "logic" of mutual assured destruction (Von Neumann and Morgenstern (1944)). But it's more intensive use in economics can be traced to the early 1980's when all hope of a viable form of general economic theory had been abandoned.

3.3.2 Heuristic tools for solving games of economic behaviour

As Fisher (1989) pointed out this shift in modelling strategy has not challenged the constraints on achieving theoretical results of general application. Indeed often the most studied game–theoretic results almost mock the possibility of making statements of general application.

One such result is the so called "folk theorem" which states that in an infinitely repeated game, with a low enough discount rate, any outcome that is individually rational can turn out to be a Nash Equilibrium. As Franklin Fisher puts it "anything that one might imagine as sensible can turn out to be the right answer" (Fisher, 1989, p. 116).

One aspect of imposing some much needed structure on general theories of economic/financial behaviours is to recognise socio–economic systems may need different models, as Karl Marx did with various "stages" of economic development or as the varieties of capitalism literature has done more recently (Hall and Soskice (2001)) in exploring how different tributaries of the capitalist economy have developed.

Hodgson (2001) points out while this problem of mapping the flow of history is now "forgotten", or simply dismissed as a naïve cry for a purely empirical approach, it featured heavily in the works of scholars of the German Historical School and the American institutional economists before the 2nd World War.

3.4 Adaptive regulation: the policy implications of accepting the AMH

For a contribution to financial debate be regarded as timely today it must shed some light on the defining event of the 2007/8 global financial crisis. Lo's book *Adaptive Markets* is certainly useful in alerting us to some seeming "fake news" regarding the roots of that Crisis. Lo rather debunks theories based on managerial greed, engorged by huge salary bonuses, and the relaxation of prudential regulations.

Lo points to a number of frustrated Cassandra like figures in the run up to the Crisis. Amongst academics the Nobel Prizewinner Robert Shiller and Ragu Rajan provided separate, but equally dismissed, warnings. Similarly, amongst senior risk managers both Madelyn Antonic at Lehmans and Paul Moore at HBOS were belittled and marginalised by their respective employers prior to their subsequent collapse, as they had predicted (MacDonald and Robinson (2009), Moore and Haworth (2015)).

A commonly advanced cause of the Crisis, which Lo accepts, is the evaporation of liquidity in securitised debt, and subsequently, equity markets, especially in the summer of 2007. Here Lo points to the market impact of the SEC's reform to make price quotes on the NYSE move in single pennies, rather than eighths/12 $\frac{1}{2}$ penny, segments. This move allowed hedge funds to post keener prices, with lower bid–ask spreads, than traditional market–makers.

But market–makers have an obligation to trade, regardless of market conditions; whereas hedge funds can run for cover, simply withdrawing from the market, or reduce trading volumes, in periods of market turbulence. Not surprisingly, given the competition they faced from hedge funds, who cherry–picked trades in good times, but quit the market in bad, many market–makers simply ceased to exist between the introduction of decimalisation of spreads in 2001 and the initial stirrings of the Crisis in 2007. A regulatory change had an unforeseen effect, producing an imbalance in the equity markets, with too many players, with high deal–flow, but not enough capital, compared to liquidity providers/market–makers willing to serve their needs.

If the AMH can help us diagnose the causes of the Crisis can it also help with developing a cure, or devise an early warning station, for future Crises? Lo points out both the growing importance of the financial sector as a whole and the failure of regulatory structures to adapt to the finance sector's importance. Lo shows how reports investigating the Crisis show the SEC was both underfunded, bureaucratic, and risk adverse in its prosecution strategy, fearing public criticism that might lead to even deeper funding cuts.

In discussion similar to much of that in the UK's Turner (2009) Review, Lo points out the laissez-faire view that markets were their own best healer, with bad practice being punished by clients, was pushed too far in the years running up to 2008. Politicians primary concern were growing regulatory burdens in an era when the basic conditions for market stability were being eroded.

Lo reviews evidence that both accounting fraud and Ponzi schemes are strongly pro–cyclical (Dyck et al. (2014), Deason et al. (2015)). So it appears financial regulators are encouraged to back off in boom markets, despite the fact that these are the times when their attention is most needed. This implies political control might be inducing a failure by financial regulators to adapt to the environment in which they operate.

3.5 How market, technological and regulatory environments interact

Another aspect of the changing environment in financial markets, on which Lo is well qualified to comment, is how technology, especially cheap computing power, has facilitated the growth of financial markets. To illustrate this Lo explains how the fortuitous arrival of the SR-52 programmable Texas Instrument hand-held calculator, at the same time as the opening of the Chicago Board of Trade (CBOT), and the Black–Scholes formula, that priced the options traded on the Chicago Board of Trade, hugely expanded derivatives trading. While derivatives markets certainly existed before computing tools to price the contracts traded upon them their growth has been hugely enhanced by that technology's power.

Lo points out such hugely empowering technology brings its own limitations in the form of hidden unintended consequences, illustrations of which include the "Flash Crash" of May 6th 2010 and in an earlier age the

1987 financial crash, when orders embedded in portfolio insurance computer programs served to turn a drama into a considerable Crisis; albeit one with little long-run effect (MacKenzie (2008), Garret and Antoniou (1993)).

Lo points out that Moore's law of the rapid progression of computing power here meets Murphy's law that "what can happen will happen". This reminds us of the hidden depth charges in the digital technology that enhances our daily lives. So while technology empowers financial professionals it also exposes them to, often concealed, dangers in an environment changed in a way none intended and perhaps no–one fully understands.

At the end of his book *Adaptive Markets* Lo asks what is the value-added of the AMH in preventing, rather than just understanding, a financial crisis? Once again the image of an ecological system prevails. We cannot understand individual events, the evaporation of liquidity in the asset–backed commercial paper market in late 2007, the collapse of Lehman's in late 2008, in isolation but rather as moving parts in an inter–locking financial system.

Locating blame in individual actors, greedy bankers, or clueless regulators, ignores the financial systems own dynamics and replicating mechanisms. A core regulatory concept has to be the sustainability of the financial system as currently constituted.

A central issue is the financial system's ability to generate systemic risk. While systemic risk is at the core of standard asset–pricing models, in the form of weightings on the market premium, the small–minus–big and "value" premium, all these measures assume deeply liquid markets in which investors are price-takers. But in reality in a financial crisis the first victim is market liquidity, this is because of the sudden evaporation of liquidity often appears in over-the-counter markets dominated by a relatively small number of traders for whom trust in their counter-parties is vital.

New measures of systematic risk

Hence Lo and colleagues are exploring new measures of risk based on connectedness and proximity (Billio et al. (2012)). Since what gets measured gets managed we might expect such systematic risk metrics to be of increasing interest to market regulators. Based on their current evidence Lo concludes that the "connectedness" of financial institutions, especially banks, has been increasing in recent decades, rendering atomistic, price-taker, models of price–formation of doubtful worth. An aspiration for such models of connectedness is that they might be used to predict critical points of exposure from which a "liquidity spiral" might emerge (Brunnermeier (2009)).

Lo argues that such control of systematic risk cannot be delegated to individual financial institutions, because this ignores the fact that in taking on higher risk in the "search for yield" each individual institution generates an externality, of a contribution to systematic risk, that needs to be controlled; and perhaps more controversially taxed, and thereby priced. By doing so a regulator can bestow the "gift of pain" which serves as a natural curb on excessive risk-taking.

One of the most common narratives of the Crisis is that financial institutions behaved as you might expect given the regulatory system they faced (Roberts (2010)). One reason for this is just the bewildering complexity of the system of laws in place to regulate financial transactions. This allows redundancy and contradictions to enter the legal treatment of financial transactions a skillful lawyer, or compliance officer, can exploit.

To try to reduce these unintended regulatory consequences Lo suggests evaluating "Law as Code" and looking for inter-connections between legal provisions that might serve to frustrate the original regulatory/judicial intent. To do this Lo and co-authors use the tools of network analysis, originally used by transport/engineering specialists, to investigate regulatory underlap, overlap, and contradiction (Li et al. (2015)).

One piece of legislation Lo and his colleagues examine in this regard is the Dodd–Frank Act of 2010, issued as a response to the 2007/8 Crisis. This reveals that legislation to be rife with implicit connections and dependencies, ready to generate unintended consequences, or simply frustrate the genuine intent of those who passed the legislation.

3.5.1 Evidence of intensifying systematic risk

While being in awe of the theoretical sophistication of models of the transition and accumulation of systematic risk within the financial system one may wonder how great this problem is in practice? Billio et al. (2012) present evidence that the degree of connectedness between key financial institutions is both large and increasing, as financial innovation and the need to comply common regulatory regime, intensifies financial connectedness and consequent dislocation in times of market downturn.

The authors point out that when we think about systematic risk/contagion we might focus on the "four L's" (Billio et al., 2012, p. 537); these being

1. leverage,
2. liquidity,
3. losses, and,
4. linkages.

Billio et al. note while measures of the first three factors in systematic risk/transmission already exist much less is known about how to measure financial linkages that might serve to propagate losses during a market downturn. A common feature of existing measures (such as CoVaR developed by Adrian and Brunnermeier (2016)) is that they rely on patterns in previously realised losses across competing/connected financial institutions.

Billio et al. (2012, p. 536) argue the major losses in monoline insurance companies were not at all correlated with those of hedge funds prior to 2007. That such monoline insurer losses became predictive of hedge fund losses resulted from the movement of hedge funds into trading on credit default swaps which underwrote potential defaults on mortgage–backed securitised debts.

Major inflections in the stock market coincide with volatility spikes, compared to the tranquillity of intervening periods. Billio et al. try to circumvent these problems by modelling financial linkages between the returns to the largest 25 institutions in four important types of players in financial markets; these are hedge funds, banks, broker/dealers, and insurance companies over five three–year time–periods that seem somewhat similar in terms of systemic risk bracketed by the years 1994–2008.

Concluding their analysis Billio et al. (2012, p. 555) state

> "the financial system has become considerably more complex over the past two decades ... While such complexity is an inevitable consequence of competition and economic growth, it is accompanied by certain consequences, including much greater interdependence."

The limits of disclosure remedies

While clarity regarding the causes of past crises may help with avoiding future needless loss it is also true the "crime scene" of a national/global financial collapse may be less clear than in an airplane crash, or terrorist attack, given the nature of the accumulation of systematic risk Lo explains so well earlier in his book.

Nor will a simple revelation of the facts deter those who stand to profit from an impending crisis, by taking the other side of the trade to those in the grip of the prevailing market frenzy (Lewis (2010)). So such disclosure, while certainly useful, cannot be regarded as a fully effective buttress against future financial crises.

A further objection to such candid disclosure by financial institutions is that they nearly always regard their trading model, strategies, and positions, as proprietary and may go to huge lengths to avoid the very disclosures a CSI of financial crises requires. Here advances in computerised multi–party computation methods may allow for the very pooling of information, on an anonymised basis, any effective oversight of the build up systematic risk must require (Abbe et al. (2012)). So while advances in computational ease have certainly served to enhance the volatility of financial markets, that very technology may yet supply its own cure to the instability it generates.

But Lo is clear that while regulatory tweaks can enhance financial stability radical change will require major changes in the way financial institutions are governed. One such reform is giving the Chief Risk Officer the right to suspend a CEO's authority, if they ignore written requests to reduce critical risks. Another is that CEOs might be held criminally liable for any broader societal damage their actions cause.

Lo notes that the excessive risk-taking of financial institutions is mirrored in the timidity/risk-aversion of regulators, fearing unjustified prosecutions will cause their political masters to cut their funding. Further regulators have to be willing to be more aggressive when markets are rising and any problems are not yet obvious.

Thus traders and regulators need to adapt their strategies to evolving market conditions, with financial institutions becoming less risk–loving and regulators less risk-averse. But this call for adaptive regulation seems in tension with a liberal view that emphasises the stability of legal restrictions; that allow agents to order their affairs to anticipate the effect of legal challenges and, if desired, offset the impact of such unwanted interventions (Epstein (1995)).

Lo states

"Like Darwin's theory of evolution, the Adaptive Market Hypothesis is a predictive theory. ... its sometimes difficult to think in evolutionary and ecological terms, but sooner or later this way of thinking will be domesticated, and will become a standard tool for economists to use."

(Lo (2017), p. 245)

3.6 Evolutionary rationality versus rationality

While it is a central tenet of the EMH that current prices are independent of past ones the reverse is the case under the AMH. The AMH sees current price/quantity choices as the outcome of both past choices/trade-offs and anticipated ones. So under the AMH "history matters", because we are the product of past evolutionary selection.

But, uniquely mankind is not just the product of the mindless evolutionary refinement of our forebears to their environment; but also of the selection, adaption, and abandonment of ideas by others facing similar choices to ourselves now. So while not smoking certainly enhances my evolutionary fitness I do not have to wait for that evolutionary selection process to occur if I allow myself to be guided by the academic consensus that smoking is a serious health danger that was already in place when I was born.

One laboratory in which Lo suggests we might see the adaptive market hypothesis at work is the hedge fund industry. Lo describes this as containing about 9000 funds worthwhile with $2 trillion under management (in 2017, when *Adaptive Markets* was published). The industry covers a wide variety of trading strategies and asset portfolios, with some huge successes, like George Soros or John Paulson, but many more transient failures.

The evolution of trading strategies

While any one individual billionaire might simply be "lucky" it is more difficult to understand the development of a whole industry based on a fortunate few. For Lo the hedge funds industry is the "Galapicos islands" of finance, where high leverage and frequent failure allows us to see financial evolution in all its savagery. Indeed Lo suggests hedge funds fortunes might even be predictive of broader changes in market sentiment.

While early funds relied on chartist methods later incarnations relied on the divergence in prices induced by "paired" block trades, when one stock is shorted to cover another block purchase. Perhaps the high point of hedge fund power was LTCM, formed in 1994, by John Meriwether the legendary bond trader with two future Nobel Prizewinners on the staff.

LTCM exploited small differences in bond prices which were unlikely to persist based on observed fundamentals. LTCM was unusual largely in its scale and breadth of operation, which meant its collapse in 1998 was a matter of public policy concern. Lo points out that LTCM's collapse had the beneficial effect of causing hedge funds to rejig their business models, reducing the dislocation caused by the implosion of subsequent hedge funds during the 2007–2008 Crisis; surely a useful evolutionary adaption from a societal viewpoint.

A more recent species of traders to progress along their evolutionary path are high-frequency traders (HFT), who initially swept all before them due to their ability to execute arbitrage trades before a human mind could even conceive of that trade as a possibility. Over time the increased capitalisation of the industry has meant HFT traders square–off against each other in an increasingly pointless arms race to lower trade execution speeds. Financial evolution has by now exposed the evolutionary limits of HFT trading.

Another type of observed differentiation in trading strategy is amongst passive investors, especially mutual funds, amongst whom initially indices constructed using equally–weighted constituents were usually favoured. Recent reductions in the cost of recalculating constituent weights and executing the necessary portfolio rebalancing now mean a much wider variety of weighting schemes, based on ethics or sovereign risk, can be easily implemented.

3.7 A new theory for a new time

In the latter part of his book *Adaptive Markets* Lo addresses to "so what" question, AMH/EMH who cares really? He begins by pointing out how an evolutionary finance perspective goes to the root of Finance theory and received wisdom regarding investment practice.

If we regard the core of Finance as being five principles; a risk/reward trade-off, the CAPM model, portfolio theory, the centrality of asset allocation, the dominance of equity as an asset class in the long-run, the AMH reminds us of the sensitivity of the undoubted wisdom contained in these principles to the environment into which they are deployed.

So while the CAPM's, α's, and β's are commonly estimated under the assumption of a stationary stock price distribution we know that assumption is unrealistic. While all models, including the AMH, require assumptions to make them workable Lo argues that observed deviations from the assumptions of standard financial models have been growing in recent years.

New models for new markets?

While the U.S. data drawn from 1930 to 2005 or so seemed to very much accord with the principles of standard finance, stated above, recently there have been problems; with greater volatility, both over time and at any point in time. Is this a blip? Lo argues it is not and the environment in which financial markets operate is fundamentally changing, necessitating a change in our theorisation of it.

Lo points out you can trace changes in required equity investor margin requirements into subsequent volatility changes, with increased margins dampening stock market volatility, suggesting how sensitive equity markets are to changes in the regulatory regime. Even the risk/return trade-off, which underpins nearly all financial discussion, is revealed by Lo to be largely a long–term phenomena with considerable periods when returns rose but stock market volatility fell lying along that long-run path. The stock market's bipolar swings in this regard accord with the thoughts of many investors who see only good stocks, offering high returns and low risk, and bad stocks that offer the reverse (DeBondt (1998)).

Financial markets, like any other, are a complex web, of counter-parties who stand willing to trade contingent assets/liabilities. Such a supportive trader ecology is unsurprisingly brittle and prone to breakdown. Evidence exists of the recent financial crisis being triggered by the need of highly leveraged hedge funds "unwinding" their equity portfolios in early August 2007 because their need to cover positions in credit securitised debt instruments.

In June 2007 two of Bear Stearn's funds trading credit derivatives had folded and in July Solwood Capital Management sold its portfolio to Citadel, after losing half its value (Khandani and Lo (2007), p. 5), by early August signs of distress began to spill over into equity markets. Khandani and Lo (2011) state

> *"[our] results suggest that the Quant Meltdown of August 2007 began in July with the steady unwinding of one or more factor driven portfolios and this unwinding caused dislocation in August because the pace of liquidation increased and liquidity providers decreased their risk capital during the second week of August."*
>
> **(Khandani and Lo (2011), p. 3)**

While the market distress was short lived, between August 7th and 10th, many funds liquidated their portfolios before the market rebound occurred. The sharp growth in the funds allocated to contrarian equity portfolios caused their return to decline dramatically in the early naughties, leading those trading such portfolios to heavily lever their market positions. This made them more exposed to temporary market declines.

Such large average losses, of the order of 15.98% on average to long/short equity portfolios, over the two day period August 7th and 8th, according to the calculations of Khandani and Lo (2007) (p. 16), were very likely to cause further liquidations elsewhere. This triggered further losses on the 9th of August, of 11.43% according to Khandani and Lo's calculation.

While the market reversal of the 10th of August largely unwound these losses it was no doubt too late for many funds forced to liquidate their high leveraged portfolios (Shleifer and Vishny (1997)). Such an unravelling of market liquidity was perhaps to be expected given the increasing correlation of hedge funds returns (Khandani and Lo (2007), p. 33).

3.8 Conclusion

The AMH offers a coherent and in many ways compelling alternative to the dominant EMH in whose shadow we have all studied and practised financial decision-making. Its appeal has been enhanced both by the decline in standard finance theory's status following the 2008 financial crisis and by indicators that financial markets are set for even more dramatic change. The impact of technological and regulatory reform means the degree of connectivity and possibilities for network failure, such as the flash crash of 2010 (Easley et al., 2011) will increase. Such interdependence will make the focus on the evolution, emergence, and abandonment of alternative trading strategies even more attractive. The connection between heuristic decision-making and financial regulatory environment is discussed in Chapter 4.

In the longer–term the AMH might answer the "its takes a theory to beat a theory" challenge of standard finance scholars. It can do so by replacing the dominant classical definition of investor rationality with an ecological one which is more congruent with fast-and-frugal reasoning. This might allow a common set of modelling techniques, capable of general, application to emerge. The conditions under which this transition might arise are discussed below in Chapter 5.

CHAPTER 4

Financial regulations and heuristics*

4.1 An unlevelled playfield

Regulators play an impossible game in a volatile uncertain environment. They must collect an enormous amount of information, consider various aspects of every possible case, and provide clear guidelines for prudent practices in financial and other markets. On the other side of a drastically unlevel playfield, financial institutions only have to deal with the challenge spelled out for them. Their sole task is to find ways of circumventing some clearly outlined regulations in order to achieve their own goals. It is a task they perform efficiently and skillfully every time, leaving regulators almost immediately with new problems to tackle.

This familiar cat-and-mouse chase continues over cycles of regulation and deregulation. The cycle moves and repeats in this order: economic turn-down and/or crisis creates angry crowds who pressure legislators for remedy and revenge; legislators pass new financial regulations; firms fight back by lobbying and eventually get their way once the turmoil subsides and pressure from constituents lessens so that legislators can, at little risk of losing reelection votes, please the interest groups ((Shefrin and Statman, 2009) and (Shefrin, 2010)).

In a playing field where the regulators' act is constrained by mandates of transparency and justification, regulations are slowed down and eventually defanged. This might be an inevitable result emanating from the central principle of democracy wherein public servants must always be tamed and contained so they cannot exploit social resources for their own benefit. But if regulators must have restrained power, the only way to save society from the eminent danger of exploitation by interest groups will be to limit their power to influence law and regulation making. An important source of power in the hands of interest groups is the amount they are allowed to spend on lobbying, as well as on campaign contributions and other forms of offerings to legislators. Alarmingly, the developments after the great reces-

* This chapter is written by Shabnam Mousavi.

A Fast and Frugal Finance
https://doi.org/10.1016/B978-0-12-812495-6.00011-2

sion of 2008 have by and large taken the opposite direction of constricting interest groups' influence.

A major blow to democratic processes of the society at every imaginable level was enacted in 2010 when the case of Citizen United vs. Federal Election Commission led to a final 5 to 4 vote by the Supreme Court of the United States[1] allowing unlimited spending of private money on political pursuits. The ensuing domination of the political arena by super PACs[2] (political action committees) and their effect on the political outcomes today undermines the spirit of democracy by steering public opinion through spending, in unprecedented ever-magnifying scales, for or against any candidate who runs for public office. In 2018 so far (October), the existing 2,127 super PACs have raised together a whopping $791,752,477.3.[3] Against this superbly well-fuelled machinery of opinion making by money, regulators have been hard at work to craft safety and stability structures for the financial practices in society. Their work has both calculative and behavioural aspects, with the second being less explicitly explored ((Mousavi and Shrefrin, 2010), (Mousavi and Kheirandish, 2017), (Viale et al., 2018)).[4]

The goal of this chapter is to elaborate on some behavioural aspects involved in the making and enforcement of financial regulations. The behavioural principles that guide our discussions are the following. Behaviour, in general, is shaped in interaction with the environment in which it emerges. In particular, the financial environment is shaped initially by regulators and then continuously reshaped and modified through the efforts of interest groups. At any given time, the shape of regulations can be viewed as a result of who has "captured" whom among the main three players: politicians, regulators, and interest groups (Stigler, 1971). At the societal level, regulators can be viewed as risk managers, where the nature of risk they are tasked to curb is highly uncertain ((Shrefrin, 2013), (Shrefrin, 2016)).

---

[1] https://www.publicintegrity.org/2012/10/18/11527/citizens-united-decision-and-why-it-matters.

[2] https://www.merriam-webster.com/dictionary/super%20PAC.

[3] https://www.opensecrets.org/outsidespending/summ.php?chrt=V&type=S.

[4] Shefrin (2010) in Chapter 7. Behaviouralizing the Approach to Financial Market Regulation, provides a rigorous approach to behavioural elements of financial regulations and a juxtaposition to the traditional framework. Mousavi and Kheirandish (2017) provide an overview of the initial steps taken by the Obama administration for informing policymaking through incorporation of behavioural science. And Viale et al. (2018) provides an edited volume that brings together practitioners, banks/regulators, and scholars for finding methods to improve financial security.

One set of tools for dealing with such uncertainty are heuristics (Mousavi and Gigerenzer, 2017), which are frequently called upon under situations of limited resources, including time. As we saw in Chapter 1, a given heuristic is signified by limited search for information and reaching a decision based on incomplete information; it is frugal. Hence, the understanding of heuristic decision making is relevant to better understanding the processes involved in regulation making and most other public administration tasks faced with similar conditions. Furthermore, heuristic-based modelling techniques can make effective tools for delivering results in public sector. We illustrate these connections by reporting some research that has been generated in such framework.

Two major financial regulation platforms recently developed in the Western world are the 2010 financial regulation overhaul in the USA and the Basel Accords in Europe.[5] In what follows, we first look at an exercise of predicting the outcome of 2010 financial overhaul in the USA, which combined behavioural principles with game theoretic operational power and resulted in a highly accurate prediction (Mousavi and Shrefrin, 2010). Then we provide an overview of a project on financial stability from the Bank of England, which used fast-and-frugal decision trees to identify the vulnerability of banks and performed better than information-exhausting techniques (Aikman et al., 2014). The chapter closes with a summary.

4.2 Predicting the configuration of financial regulations

In 2009, when the US congress was working on the financial regulation overhaul later known as the Dodd–Frank Bill, Shefrin, and Mousavi developed an exercise to predict the final configuration of the legislation. They adopted the game theoretic platform of negotiations, the Predictioneer's Game, developed by de Mesquita (2009) (2009, BdM hereafter) and designated six main players involved in shaping the financial regulations overhaul: House Democrats, House Republicans, Senate Democrats, Senate Republicans, Administration/President Obama, interest groups/industry (see Table 4.1). For each player the input parameters for the BdM

[5] An elaborate and accurate review and assessment of bank regulatory structures commissioned by the European Commission was executed by a group of experts under Erkki Liikanen of the Bank of Finland. The report including their notable recommendations, released in 2012 in Brussels, can be found at: https://ec.europa.eu/info/system/files/liikanen-report-02102012_en.pdf. (Credit is due to Markus Schuler for bringing this to my attention.)

Table 4.1 Players and inputs for the BdM Predictioneer's Game.

Name	Position	Salience	Influence	Flexibility	Veto
Senate Republicans	50	30	50	50	N
Senate Democrats	85	80	80	60	N
House Republicans	40	30	20	40	N
House Democrats	70	80	80	60	N
Obama Administration	65	70	30	90	Y
Financial Firms	30	99	70	20	N

Source: Mousavi and Shrefrin, 2010.

game were assessed based on our take on public announcements and media reports on a linear scale between 10 and 100.

The five input parameters of the BdM game are defined as follows.

Position which indicates the value of players' respective most preferred outcome, with 100 indicating a complete change of the status quo; Senate Democrats desired the highest amount of change, whereas House Republicans aimed for the least change.

Salience reflects the resources each player devotes to negotiation on the matter, with 100 meaning the highest priority on the list; firms have the highest score because they drop everything else to attend to this negotiation.

Influence measures the degree to which a player can persuade others to shift their positions; Democrats have the highest scores because they held the majority in the House and the Senate.

Flexibility indicates the amount of compromise that can be expected for achieving an agreement instead of no agreement; the Obama administration held the highest desire to make this overhaul come through, instead of retaining the status quo.

Veto right, a binary variable, is held by only one of the players, the administration.

4.2.1 Dodd–Frank Bill of 2010: the financial regulation overhaul

Prompted by the financial crisis of 2008, President Obama initiated in June 2009 the legal procedure for a new regulatory framework that would provide centralised oversight (mainly under the Fed) as well as elaborate provisions for consumer protection. The House passed the *Wall Street Reform and Consumer Protection Act* of 2009 in December with no support from Republicans (223 to 202). This Act was then negotiated and modified at the Senate, which passed in May 2010 (59 to 39) under the *Restoring Amer-*

ican Financial Stability Act of 2010; with the following four major provisions (Mousavi and Shrefrin, 2010):

1. *Consumer Financial Protection* (**CP**): A bureau to be housed within the Federal Reserve; to crack down on swipe fees that retailers pay when customers use debit cards.

2. *Derivatives/Financial Risk* (**DER/FI**): Trades of derivatives to take place in regulated exchanges; the so-called "Volcker Rule" prohibiting proprietary trading; the Lincoln Provision's requiring banks to spin off all their derivatives business into subsidiaries; banks with more than US$250bn in assets must meet capital standards at least as strict as those that apply to smaller banks.

3. *Too Big to Fail* (**TBF**): Banks will be taxed to pay for unwinding banks after a collapse; the GAO (Government Accountability Office of the USA) would conduct a one-time examination of the Fed's emergency lending to financial institutions in the months surrounding the 2008 financial crisis.

4. General Issues (**GI**): Creates a nine-member Financial Services Oversight Council; shareholders would have the right to cast non-binding votes on executive pay packages; the Fed sets standards on excessive compensation that would be deemed unsafe and unsound practice for the bank; an independent board would select ratings agencies to assess the risks of new financial products, replacing a long-standing practice where banks select and pay ratings agencies to rate their new offerings; lenders would be required to obtain proof from borrowers that they can pay for their mortgages.

Each one of these four provisions could have ended up more or less pronounced in the final bill. We decided to view each provision in terms of its main elements, which Table 4.2 lists under each provision in column 1. The other columns provide an ordered summary of final combinations, from the strongest possible version of each provision and its composing elements, extracted from the initial bills of the House or the Senate, in the first column to the weakest version imaginable in the last column. The columns in between these two extremes include the actual initial bills produced by the House of Representatives and the Senate, along with two other possible compromised final outcomes.

Table 4.2 reflects that in provision 1 above, the strongest version of consumer protection entails a stand-alone agency (placed in column 1), which means that a bureau under the auspices of the Federal Reserve Bank would relatively weaken this provision. The other items listed under consumer

Table 4.2 Listed from weak to strong: possible outcomes for the financial regulation bill.

		Strongest	Senate Bill	House Bill	Strong CP, NL/NV, weak TBF	Weak CP, NL/NV weak TBF	Weak CP, NL/NV, weak TBF, weak exchange, weak capital Stds	Weakest
CP	Consumer protection body	Standalone agency	Bureau in Fed	Standalone agency	Standalone agency	Bureau in Fed	Bureau in Fed	Bureau in Fed
	Auto industry exemption	No	No	Yes	No	Yes	Yes	Yes
	Restrict debit card swipe fee	Yes	Yes	No	Yes	No	No	No
	Mortgage proof of income	Yes	Yes	Yes	Yes	Yes	Yes	Yes
Der/FR	Lincoln Provision	Yes	Yes	No	No	No	No	No
	Volcker Rule	Yes, strong	Yes, strong	Yes, weak	Yes, strong	Yes, strong	Yes, weak	Yes, weak
	Der clearing/exchange	Yes, big like small banks		Yes, big and small	Yes, big like small banks	Yes, big like small banks		
	Capital standards		Yes, 15% cap				Yes, 15-to-1 D/NC	Yes, 15-to-1 D/NC
TBF	Too big to fail	$150bn fund ex ante	ex post tax	$150bn ex ante	ex post tax	ex post tax	ex post tax	ex post tax
GI	Executive pay	Investor say	Fed standards	Investor say	Investor say	Investor say	Investor say	Fed standards
	Pre-emption	Little	More	Little	Little	Little	Little	More
	Rating agencies	Chosen for banks	Register with SEC	Chosen for banks	Chosen for banks	Chosen for banks	Chosen for banks	Register with SEC
	Audit of Fed	Routine	One time	Routine	Routine	Routine	Routine	One time
	Oversight council	11 members	9 members	11 members	11 members	11 members	9 members	9 members
Position		100	85	70	60	50	40	30

Source: Mousavi and Shrefrin, 2010.

protection include exemption of the auto industry from new regulations and imposing restrictions to debit card fees.

With regards to provision 2 (derivatives/financial risk) above, in Table 4.2 **NL** denotes no Lincoln Provision, and **NV** no Volcker Rule. The other elements of the second provision listed and evaluated are derivative clearing/exchange, and capital standards (Capital stds). For the third provision of Too Big to Fail, the House bill was the strongest in requiring a large initial fund, as opposed to the Senate bill that only required taxes afterwards. For the last and fourth provision we considered the following general issues: executive pay restrictions, pre-emptive requirements, designation mechanism for rating agencies, audit of the Fed itself, and the number of members who will sit in the oversight committee.

The last row in Table 4.2 gives a score between 30, for the weakest overall final outcome, to 100, for the strongest possible one. It is clear that firms would want the position of 30 or the weakest possible outcome (as was seen in Table 4.1). Also, it appears that overall, the Senate bill (85) is assessed as stronger than the House's version (70) across all these elements together.

4.2.2 Modelling the Frank–Dodd legislation using the BdM Predictioneer's game

To predict the final form of the financial overhaul, we ran the BdM game, which involves consecutive bilateral negotiations between the players, using six players and their assessed input values. We wanted to predict the final form of the emerging bill that would be sent to the President for approval. In reality, several rounds of negotiations were held between the House Democrats led by Congressman Barney Frank and Senate Democrats led by Senator Chris Dodd. Meanwhile, our model, which we continuously fed with updated input based on the media reports, consistently predicted a final outcome weaker than Democrats' propositions overall.

We reported how our final prediction faired in comparison to the actual outcome in Mousavi and Shrefrin (2010):

Consumer Financial Protection   The regulator for consumer protection will reside within the Fed. This was in line with our prediction, as was the stipulation that the regulator would not oversee auto dealers who make auto loans. With respect to debit card fees, Dodd–Frank indicates that the Fed can place a cap on these fees, a possibility that was regarded as plausible but was not predicted. In line with our predictions, the bill requires that, before originating mortgages, lenders document borrowers' incomes and verify borrowers' ability to repay loans.

Derivatives/Financial Risk   As predicted, the trading of many derivatives will move from being OTC (over-the-counter) to being exchange-traded with clearing, albeit with significant exemptions. In terms of the Volcker Rule, we accurately predicted that Dodd–Frank would permit banks to engage in proprietary trading and own hedge funds. Nevertheless, Dodd–Frank also places limits on these activities, which was not specifically predicted.

In terms of the Lincoln Provision, we predicted that financial firms would be able to continue their derivative operations, rather than spinning these off. And they can; however, we failed to predict the qualifying language of the bill, which requires that the derivatives not be deemed excessively risky. Therefore, although the strongest elements from the Volcker Rule and Lincoln Provision were eliminated from Dodd–Frank, as predicted, weaker elements are indeed present.

Too Big to Fail   As predicted, Frank did accept the Senate version of Too Big to Fail, in which the FDIC secures a line of credit from the Treasury to pay for the liquidation of firms taken over by federal regulators. In turn, the FDIC (Federal Deposit Insurance Corporation) will recoup any costs by selling assets and, if needed, by imposing fees on large financial firms. Dodd–Frank grants regulators the power to break up firms they judge not only to be "too big" but that hold the potential to destabilise the financial system.

General Issues   As predicted for executive pay and severance packages, Dodd–Frank provides shareholders with a non-binding advisory vote. With respect to credit-rating agencies, the Dodd–Frank Bill stipulates that the Securities and Exchange Commission (SEC) has two years to develop a system to match ratings agencies with firms that want securities rated. We predicted that this provision would be part of the bill, but without any delay.

Notably, Dodd expressed concern that the provision might not be practicable. Therefore, the final bill provides for a two-year grace period to find a better alternative; if none be found, then the original provision will come into force.

In respect to the number of members on the oversight council, the House and Senate split the difference between 9 and 11 by setting the number at 10. This was an easy prediction, which in retrospect was simply missed. An important issue that was not anticipated and was not part of either the House or Senate bills is a proposed bank tax to the amount of US $19bn to pay for the costs of the reform. This would be levied on the largest financial firms, especially those taking the most risk.

Overall, our predictions lined up very well with the actual outcome announced by the conference committee as the *Dodd–Frank Bill*. Our model made accurate predictions of the dissent arising about the final compromised outcome as well, such as the objection of Republican members of the committee that consumer protection and derivative regulations are too strong.

In sum, we used a game theoretic framework and fed it with parameter values based on our interpretation of the media reports to predict the final outcome of financial overhaul negotiations. The number of players (six) was too small for this type of game configuration requiring a considerable amount of aggregation, such as viewing all Democrats in the House as one player, which entails ignoring their within-group differences in position. Nevertheless, the simplicity of our method was not costly in terms of accuracy of prediction. This "less-can-be-more phenomenon" is precisely the topic we discuss next in the context of another project related to financial regulation, this time in England.

4.3 How complex regulations need to be?

"Modern finance is complex, perhaps too complex. Regulation of modern finance is complex, almost certainly too complex. That configuration spells trouble. As you do not fight fire with fire, you do not fight complexity with complexity. Because complexity generates uncertainty, not risk, it requires a regulatory response grounded in simplicity, not complexity."

Thus reflected Haldane (2012), Executive Director of Financial Stability of the Bank of England, on the status of financial regulations at the Federal Reserve's annual policy conference in August 2012[6] Haldane was reflecting on the requirements of implementing the Basel III Accord. First, a bit of background[7]

The Basel Committee – initially named the Committee on Banking Regulations and Supervisory Practices – was established by the central bank governors of

[6] In 2013, the Wall Street Journal hailed this talk as the speech of 2012.
[7] Source: https://www.bis.org/bcbs/history.htm.

the G10 countries at the end of 1974 in the aftermath of serious disturbances in international currency and banking markets (notably the failure of Bankhaus Herstatt in West Germany).

The Committee, headquartered at the Bank for International Settlements in Basel, was established to enhance financial stability by improving the quality of banking supervision worldwide and to serve as a forum for regular cooperation between its member countries on banking supervisory matters. The Committee's first meeting took place in February 1975, and meetings have subsequently been held regularly three or four times a year.

Since its inception, the Basel Committee has expanded its membership from the G10 to 45 institutions from 28 jurisdictions. Starting with the Basel Concordat, first issued in 1975 and then revised several times, the Committee has established a series of international standards for bank regulation, most notably its landmark publications of the accords on capital adequacy, which are commonly known as Basel I, Basel II and, most recently, Basel III.

In numbers, *Basel I: the Basel Capital Accord*, published in 1987 and released to the banks after G10 approval in 1988, comprised only 30 pages. The revised set of regulations, *Basel II: the new capital framework*, from 2004 consisted of three pillars;
1. minimum capital requirements,
2. supervisory review process, and
3. market discipline and was 284 pages in length.
4. Finally, *Basel III: responding to the 2007–09 financial crisis*, published in 2010, came in at 616 pages[8] and was then revised and amended in 2014, adding 79 further pages (for a history of Basel Accords, see (Penikas, 2015))

A summary of Basel III is provided in Fig. 4.1.

The implementability of Basel Accords has been criticised theoretically as well as pragmatically (e.g., see (Lall, 2009), (Lall, 2012)). Over the years, Haldane, since risen up in rank[9] at the Bank of England, remains an advocate of simple rules and regulations instead of complex ones for establishing financial stability as a main criterion for societal safety.

The less-is-more phenomenon, he argues (see the opening quote of this section), is understood in light of the distinction between risk and

---

[8] https://www.ft.com/content/8a5e61b2-f34a-11e1-9c6c-00144feabdc0.

[9] Presently, in 2018, he is the Chief Economist and Executive Director until 2020. For his biography and publications, see https://www.bankofengland.co.uk/about/people/andy-haldane/biography.

Basel Committee on Banking Supervision reforms – Basel III

Strengthens microprudential regulation and supervision, and adds a macroprudential overlay that includes capital buffers

	Capital				Liquidity
	Pillar 1		Pillar 2	Pillar 3	
	Capital / Risk coverage	Containing leverage	Risk management and supervision	Market discipline	Global liquidity standards and supervisory monitoring

All Banks

Capital

Quality and level of capital
- Raising minimum common equity to 4.5% of risk-weighted assets, after deduction.
- A capital conservation buffer comprising common equity of 2.5% of risk-weighted assets brings the total common equity standard to 7%. Constraints on a bank's discretionary distributions will be imposed when it falls into the buffer range.
- A countercyclical buffer within a range of 0–2.5% comprising common equity will apply when credit growth is judged to result in an unacceptable build-up of systematic risk.

Capital loss absorption at the point of non-viability
Allowing capital instruments to be written off or converted to common shares if the bank is judged to be non-viable. This will reduce moral hazard by increasing the private sector's contribution to resolving future banking crises.

Risk coverage

Revisions to the standardised approaches for calculating
- credit risk;
- market risk;
- credit valuation adjustment risk; and
- operational risk

mean greater risk sensitivity and comparability.

Constraints on using internal models aim to reduce unwarranted variability in banks' calculations of risk-weighted assets.

Counterparty credit risk
More stringent capital instruments for measuring exposure; capital incentives to use central counterparties; a new standardised approach; and higher capital for inter-financial sector exposures.

Securitisations
Reducing reliance on external ratings, simplifying and limiting the number of approaches for calculating capital charges and increasing requirements for riskier exposures.

Capital requirements for exposures to central counterparties (CCPs) and equity investments in funds to ensure adequate capitalisation and support a resilient financial system

A revised output floor, based on Basel III standardised approaches, limits the regulatory capital benefits that a bank using internal models can derive relative to the standardised approaches.

Containing leverage

A non-risk based leverage ratio including off-balance sheet exposures is meant to serve as a backstop to the risk-based capital requirement. It also helps contain system wide build-up of leverage.

Risk management and supervision

Supplemental Pillar 2 requirements address firm-wide governance and risk management, including the risk of off-balance sheet exposures and securitisation activities; sound compensation practices; valuation practices; stress testing; corporate governance and supervisory colleges.

Interest rate risk in the banking book (IRRBB)
Extensive guidance on expectations for a bank's IRRBB management process; enhanced disclosure requirements; stricter threshold for identifying outlier banks; updated standardised approach.

Market discipline

Revised Pillar 3 disclosure requirements

Consolidated and enhanced framework, covering all the reforms to the Basel framework. Introduces a dashboard of banks' key prudential metrics.

Global liquidity standards and supervisory monitoring

The Liquidity Coverage Ratio (LCR) requires banks to have sufficient high-quality liquid assets to withstand a 30-day stressed funding scenario that is specified by supervisors.

The longer-term, structural Net Stable Funding Ratio (NSFR) is designed to address liquidity mismatches. It covers the entire balance sheet and provides incentives for banks to use stable sources of funding.

The Committee's 2008 guidance Principles for Sound Liquidity Risk Management and Supervision takes account of lessons learned during the crisis. It is based on a fundamental review of sound practices for managing liquidity risk in banking organisations.

Supervisory monitoring
The liquidity framework includes a common set of intraday and longer-term monitoring metrics to assist supervisors in identifying and analysing liquidity risk trends at both the bank and system-wide level.

Large exposures

Large exposures regime established to mitigate systemic risks arising from interlinkages across financial institutions and concentrated exposures.

SIBs

The Committee identifies global systemically important banks (G-SIBs) using a methodology that includes both quantitative indicators and qualitative elements. In addition to meeting the Basel III risk-based capital and leverage ratio requirements, G-SIBs must have higher loss absorbency capacity to reflect the greater risks that they pose to the financial system. The Committee also developed principles on the assessment methodology and the higher loss absorbency requirement for domestic systemically important banks (D-SIBs).

Figure 4.1 Summary of Basel III reforms. *Source*: https://www.bis.org/bcbs/basel3/b3_bank_sup_reforms.pdf

uncertainty, with the latter being prominent in the financial domain. To elaborate on this phenomenon, I next discuss the distinction between risk and uncertainty in relation to heuristic decision-making processes. Thereafter, I provide an overview of a project delivered at the Bank of England in collaboration with scientists from the Max Planck Institute for Human Development, which used the findings from the study of fast-and-frugal mechanisms and developed a fast-and-frugal tree for detecting vulnerable banks.

4.3.1 Risk vs. uncertainty: heuristics as tools for dealing with uncertainty

Institutional decisions are usually made under considerable uncertainty. Interestingly, managers of large international corporations consider about half

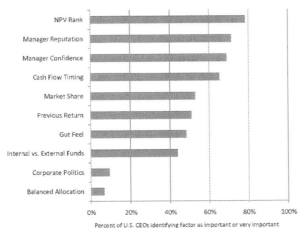

Figure 1: Survey evidence on the factors that affect capital allocation decisions within a firm. The responses in this graph are for more than 1,000 U.S. CEOs. Respondents ranked the importance of each factor on a scale of 1 to 5, with 1 being not important at all and 5 being very important. A factor is deemed to be "important" to a respondent if the ranking was a 4 or 5.

(Adopted from Graham et al, 2010 with permission)

Figure 4.2 Factors driving allocation of capital. *Source*: Graham et al. (2015), Figure 1

of their professional decisions as gut decisions, made after having considered all the data available (Graham et al., 2015), (Gigerenzer, 2014).

Fig. 4.2 shows the role of gut feel in relation to more deliberative and quantifiable procedures and factors in making budgeting decisions, for a sample of 1000 American CEOs.

Gut feelings (or intuition) are typically based on heuristics (Gigerenzer, 2007). Knight (1921) Frank Knight (1921), emphasising the role of intuition in business decision making, famously distinguished between risk and uncertainty in this regard.

Mousavi and Gigerenzer (2017) highlight this distinction:

Knight introduced three forms of probability: a priori probability, statistical probability, and estimate. Knight's conception of probability predates Savage's notion and so must be read with a fresh mind. A priori and statistical probability correspond to risk, whereas the use of what Knight calls "estimates" occurs when dealing with uncertainty. Knight argued that the last category of situations is not meaningfully reducible to statistical calculations, and he considered the associated uncertainty as immeasurable.

Table 4.3 Decision Under Risk versus Uncertainty.

Nature of unknown	Knightian probability	Decision process	Generated knowledge
Risk	Deductive	Use of probability theory to model the underlying structure	Deterministic knowledge (as in lotteries) e.g. objective odds.
Risk	Inductive (statistical inference)	Use statistical inference optimisation	Stochastic knowledge; e.g. estimates of correlations
Uncertainty	Heuristic	Select a heuristic that is ecological rational for a task; exploratory	Satisficing solutions when optimising is not feasible; intuition as in entrepreneurship

Source: (Mousavi and Gigerenzer, 2017)

His humorous characterisation of the mainstream practice of using probability measures to model all uncertain decision situations is most illustrative: "If you cannot measure it, measure it anyway"' Bernstein (1996). One main point in the business world is that entrepreneurs can generate profit in the markets, a la Knight, precisely because they intelligently deal with immeasurable, irreducible uncertainty. We argue that the study of heuristics provides a descriptive and normative framework to model how entrepreneurs and others deal–and should deal–with uncertainty.

In Chapter 2, we reviewed the study of heuristics as effective strategies in business and other fields with several examples. We argued that a science of heuristics consists of a systematical classification of the building blocks of heuristics and the structure of environments in which they solve problems effectively, and also that understanding heuristics is helpful for developing reliable knowledge in dealing with uncertainty instead of trying to reduce all uncertainty to risk.

The heuristics approach agrees with Knight's (1921, p. 311) view that "the results of human activity cannot be anticipated and then only in so far as even a probability calculation in regard to them is impossible and meaningless." Table 4.3 summarises the connection between Knight's typology of risk and uncertainty and the different forms of knowledge generated under each situation, including the heuristic-based procedures.

The point relevant to financial regulations is that financial institutions face a high degree of uncertainty. The claim then is that heuristic-based approaches can assist with taming this uncertainty to achieve financial stability. To illustrate this point, the next section summarises a project that used fast-and-frugal heuristics knowledge to develop a simple procedure for identifying vulnerable banks.

4.3.2 Calling out vulnerable banks: an exercise with fast-and-frugal trees

At the instigation of Governor Mervyn King, a Bank of England team started collaboration with Gigerenzer and his researchers at the Max Planck Institute for Human Development to explore alternative mechanisms for improving financial stability towards a safer world for all. This exploration aimed at extending the findings from the study of fast-and-frugal heuristics to the domain of banking and financial regulations. Results were summarised in a working paper by Aikman et al. (2014):

> "Distinguishing between risk and uncertainty, this paper draws on the psychological literature on heuristics to consider whether and when simpler approaches may outperform more complex methods for modelling and regulating the financial system. We find that:
> • simple methods can sometimes dominate more complex modelling approaches for calculating banks' capital requirements, especially if limited data are available for estimating models or the underlying risks are characterised by fat-tailed distributions;
> • simple indicators often outperformed more complex metrics in predicting individual bank failure during the global financial crisis; and
> • when combining information from different indicators to predict bank failure, "fast-and-frugal" decision trees can perform comparably to standard, but more information-intensive, regression techniques, while being simpler and easier to communicate."

Let us look at the steps involved in this analysis leading to the construction of a fast-and-frugal tree and its comparison with alternative techniques, using the same variables. The first step involves specification of indicators of bank failure as well as the order in which they are sequentially examined to raise a red flag. This led to the choice of variables in Table 4.4.

These variables were evaluated for a database of 116 global banks across 25 countries with more than 100 billion US dollars at the end of 2006,

Table 4.4 Select measurements for investigation of bank vulnerability.

Indicator	Definition
1 Total asset growth (per cent)[a]	$\frac{\text{Total assets in 2006} - \text{Total assets in 2005}}{\text{Total assets in 2005}} * 100$
2 Basel I risk-based capital ratio (balance sheet) (per cent)	$\frac{\text{Tier 1 capital}}{\text{Risk-weighted assets}} * 100$
3 Leverage ratio (balance sheet) (per cent)	$\frac{\text{Tier 1 capital}}{\text{Total assets}} * 100$
4 Market-based capital ratio (per cent)	$\frac{\text{Market capitalisation}}{\text{Risk-weighted assets}} * 100$
5 Market-based leverage ratio (per cent)	$\frac{\text{Market capitalisation}}{\text{Total assets}} * 100$
6 Wholesale funding ratio	$\frac{\text{Wholesale funding level (see 7)}}{\text{Total assets}}$
7 Wholesale funding level[b]	Bank deposits + senior paper + collateralized financing (via repo) + wholesale deposits + securitised debt
8 Core funding ratio[c]	$\frac{\text{Retail deposits} + \text{long–term wholesale funding} > 1 \text{ year}}{\text{Total assets}}$
9 Loan to deposit ratio[d]	$\frac{\text{Retail loans}}{\text{Retail deposits}}$
10 Net stable funding ratio[e]	$\frac{\text{Available stable funding}}{\text{Required stable funding}}$
11 Liquid asset ratio	$\frac{\text{Cash and balances with central banks} + \text{government bonds}}{\text{Total assets}}$

[a] Adjusted for significant mergers.

[b] This is oar preferred measure. For some banks, it is not possible to distinguish between retail deposits and deposits placed by non-bank financial corporations or obtain clean definitions of some of the other components. In these instances, we use close proxies as appropriate.

[c] The weighting scheme used to classify different liabilities to determine the core funding ratio on the basis of Liquidatum data is available on request from the authors.

[d] This is our preferred measure. For some banks, it is not possible to distinguish between retail deposits and deposits placed by non-bank financial corporations — in these instances, we proxy the loan to deposit ratio by (customer loans/customer deposits).

[e] The weighting scheme used to classify different assets and liabilities to determine the NSFR on the basis of Liquidatum data is available on request from the authors.

Source: https://www.bis.org/bcbs/basel3/b3_bank_sup_reforms.pdf

of which 42 failed during the recent 2007–2009 financial crisis. Failure, with some modification,[10] was assessed based on meeting four or more of the six criteria developed by Laeven and Valencia (2012) for significant intervention in the banking sector (Laeven and Valencia, 2012, pp. 6–7):

1. extensive liquidity support (5 percent of deposits and liabilities to non-residents)
2. bank restructuring costs (at least 3 percent of GDP)
3. significant bank nationalisations
4. significant guarantees put in place
5. significant asset purchases (at least 5 percent of GDP), and
6. deposit freezes and bank holidays.

Choice of variables to serve as binary cues in a decision tree were made based on "economic intuition", that is, the judgement of experts from the bank about the relative importance of the cues. As depicted in Table 4.4, the balance sheet leverage ratio is judged the most discriminating cue, with a threshold of 4.1%. Notably, passing this criterion is not judged sufficient for solvency and therefore a second cue is considered, namely the market-based capital ratio, which strongly penalises assets according to their riskiness and as such complements the first cue by highlighting an alarm that the leverage ratio can miss.

Falling below the threshold of a 16.8% market-based capital ratio raises a red flag. However, passing this second criterion is still short of being considered sufficiently solvent. The remaining cues are liquidity metrics in the order of judged importance. The third cue chosen is a bank's wholesale funding level, which must be above 177 billion US dollars. Here, passing the first three criteria is deemed sufficient for a green flag, indicating bank solvency. The authors note, however, that a conservative regulator might continue to the fourth criterion before raising the green flag. The fourth and last cue is loan-to-deposit ratio, which raises the green flag above attached to wholesale funding and the loan deposit ratio in Fig. 4.3.

Shefrin (2016) notes the structural similarity between a fast-and-frugal tree and a project adoption procedure based on sequential hurdles. As can be seen in Fig. 4.4, four categories emerge in such sequential procedures. White elephants occur when a vulnerable bank is wrongly identified otherwise, whereas false warnings refer to identifying banks that are not vulnerable as vulnerable. Winning calls is the category in which banks are

---

[10] See Aikman et al., 2014, p. 14, footnote 3 for details.

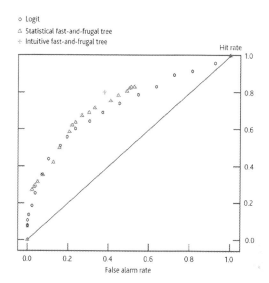

Figure 4.3 Judgement-based fast-and-frugal tree for assessing bank vulnerability. *Source*: Aikman et al., 2014

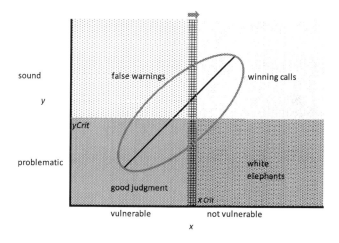

Figure 4.4 The elliptical confidence region for determining "success" or "failure". Values of y above the threshold yCrit correspond to "success." *Source*: Shefrin (2016)

rightly recognised as being not vulnerable, and good judgement indicates correct identification of a bank's vulnerability.

From this depiction, one can see that the performance of a process can be assessed based on the ratio of winning calls to all banks categorised as

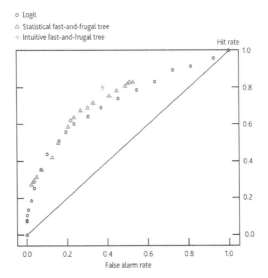

Figure 4.5 Receiver operating characteristic curves for three identification procedures. *Source*: Aikman et al. (2014)

not vulnerable, that is, the sum of winning calls and white elephants. This is referred to also as the hit rate.

The judgement-based fast-and-frugal tree in Fig. 4.4 had a hit rate of 82% and a false alarm of 48%. The Bank of England team compared this performance to a logit model and to another fast-and-frugal tree constructed based on statistical validity of cues as opposed to expert intuitive judgement. As can be seen in Fig. 4.5, the results indicate a promising role for fast-and-frugal procedures.

Finally, Bank of England team also ranked the 14 single cue heuristics in terms of their performance in predicting bank vulnerability. The central index of the Basel framework, the risk-based capital market ratio (Cue 2 in Table 4.4) unimpressively ranked sixth. Moreover, the simple balance sheet leverage based on total assets came out above its risk-weighted counterpart (see Shefrin, 2016, Chapter 13 for a detailed analysis and comparison).

All in all, the results from this project opened an exciting path for exploration of conditions under which simple procedures (and indexes) can be used successfully for dealing with important and consequential financial operations in banks and constructing fast-and-frugal diagnostic models which surpass their more complex counterparts.

4.4 Summary

"We can have democracy in this country, or we can have great wealth concentrated in the hands of a few, but we can't have both".[11] Financial regulations are safety guards for preservation of democracy by maintaining financial stability. The recent financial crisis has set the regulators on a new search for ways to improve financial stability. At the same time, big money has a persistent tendency to discover new ways for growth and dominance. The appropriation of legislators by interest groups influences the eventual shape of regulations towards less stability and more opportunities for exploitation of people. This trend has facilitated unfortunate yet not surprising sociopolitical manifestations that diminish democracy, which goes far beyond the scope of our chapter's focus. Nonetheless, our analysis of these behavioural financial aspects provides a framework that can be extended to make sense of the way in which other social and political domains are being shaped as well.

In this chapter two major financial regulation documents produced in the last two decades in the USA (Dodd–Frank Bill) and Europe (Basel Accords) were briefly reviewed. From a behavioural point of view, regulations structure the environment in which financial institutions operate. We illustrated this point by reviewing a paper that predicted on the basis of this premise the final configuration of the Dodd–Frank Bill. The message is simple: the users of financial architectures must be saved from exploitation by financial institutions, which have expertise in neutralising regulations.

We discussed regulations from a behavioural stance with respect to the distinction between risk and uncertainty, emphasising and illustrating how heuristics are tools for uncertainty. And the world of finance is a highly uncertain one. The efficacy of fast-and-frugal trees in identifying vulnerable banks was showcased as evidence for the less-is-more principle in relation to the Basel III Accord.

The idea of less-is-more is a counterintuitive one. We are routinely trained to believe that more information, more procedures, and more criteria will result in higher performance. Acceptance of the functionality of simple heuristic procedures in dealing with complex and uncertain circumstances is in its infancy. For it to become mainstream, more advocates as well as the production of further evidence are required. Our current book is one such effort and to the best of our knowledge the first of its kind in the field of finance.

[11] Louis Brandesis, Supreme Court (Source: (Warren, 2017)).

CHAPTER 5

When fast-and-frugal works best

In this chapter we discuss some of the origins of fast-and-frugal reasoning and how it differentiated itself from the "Heuristics-and-Biases" program that preceded it and which underlies almost all behavioural finance by academics such as Richard Thaler, Werner De Bondt, Nick Barberis, Hersh Shefrin, and Meir Statman. Like Cornelius in *Fight Club* we will see that fast-and-frugal reasoning was "on everybody's tongue [Gigerenzer] just gave it a name".

So while Gigerenzer sometimes speaks of a "heuristic revolution" in evangelising his approach it is also an evolution, or re-assertion, of an earlier understanding of problems in financial decision-making as lying on a continuum between risky and uncertain outcomes. In many ways the behavioural finance we have reflects a broader move in the application of psychology "from tools to theories" (Gigerenzer, 1991).

Like many revolutionaries Gigerenzer seeks to restore a prior, perhaps only imagined, order. Specifically Gigerenzer reminds us of techniques that were explored before the almost complete reliance of psychologists and economists on bayesian statistics in the belief that we have the mind of an "intuitive statistician".

Since we have had the deft hammer of expected utility theory, invoking classical probability, every problem is now a nut to exhibit some, hopefully predictable, bias. We begin by examining the history of classical probability theory, which underpins standard expected utility theory and thus so much of modern finance, portfolio theory, risk-neutral asset pricing models, binomial option pricing models, and so much more.

The Chapter examines developments both within psychology and economics to understand how behavioural finance/economics was formed and the issues it addresses. Both the behaviourist movement and neoclassical economics divorce the *process* of decision-making from decision-making's *outcomes*.

How decisions are made and their nature are separated. A fast-and-frugal finance can break this divide and potentially take new ground in explaining financial decisions. Güth (2008) suggests some ways in which this might be done, building on the notion of ecological rationality.

A Fast and Frugal Finance
https://doi.org/10.1016/B978-0-12-812495-6.00012-4

5.1 What behavioural economics does best

To isolate what fast-and-frugal reasoning can add to the behavioural finance research agenda it worth considering what current behavioural finance models aspire to at their finest. Rabin (2013), a leading scholar in behavioural economics scholarship, gives an indication of this when he calls for portable extensions of existing models, or PEEMs, which

extend   existing standard models of choice,

embeds   portability by allowing the revised model to be applied across various decision domains,

While this is the dream, Rabin (2013) (p. 618), as a master craftsman in behavioural economics modelling, is well aware of the nightmare; which he describes as follows

> *"take a current model, pick an available Greek character, toss it in with a bunch of right–hand–side variables and model away."*

In this style such models become a mere "game", in the pejorative sense, to display the author's mathematical skills, if not intuitive insight. Despite this inherent danger Rabin believes in the need to construct simple, tractable, economic models.

In setting out upon this task Rabin believes we must bear in mind first that most economics theory simply assumes the actor/investor maximises their expected wealth, future cash-flow, income, etc. Secondly, we must recall, as Rabin (2013) (p. 617) puts it

> *"the core empirical exercise in economics is not to identify the existence of phenomena, but to understand their ecological significance".*

Specifically good theories rule out many forms of behaviour, in a way that mimics the simple decision-making schemata embedded in fast-and-frugal trees. Rabin points out that while elegant, and capable of widespread application, many such models rest crucially on the interpretation, rather than merely *re–specification* of the investor/agent's utility function. So much of the power of behavioural models comes in the "story" they offer, rather than the pure mathematical mechanics of the modelling strategy followed by the author(s).

Here the behavioural agenda meets, enriches, and is enriched by, its fast-and-frugal twin. Importantly, a theory is just a theory. While all theories are wrong, the only legitimate question is whether the new theory *improves* an old one, not whether it perfectly matches reality. As we shall argue in the remainder of this book on this basis a fast-and-frugal modelling of financial decision-making has much to commend it.

So whether the model follows a standard finance theory tradition, of Samuelson and Gary Becker, or the behavioural tradition, of Thaler and Nick Barberis, the goal is to re–parameterise the model, alter its intuitive understanding, to better explain observed financial decision-making remains.

Rabin (2013) concludes his review of the behavioural economics research agenda by pointing out the ultimate test of a financial decision-making model is it's ability to accurately predict investor's/trader's responses to changes in prevailing conditions. Rabin's invocation of an ecological, rather than classical, rationality, in the quotation given above, is noteworthy. It shows an awareness of the fragility, and possibly misleading nature of, standard models reliance on classical rationality.

Rabin (2013) (p. 621) closes his discussion with a challenge to behavioural economics/finance researchers.

"With explanatory power comes explanatory responsibility: researchers developing PEEMs should ask themselves what the theories imply in basic settings outside the theoretical, or empirical, context in which they are developed."

Thus the aim for both behavioural and fast-and-frugal models is to produce, simple, easy to apply, models of general application embedding a demonstrable ecological rationality, conforming cognition with the changing contexts into which it's judgements are applied.

5.2 The classical origins of fast-and-frugal reasoning

In our rush to convince the reader of the new insights gained from reading and applying the insights of Gerd Gigerenzer and the ABC group it would be remiss of us to conceal the degree to which fast-and-frugal reasoning simply re-asserts a consensus that prevailed before neoclassical economics, as we have received it, was formed.

One could be forgiven for believing that Pierre–Simon Laplace had just put down his copy of Gigerenzer (2007) when he wrote in his *Essai philosophique sur les probabilités* of 1814 ((Daston, 1988), p. 68) *"the theory of probabilities is at best common sense reduced to calculus, it makes us appreciate with exactitude that which exact minds feel by a sort of instinct without being able ofttimes to give a reason for it."*

Indeed it is striking how influenced early probabilist reasoning was by the actions of "reasonable men", for example Judges and successful merchants. In particular the predictions of classical probability calculations were judged against what "reasonable men" did.

Rather than regarding "anomalies" as a failure of reasonable men they simply regarded them as motivation to recast/improve the probabilistic model being advanced. Gigerenzer and the ABC group are attempting this, advancing their PMM models of decision-making under uncertainty, which we will discuss later, to make such a reconstruction possible.

In the mainstream of behavioural finance anomalous human behaviour is regarded as a justification for changing the investor/agent's, utility function and by implication what they want or who they are (Berg and Gigerenzer, 2010).

The idea of challenging the fundamental calculus of investor/agent utility never arises in most behavioural finance discussion. But this inverts the logic by which the original 18th Century probabilists developed concepts of risks and expected values deriving from risky outcomes.

Daston (1988) (p. 108) concludes her discussion of the link between expected value and the judgement of a reasonable man thus

"Throughout the 18th Century, probabilists regarded expectations as a mathematical rendering of pragmatic rationality. The calculus of probabilities reflected the thought and practice of a small elite of perspicacious individuals who exemplified – rather than defined – the virtue of reasonableness."

Part of the reason why this link between the mechanics of calculating probabilities broke down was precisely because deciding whose behaviour was a benchmark for reasonableness proved difficult after the French revolution, so inspired by reason, began to eat its own children. But in its earliest days a link between the common law definition of "reasonable man" and that used in deciding on attitudes to conjectured risks was clear. This engagement with legal reasoning has been a strength of the fast-and-frugal/ABC research tradition (Engel and Gigerenzer, 2006).

5.2.1 The origins of classical probabilities in contract law

Early classical probabilists relied upon legal definitions of a "reasonable man's" actions because the practical context in which the calculation of expected values arose where disputes over aleatory contracts, which involved some element of risk, insurance and hence perhaps the payment of interest as a compensation for bearing risk.

Such interest payments always ran the risk of challenge by Ecclesiastical courts for being a form of usury. Such aleatory contracts, requiring a future division of goods, arose naturally in insurance contracts, games of chance, and in the valuation of a future inheritance, when the inheritance date is unknown and the chance of a frustrating event, like the demise of the party set to inherit, was unknown. But at the centre of all such legal disputes of what was reasonable was some notion of fairness.

This reflects a broader relationship between law and social norms (Benabou and Tirole, 2012). As Gigerenzer (1996) (p. 593) points out the general applicability of probabilistic thinking is not unproblematic, stating

> "Many demonstrations of biases in probabilistic reasoning are founded on this practice... Content–blind norms are appropriate for textbook problems in probability theory, where the content is only decorative, but they are not appropriate either for evaluating human judgement or as a research tool to uncover underlying processes... In contrast, I believe sound reasoning begins by investigating the content of a problem to infer what probable means."

So the technique of determining probable cause cannot be separated from the nature of the problem itself. This aligns with the concept of *stare decisis*, in the common law, by which a legal solution is advanced as attractive by analogy to other cases of a similar type, or those raising similar legal distinctions.

5.2.2 If the mind is an "intuitive statistician" what type of statistician is it?

Observed "reasonable behaviour" clearly affects our understanding of what is "rational". As Gigerenzer (1991) (p. 2) observes

> "More recently, Bayesian statistics, rather than Fisherian statistics, has been used as the yardstick, [by which] many subject's judgements seemed flawed by fallacies and errors in statistical reasoning."

This realisation led to something of a crisis in social psychology that Kahnemen and Tversky's "heuristics-and-biases" program seemed to, at least partially, solve. The heuristics-and-biases program did this in two ways, (Gigerenzer, 1991) (p. 2)

1. developing a list of what are termed biases/fallacies, deriving from apparent errors in probabilistic reasoning,
2. proposing explanations of such cognitive biases/fallacies based on heuristics, such as availability, representativeness, anchoring, etc.

Gigerenzer (1991) (p. 2) raises doubts about the efficacy of these problems pointing out

> *"most so-called errors or cognitive illusions are, contrary to the literature, in fact not violations of probability theory. In their normative claims, Tversky and Kahneman, and social psychologists following in their footsteps, have neglected conceptual distinctions that are fundamental to probability and statistics."*

One problem with the heuristics-and-biases research program is that it assumes there is just one form of statistics, bayesian statistics, that captures the correct/right way to think. After revisiting a number of alleged cognitive errors/illusions on the heuristics-and-biases list, representativeness, optimism and base rate neglect, Gigerenzer (1991) concludes that (p. 22)

> *"To move towards a theoretically deeper understanding of judgement under uncertainty we must first abandon the narrow concept of 'bias', and the program of explaining 'biases' by largely undefined 'heuristics'. Then we might find out what kind of statistician the intuitive statistician is. My guess is a frequentist."*

So Gigerenzer argues much confusion has derived from allowing bayesian inference to become the default, if not the exclusive, definition of what is rational. Those who deviate from its calculus are judged "anomalous", problematic, or perhaps just "dumb".

But maybe they just inhabit a different context, or perceive a given context differently. For that reason an understanding of where the probability calculus came from, and how that history impacts it current usage in financial modelling, is useful.

5.2.3 Fermat/Pascal's correspondence on the "problem of points"

The most famous discussion of an equitable distribution of spoils based on an uncertain future outcome is the "problem of points" discussed in correspondence between Blaise Pascal and Pierre Fermat between July and October 1654. The problem, posed by Chevalier de la Mérè, is stated as arising from a game of chance where two players, A and B, gamble 32 pistoles (we can say dollars maybe) on a game where attaining 3 points wins the game. Unfortunately the game is interrupted when Player A has already won 2 points and Player B has 1. If the game cannot be resumed how should the stakes of $ 32 stake now be divided?

Fermat's proposed solution to the problem invoked a complete elaboration of all possible outcomes, if the game had continued, and the resulting pay-offs to each possible outcome elaborated. Pascal felt this was too messy and suggested Player's A's pay-off could be calculated as being:

$$\frac{1}{2} \times 32 + \frac{1}{2} \times 64 = 48 \tag{5.1}$$

where Player A is given a pay-off based on an equal probability of holding on to his stake and doubling it; the latter being the upside deriving from being on 2 points, compared to Player B's 1. Thus A's 1 point lead in a game requiring 3 points to win, is captured in Pascal's calculation as the player having a 50%. chance of ultimately winning the game.

So Pascal regards the $32 A has waged as being secure in their grip, it is the remaining pot of pooled stakes that is uncertain. Hence the A's expectation of A's winnings can be restated as

$$1 \times 32 + \frac{1}{2} \times 32 = 48 \tag{5.2}$$

Here A retaining their stake is regarded as already certain, all that A wagers is their 50% chance of taking B's stake as well. So while Fermat and Pascal's solution rendered the same result, an expected pay-off of $48 to Player A, Pascal excised probabilities from as much of that calculation as he could, while Fermat was happy to make all aspects of the calculation of final expected pay-offs to the players dependent on correctly calculating the probability of all possible outcomes.

Both solution methods, both the full enumeration of Fermat and the contracted calculation of Pascal, yield the same expected pay-off/expected values, despite their very different use of probabilities. So are they different or not?

For classical probabilists it was equal value, evaluated over all prospective, outcomes to the various parties to the contract, or players of the game, that constituted equity and not equal probabilities of individual prospective outcomes.

So for Hugo Grotius in his *De jure belli ac pacis* of 1625, ((Daston, 1988), p. 23), stated

"In all contracts natural justice requires that there are equality of terms."

This led Grotius to examine a series of legal decisions in contract and international relations where juristic practice might be defined. But the emphasis was on making calculative method conform to what reasonable folk regarded as righteous. Often today the righteous path seems to be dictated by received statistical method; with any deviations being regarded as "anomalous", triggering a reformulation of an investor/agent's utility function.

5.2.4 Proposed resolutions of the St Petersburg paradox as guidance to improved risk evaluation

A standard example used to discredit the received wisdom of expected utility theory is a game offering a doubled pay-off of 1, 2, 4, 8, 16, etc., at successive tosses of a fair coin. Thus the prospective gamble's prospective pay-off can be stated as

$$\frac{1}{2} \times 1 + \frac{1}{4} \times 2 + \frac{1}{8} \times 4 + ...$$
$$\text{Or}\ \ 0.5 + 0.5 + +0.5 + ... = \infty \tag{5.3}$$

But one might ask would anyone really pay an infinite amount to enter such a gamble? This disturbing example of the limits of expected utility was first raised by Nicholas Bernoulli, the younger brother of Daniel, who while living in St Petersburg, wrote a letter to Pierre Montfort, who later published it in his *Essai d'analyse sur les jeux de hazard* of 1713 (Daston (1988), p. 69).

Daniel Bernoulli suggested a solution to his brother's paradox by noting simply that each increment of gains, earned by successive wins, is less valued by gamblers. The huge generosity of Bill Gates, or Warren Buffett, seems

Table 5.1 Calculating the utility of wealth for a logarithmic utility of wealth function.

Winnings	Winnings × 2	Utility of winnings, Ln (Wealth)	Utility of cumulative winnings
1	2	0	0
2	4	0.1733	0.1733
4	8	0.1733	0.3466
8	16	0.1300	0.4476
16	32	0.0866	0.5632
32	64	0.0542	0.6173
64	128	0.0325	0.6498
128	256	0.0190	0.6688
256	512	0.0108	0.6796

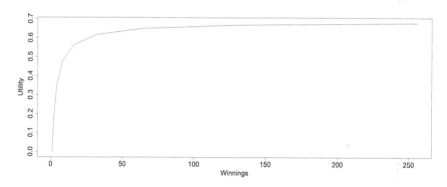

Figure 5.1 Plot of log utility function. *Note*: Based on data in Table 5.1.

consistent with this. Money just means less to them after the first $30/40 billion.

Daniel Bernoulli captured this idea of the diminishing returns to increments in prospective wealth by employing a natural logarithmic utility of wealth function, such as that represented in Table 5.1 (see also Fig. 5.1).

Daniel Bernoulli's invocation of a logarithmic utility of wealth, reflected a broader social discussion in his lifetime about the morality of luxuries and the high life. His treatment of exorbitant wealth seems to have been influenced by Bernard Mandeville's claim in his *Fable of the Bees* of 1727 that the sort of capricious "private vices" we might chuckle about, or even resent, contain "public virtues" we can all benefit from.

So while it may be vain for the singer Beyonce to post photos of herself garlanded with a headdress of flowers, her choice to do so gave work for photographers, florists, fashion magazine writers, etc. Thus the eccentricities of the rich may yield the necessities of the less fortunate masses.

So while the utility of wealth to the individual may decline to almost zero, its value to society may not. This is a clear example of Simon's teaching that cognition and context can never be separated.

Here our wealth, conditions our response to increases in it. The adoption of diminishing marginal returns, embedded in the logarithmic utility function, reflected an engagement of the classical probabilists with broader trends within political economy.

Calculated expected values were not taken to be the "correct" values to inform investor decisions. But rather provisional calculations to be revised as and when observed reasonable behaviour contradicted its predictions.

Daston (1988) (p. 106) outlines how this consensus regarding the need of probabilist reasoning to conform to the behaviour of reasonable men held up until the French revolution when the idea of men, even of high status and education, acting reasonably seemed almost farcical. Simoén Denis Poisson and Pierre–Simon Laplace began the transition of raising probabilistic reasoning to the level of a normative standard for human–reasoning to be judged by. This trend is most obvious in the development of the Bayes-Laplace development of a notion of an investor/agent's subjective probability, based on the revision of a previously held *prior* probability; suitably revised in light of the observed likelihood of the outcome.

Laplace believed that the St Petersburg paradox, and many other "anomalies" in human–reasoning would be quickly resolved once a subjective/bayesian probability calculus was adopted. In particular he believed any provisional assumption of the equiprobability of future events should be carefully adjusted for the observed asymmetry in the relative likelihood of future events.

So once a prior probability of the independent outcome of each gamble, in the St Petersburg paradox, had been adjusted for the fact that long streaks of wins are rare, the paradox resolves itself. A pay-off of 128, earned on the eighth consecutive win, are just not that common and so the investor/agent set its subjective probability to zero, even though its objective probability is not quite zero.

Table 5.2 The three realms of rationality.

Realm	Type of problem	Type of inference	Appropriate tool	People are..
Certainty	All options and consequences are known for certain (known knowns)	Deductive Inference	Logic	Intuitive logicians
Risk	All options and consequences are known, and their probabilities can be calculated	Inductive Inference	Probability theory, statistics	Intuitive statisticians
Uncertainy	Ill–posed or Ill–defined problems (unknown knowns)	Heuristic inference	Heuristics, ecological rationality	Homo heuristicus

Note: Source: Table 1 of Neth and Gigerenzer (2015), p. 3

5.3 Heuristic tools as a response to an uncertain financial landscape

Often researchers in behavioural finance have regarded such heuristic tools as a coping strategy; when an investor has cognitive restrictions and limited time and resources to make decisions under *risk*. However Neth and Gigerenzer (2015) argue that in truly *uncertain* environment such heuristics tools may simply do a better job. The adoption of such heuristics arises out of an emergent ecological rationality, which reflects the adaption of cognition to a changing stock market context.

Applying a single, probability based, formal logic to all decision-making problems has huge academic appeal for anyone with a tidy mind. But in the uncertain, changing, world of decision-making in the field, as opposed to the experimental lab, or the thought–experiment, such methods can seem almost irrelevant. Neth and Gigerenzer (2015) argue for a division of decision-making space into three realms, or territories, as illustrated in Table 5.2.

Neth and Gigerenzer (2015) divide decisions into those made under certainty, risk, and uncertainty. Picking stocks seems a lot closer to decision-making under uncertainty than risk. So much turns on Elon Musk's latest musing, or President's Trump's early morning tweet, that it seems impossible to anticipate all outcomes.

In this world (Neth and Gigerenzer (2015), p. 4)

"of 'unknown unknowns', finding the best solutions by means of statistical optimisation techniques is, by definition, no longer feasible. Instead heuristics can be useful to find good solutions."

In this alternative, fast-and-frugal, mode of reasoning, heuristics can be adaptive tools, requiring limited information cues, that enable robust predictions regarding the appropriate best behaviour for the market environment the investor inhabits. Thus heuristic tools provide simple decision-making algorithms, requiring little information and providing clear, unambiguous, guidance for the investor.

Heuristics tools must be carefully crafted to the decision-making context, into which they are deployed, and sensitive to adaptations motivated by changes in that context. Such ecological rules of reasoning will work best whenever *ecological* rationality works best, and by implication *classical* rationality worst. This is when

1. the heuristic is closely matched to the decision-making environment,
2. an investor/analyst has capacity to apply that heuristic well.

So financial accounts which are examined from many perspectives, using a variety of valuation models, seem ideally suited to a deployment of an ecological rationality perspective, with the heuristic tools that perspective brings.

5.4 Knightian uncertainty

A key justification for fast-and-frugal reasoning is the fact most financial decisions we make occur under conditions of uncertainty not risk. Where risk is both present and capable of accurate calculation fast-and-frugal reasoning is both less useful and less required.

In the first chapter of his classic text *Risk, Uncertainty, and Profit* Knight points out much of standard finance offers a trade-off between the comparative exactness of economics as a social science and the "unreality" of its predictions (Knight (1921), p. 3).

It is this unreality that fast-and-frugal reasoning breaks through so well, recognising the realities of investor choice. Knight captures some of the stylisation of decision-making fast-and-frugal trees invoke. He states (Knight (1921), p. 4) the essence of economic modelling to be the recognition

*"in large groups of problem situations certain elements are common [they]...
are both few in number and important enough to largely dominate situations."*

Knight praises Marshall's treatment of competition for his focus on con-
creteness and his focus on "representative" conditions. Knights recall the
importance of context for competitors' cognition as follows (Knight (1921),
p. 16)

*"We have no way of discussing a force or change except to describe its effects
or results under given conditions".*

One crucial environmental characteristic for Knight is the presence of
uncertainty rather than risk. For Knight only contexts of unquantifiable
uncertainty, as opposed to risky ones, support the presence of profit in a
competitive economy. Under conditions of risk we might expect competition between highly motivated traders, to eliminate profit (Milgrom and
Stokey, 1979).

Knight gives the example of Champagne manufacturers, who estimate
that a proportion of their bottles will burst as the wine "breathes" in the
bottle (Knight (1921), p. 213). Estimates of spillage, due to burst bottles,
simply becomes part of the fixed costs of champagne production. This
might rightly be regarded as a business "risk".

Knight contrasts this with case of an insurer who knows each year an
unknown number of insured properties will burn down. Here past probabilities might be both hard to calculate, if some do not claim to keep their
no claim bonus, and perhaps not that useful for prediction; even when
a calculation of burn-down rates is possible. Insurance companies seek to
classify the properties they insure into specific types, to capture those who
burn down their restaurant, in response to losing money and being threat-
ened with bankruptcy.

5.4.1 The ubiquity of uncertainty

So no uncertainty, means no profit/loss, in Knight's vision of a "static economy". So he asks what delineates the difference between uncertainty and
risk in Table 5.2 above. Knight goes beyond making this distinction to
pointing out how much unquantifiable uncertainty dominates our life. He
states (Knight (1921), p. 210)

"The ordinary decisions of life are made on the basis of "estimates" of a crude and superficial character. In general the future situation in relation to which we act depends on the behaviour of an indefinitely large number of objects, and is influenced by so many factors that no attempt is made to account for them all, much less separate and summate their separate significance."

Knight differentiates between "statistical" and "a priori" probabilities. A statistical probability might be that of a fair dice landing on six, almost regardless of outcomes in testing we know this to be $\frac{1}{6}$. But the chance of an insured building burning down, in a specific postal/zip code area, is not like this.

Our success in estimating a statistical probability often depends on the comparisons made over the time, geographic area studied, being the same. So we might wonder if restaurants that employ waiters and fast–food restaurants, or those that serve wine at table and those that do not, are the same. If such a regularity cannot be found speaking of "trends" in burn-down rates seems misleading.

Knight points out such statistical regularities are so rare. Hence investor/agents are pushed back on "common sense", which sometimes just doesn't seem that common at all (Knight (1921), p. 22). Heuristic tools, fast-and-frugal trees, and other elements of the "adaptive toolbox" of heuristic methods, might be seen as a structured description of such "common sense".

For Knight (1921) (p. 222)

"We act upon estimates rather than inferences, upon "judgement" or "intuition", not reasoning, for the most part."

For Knight risky situations are quite rare in business and uncertainty is the norm. In general we seem happy to live with a great deal of ignorance regarding future events, other's action, and intentions towards us. Knight points out conscious thought, as when we struggle to recall the name of a good book/film, can simply hinder our attempts at achieving a cognitive goal.

Similarly, prophetic vision/revelation seems to be given by serendipity rather than intense focus on the task. For Knight the mental process by which business men attach subjective probabilities to future are "mostly subconscious" (Knight (1921), p. 230).

In a phrase reminiscent of Hayek elsewhere, (Hayek, 1948), Knight states (Knight, 1921), (p. 261)

"The collection, digestion and dissemination of economic information in usable form is one of the staggering problems associated with our large scale organisation.... there is no satisfactory solution to this problem... and it safe to predict none will be found in the future."

While big data and business analytics hold out the solution to this problem Gigerenzer's "less is more" in predictive modelling principle suggests real limits to such predictive tools. These limitations arise both because it is hard to know which variables are truly predictive of future outcomes and the cumulation of predictive errors, relative to the bias ignoring variables with alleged predictive value, brings.

Knight notes that the rise of information/data as a source of value has led to a proliferation of areas of supposed expertise, beyond medicine and the law, to new specialisms in regulatory compliance, governance, and financial analysis. Such professions, which many business school students will later join, attract our interest in later chapters of this book.

5.4.2 Sources of probabilities for inference

While statistical probabilities can be inferred from general principles, such as the law of large numbers, "estimates", used for inference under uncertainty, can only be guessed at empirically, making these judgements far more contextual.

Knight proposes a three-fold classification of probabilities in decision-making

1. *a priori* probabilities applicable to recurrent situations which the decision-maker regards as identical, this might be appearance of complete lunar eclipses or the return of Hayley's comet. These are recurrent events which are as yet to occur but, barring an apocalyptic event, will occur with a known frequency

2. *statistical* probabilities inferred from frequency of occurrence, say rainy days in July in London. Here the value of the classificatory mechanism to days in July, in London, is key. So here the definition of the "reference class' of comparable objects is key to predictive value.

3. *estimates* where the classificatory mechanism is fraught or even impossible, say looking for the next great writer, or "face", of the future, where nothing but the unexpected seems to have any hope of succeed-

ing. Often the very unreadability/apparent ugliness of the new "find" is regarded as evidence of their depth/inner beauty. Such unique events give rise to what Knight calls "true uncertainty".

Obviously statistical probabilities are more useful for more clearly delineated the types of risk. So we might view statements about all Nigerians, or all women, as being innately estimates, as there so much within group variation. While Nobel Prizing winning writers in Ireland and Nigeria may have much in common, Dubliners and Kerry men may not.

The extent to which risk applies depends on the degree to which a transaction/trade is unique. The more unique it is the less relevant trends from statistics are. But even in the most unique of circumstances, say the "big short" ((Lewis, 2010)) of securitised debt, secured on mortgage re-payments, or George Soros' shorting of sterling in the 1992 "shadowing" of the European Monetary system, probabilities of success, and even confidence in their accuracy must be, and routinely are, inferred.

Indeed this ability to act/venture, into the most unknown territory is part of the essence of our humanity. As Knight phrases it

"We are so built that what seems to us reasonable is likely to be confirmed by experience, or we could not live in the world at all."

So facing true uncertainty, and forming estimates of likely outcomes, which such uncertainty might bring forth, is just the reality of our daily lives. While perhaps no event is truly unique, the 2008 Crash is "like" 1929 in some aspects. No two events are truly the same because "no man steps in the same river twice". The inter–temporal nature of financial choices make them both, forward–looking, and more often than not uncertain, unless an unusually precise grouping for the purpose of a risk–class calculation is possible.

When a firm basis of comparison is possible in the limit "risk" becomes almost perfectly manageable and thus in no substantive way different from a fully deterministic world. Yet often the basis of comparison between events may not be that obvious.

The Crash of 2008 was a decline in asset prices, but only after it was an evaporation of liquidity, in August 2007. This might lead us to compare the 2008 crash to other thinly traded assets, like the market for the highly prestigious residences on the Rue De Paix, Paris, or Park Lane, New York, or flight slots at Heathrow Airport. Such analogies, while reasonable, never seem to convince us that the market conditions are truly "the same".

5.4.3 Strategies for an uncertain world

But the inherent uniqueness of many financial decisions does not prevent the pricing a trading of insurance risks. Knight discusses the role of Lloyds syndicates of wealthy members in insuring unusual risks, such as those associated with Royal Coronations ((Knight, 1921), p. 250).

Such bespoke insurance contracts reflect an exercise of judgement, based on experience, no actuarial table can embed. Further such insurance must reflect both objective risk and threats induced by moral hazard, and hence the character/integrity of the person/business seeking to buy such insurance.

Knight points out this fact drives clear economies of scale, due to the ability to self–insure, over multiple trades/contracts, larger size brings. Knight saw this as motivating much of the industrial consolidation occurring in the post World War One world his book was published into. Knight states ((Knight, 1921), p. 252)

"It is undoubtedly true that the reduction in risk to borrowed capital is the principle desideratum leading to the displacement of individual enterprises by the partnership..."

By extension one can see the most grave threats to mankind today, say global warming and anti-biotic resistance, as justifying State intervention. The State is perhaps the greatest risk consolidator of all.

As some have pointed out if our native banks are now perhaps too internationally competitive, they must replicate the risk–bearing tastes of the Bank of China, backed as it is by some 1.4 bn people. This may make our native banks "too big to save", when they fail next time.

Knight (1921) points out an upside of living in an age of billionaires (say Elon Musk or Jim Clarke, see (Lewis, 2000)) is that some, visionary individuals can personally assume the risk of bringing potentially life–changing technologies to the market. Such, "blue sky creativity" investments can only emerge from those willing to risk a substantial part of their fortune on a technology, product, life–style, in which they truly believe.

5.4.4 Management of uncertainty

Knight points out that even if we could purge uncertainty from our lives it is not clear if we would want to. Knowing, or estimating, the hour of death, we would simply sit and "counts down the days" of our life. Much of life's joy is the unexpected challenges, diversions, and amusements, it throws up.

But insofar as we must face uncertainty our ability to bear it depends on the efficacy of three, often complimentary, strategies (Knight (1921), p. 241). These are

consolidation of risks, so that risk associated with holding a futures contract on Brent crude, expiring in December, can be calculated by averaging the risk across all similar such contracts. Once risk exposure is known its can be priced and insured.

specialisation of risks, to allow hedging/offsetting of the risk assumed. So if I expose myself to $\$/£$ risk in the currency futures market I can hedge with trades in the $£/\$$ spot market. Only if I can calculate a risk can I plan a diversification strategy to mitigate it.

dispersion or what we call today diversification, usually implemented today in portfolio formation mechanics, as discussed in the next chapter on asset pricing (Knight, 1921), (p. 254).

A frustrating element of predicting future market price is that it requires not only predicting/planning the investor's own trades, but also how other traders will respond to these. This raises the problem of individual investors having a "theory of mind" and correctly anticipating how others will react to our trades, you to theirs, their to yours, ... and so on in a potentially infinite regression ((Lewis, 2002), pp. 27–36 discusses this problem). To do this an investor must predict/plan for both their own and the market's aggregate demand.

One aspect of specialisation in risk–bearing is speculation, with all its dangers, this involves trying to counter-trade the market's sentiment, to buy cheaply, and sell out at the peak. Needless to say this requires rare intuition and commonly leads to ruination.

But the scale and repeated use of hedging instruments by speculators at least offers them some diversification of risk, as compared to an enterprise entering the futures/forward market to hedge a specific/one-time risk ((Knight, 1921), p. 256).

Such a speculative investor groups his "estimates"/hunches in the hope that they may display some of the regularity of risks, when averaged over all their trading activity. As Knight ((Knight, 1921), p. 258) describes this speculative process

"he does not "expect" to have his "expectations" verified by the results in every case; the expectations on which he really counts are an average, on an "estimate" of the long-run value of his estimates."

This very fragility of financial markets inspired Minsky to emphasise the vulnerability of financial markets to collapse. Minsky (1986) envisages financial markets as passing through five stages of credit expansion and contraction, including rapid implosion. These are

displacement,
boom,
euphoria,
profit-taking,
displacement.

One interesting aspect of Minsky's work is the evolutionary, cyclical, nature of the financial instability hypothesis. The fruit of each stage in the credit cycle creating the conditions for the arrival of the next stage. So good market conditions encourage lending for the future. To satisfy demand to borrow banks erode their lending criteria, exposing banks to risk, etc.

5.5 Fast-and-frugal reasoning and behavioural economics

Behavioural finance is already well established as a subject both for research and teaching ((Thaler, 1993), (Thaler, 2005), (Akert and Deaves, 2010), (Forbes, 2009)). An obvious question arises what can fast-and-frugal reasoning add to this already well-established research program?

Berg and Gigerenzer (2010) argue that, despite the many insights of the current behavioural finance research program that so many of us, including the current authors, have enjoyed participating in is that it is unusually conservative in many ways. Specifically it has largely been content to adopt classical rationality as it benchmark for what is rational/normal/correct behaviour, rather than an ecological rationality that reflects the ever–changing context in which investors must trade, markets operate.

Berg and Gigerenzer (2010) point out the adoption of unrealistic assumptions about how choices are made does not condemn the behavioural finance program in and of itself. No less an authority than Freidman (1953) established that the validity of a theory is best judged by its predictions and not its assumptions.

5.5.1 What a difference an assumption makes

Altman (2015b) points out, following Herbert Simon, that what distinguishes a behavioural from a purely economic approach is a focus on the reality, and crucially the reliability, of the underlying assumptions made in investigating the behaviour discussed. Elsewhere Altman (2015a) points out the importance placed by the founders of economics, Adam Smith, John Stuart Mill, and Alfred Marshall on building their economic models upon credible assumptions which accorded with observed social and business practice.

Altman (2015b) cites Leibenstein's comments, which has much intuitive appeal, that:

"counter-factual postulates are unlikely to lead to coherent explanations."

(Leibenstein, 1983), p. 840.

For Altman, inspired by Herbert Simon, this reflects an undue focus on choice *outcomes*, as against the *process* by which a choice is made. Later reflecting on Vernon's Smiths research on experimental economics he asks

"If you could choose your ancestors would you want them to be survivalists or wealth-maximisers?"

Hopefully we all know which to choose. Survival is a minimal, if not entirely noble, objective if a trait, behaviour, or culture is to persist in future generations.

The law of gravity assumes a frictionless universe, a ridiculous assumption. But it predicts the trajectory of spacecraft pretty well, so what's not to love? Problems arise when models based on flawed assumptions predict badly the economic/social phenomena they address. This may become a problem when the environment changes, as it did during the 2008 crisis, as new trading strategies, regulatory arbitrage and new market actors, in the form of the shadow banking system, wreaked their effects.

5.5.2 Behavioural finance: applications and their limitations

Berg and Gigerenzer (2010) examine three examples where the explanatory power of behavioural finance models, invoking, classical rationality as a normative guide to investor agent behaviour, has come up short. These are
1. models of loss-aversion, especially (Kahneman and Tversky, 1979), (Barberis et al., 2001b),
2. models of time–inconsistent choice, especially (Laibson, 1997),
3. models of choice which includes other's benefit as well as the chooser's, especially a model of fairness proposed by Ernst Fehr (Fehr and Schmidt, 1999).

Each of these applications shares a common modelling strategy. First a standard investor/agent's utility function is augmented to reflect deviation between observed behaviour/practice and the model's predictions, say losses hurt twice as much as gains please, or an observed "present bias". Secondly, the model retains classical rationality, expected–utility with rational expectations.

Kahneman (2011) (p. 272) in introducing a discussion of his development, together with Amos Tversky who tragically died before sharing the Nobel Prize with Kahneman, of prospect theory states

"During the first few years we spent looking at how people make decisions we established dozens of facts about choices between risky options. Several of these were in flat contradiction of expected utility theory... We then constructed a theory that modified expected theory just enough to explain our collection of observations. That was prospect theory."

Berg and Gigerenzer (2010) see this sort of reasoning as falling into a pattern behavioural economics/finance scholars follow of adopting a revised investor/agent utility function and proceeding as normal with neo-classical economics modelling. Rabin (1998) in reviewing literature on behavioural economics explicitly states that the contribution of psychology to economics works though a better specification of the investor/agent's utility function.

We shall discuss one very elegant and illuminating example of such an approach by Rabin himself in the Chapter on the "law of small numbers". This approach to behavioural finance simply accepts the tools in the economic theorists toolbox, expected utility, rational expectations, transitivity, etc.; even when they seem almost absurd in their implications. They do so in the hope of yielding simple, elegant, models with high explanatory power.

Berg and Gigerenzer (2010) point out adding additional parameters to an investor's utility function can just lead us to overfit the model to in–sample data, at the cost of compromising out–of–sample predictions. One example of this they give is the ability of the lexicographic, "priority heuristic", (Brandstätter et al., 2006), which has no adjustable/estimated parameters, to beat a standard "prospect theory" prediction of a gambler's choice across gambles.

There is a danger researchers are unwittingly drawn into adopting models that raise estimated R-square in sample, but serve the investor/agent badly as a predictive tool. If we agree with Freidman (1953) that a model's predictive power is the central trait on which it must be evaluated this would be a very unfortunate path to enter upon.

Behavioural finance research simply accepts the normative implications of received neoclassical theory. This may have been wise in a brand of scholarship that was not initially welcomed with open arms by mainstream finance scholars (Fama, 1998).

Thaler (1994) (p. 138) was quite explicit about this acceptance of the modelling framework of neo-classical economics stating[1]

"A demonstration that human choices often violate the axioms of rationality does not necessarily imply any criticism of axioms of rational choice as a normative idea. Rather, the research is simply intended to show that for descriptive purposes, alternative models are sometimes necessary."

So at its first incarnation the behavioural approach was value free and purely descriptive. Yet as Berg and Gigerenzer (2010) argue this does not seem to have stopped behavioural economists advocating quite defined policy positions, perhaps most famously the "Nudge" behavioural guidance initiative (Thaler and Sunstein, 2008). This type of advocacy seems to wish to expand models of choice to encompass commonly observed "mistakes"; without ever reflecting on whether these are truly mistakes, rather than the product of an alternative, ecological, rationality.

Thus ecological rationality may dictate eating more in cold climates, where body fat can help retain body heat, than in warm ones. Or saving more when I have dependents to inherit my estate. The "correct" choice depends very much on the environment into which it will be deployed. Berg and Gigerenzer (2010) remain sceptical that non-expected utility maximisers, or those who deviate from bayesian inference, can by default be classified as "irrational".

5.6 Is behavioural economics behavioural? If not how can it be made so?

A fairly basic problem with behavioural economics is. "If we accept the, straw man, interpretation of behavioural finance as changing the utility function and carrying on as usual with neo-classical economics modelling

---

[1] Cited by Berg and Gigerenzer (2010), p. 145.

techniques, can behavioural economics/finance research really add much to understanding investor behaviour?". Güth (2008) considers behavioural models of "fairness" which seek to explain results from ultimatum games which suggest players reject lowball offers offering below a third of the shared pot, despite the fact this is costly to them (because they then lose out on their, derisory, share of the pot they are offered).

Such, self–defeating, indignation has been termed "inequality aversion" by behavioural economics theorists. Güth wonders whether this advances the debate on what justice is, or how it is established, that much. It can rather seem like an exercise in fancy labelling, without any serious attempt to explain the phenomena.

The danger is such labels become so blithely applied that they effectively become meaningless (Gigerenzer, 1996). Gigerenzer (1996) (p. 592) explains the problem thus

> *"The problem is with these heuristics is that they explain too little and too much. Too little, because we do not know how these heuristics work and how; too much, because, post–hoc, one of them can be fitted to almost any experimental result."*

One is left feeling that such trading in behavioural labels simply diverts us from any serious attempt to model the financial decision-making process. In place of this Gigerenzer (1996) (p. 594) points to two typical strategies used by behavioural economics/finance theorists

1. the application of one–word labels, like representativeness, optimism, herding, to broadly describe rather than explain a finding,
2. explanation as redescription, so calling retaliation for injustice "inequality aversion". Sometimes just presenting a problem, which demonstrated decision-maker bias when discussed in probabilities, in frequency of occurrence terms, serves to resolve the apparent "bias". It is hardly then satisfying to explain this by stating that the correct answer is rendered more transparent. This simply serves to restate the problem without resolving it.

5.6.1 A reformation or a revolution? Repair programs and game–fitting standard finance models

Güth (2008) points three different ways of adapting standard finance/economic models to a behavioural purpose. These are by changing assumptions regarding

1. preferences,
2. choice sets,
3. what is best/optimal for the individual, that is their utility function.

Güth calls behavioural models that rejig standard models of individual choice "neoclassical repairs" for a behavioural purpose and analogous behavioural models of group choice, "game–fitting". It is worthwhile considering some examples of these models in action. He notes it is rare to find anyone asking "Why do investors behave this way?" or "Why is this the choice set on offer?" and not some expanded/contracted one? For a behavioural approach often the behaviour being considered almost passes without comment.

As already discussed in Chapter 3 above a major feature of the fast-and-frugal approach has been its preference for *ecological* over *classical* definitions of rationality. Such Darwinist forms of modelling embed the notion that "history matters", if I notice my peers are getting rich adopting, contrarian/momentum strategies I may imitate them. If I get burnt by following a particular analyst I may shun their advice in future. A central insight of the EMH is the *forward* looking nature of financial markets and it is hard to fault the wisdom of that approach. But our intuition suggests history matters too.

5.6.2 The properties of adaptive dynamic models

So replicator dynamics type models, that extrapolate current from past behaviour alone are polar case models requiring balancing by some forward–looking element. Re-enforcement learning/RL models are subject to a similar objection. Güth considers a range of such adaptive models and their respective properties, see Table 5.3, and stylises these models according to three attributes

1. what the decision-maker must know about their environment,
2. which feedback information the decision process requires,
3. the degree of rationality required of the decision-maker by the decision-making process.

Note the first two candidate models in the adaptive dynamics group, replicator dynamics and re-enforcement learning models, suppose we *solely* look backwards in making current decisions; perhaps an incredible case. Directional learning models extend the decision-maker's rationality by supposing they make inferences about how one's choices now impacts one's future success, but without considering how other traders/players will respond to, imitate/shun, my successful/failing strategies.

Table 5.3 Adaptive dynamics models properties.

Type of adaption	Awareness of decision environment	Feedback information	Rationality request
Replicator dynamics	None	None	None
Reinforcement learning	That our own and other's behaviour are the same. Directional learning	Full	What was good in past will be good in future. About our own past outcome retrospective decision analysis
Imitation		About other's past behaviour	
Full rationality in	Full		Rational forward
Best reply dynamics			looking deliberation

Güth reports such directional learning models as having mixed success. He finds this sort of mechanical, adaptive dynamics models somewhat shallow as explanations, as opposed to possible descriptions, of behaviour. He states (p. 247)

"In our view, the new tradition of behavioural economics, also requires a new toolbox. There is nothing truly behavioural about maintaining people optimise more or less complex "utilities", that interacting parties will be able to derive equilibria requiring circular reasoning, or when claiming the opposite, namely that people are dumb, as supposed by some of the popular adaptive dynamics [models]."

So Güth is despondent about much current "behavioural" economics/finance and asks what are possible areas for truly behavioural models of financial decision-making? Güth (2008) (p. 250) identifies four fertile areas

1. heuristics, fast-and-frugal decision-making tools, requiring little information or prolonged reflection,
2. routines, standard rules for how to change behaviour in response to a change in environment, which are commonly encountered, so say keeping a fixed pay-out ratio out of retained earnings each year.
3. searches for similarity in the decisions we regularly make, so all biotech start-up IPOs, which can be dealt with in the same way, or at least can have their prospective value analysed according to a common schemata. This is the important task of constructing a "reference class" for judging event frequencies. Such rules must be clear and tightly defined, so as to be easily implemented.
4. aspects of cognitive psychology that tell us *how* decisions are made, offering decision templates which might be represented as fast-and-frugal trees.

Ideally a true behavioural economics will not only *explain* investment behaviour but also *improve* it. Güth (2008) states the case thus (p. 250)

"Behavioural economics has to offer a truly behavioural perspective on how behaviour can be improved by teaching, learning and advice."

Indeed this has been the increasing orientation of Gerd Gigerenzer himself in addressing health choices and medical decisions and ameliorating the effects of poor financial literacy in his most recent work at the Harding Centre ((Gigerenzer, 2002), (Gigerenzer, 2015)).

5.6.3 Irrational choice: now you see it, now you don't

As stated earlier once we reject the heuristic and biases tradition's exclusive focus on bayesian rationality as the only true rationality what counts as a cognitive error starts to change. Gigerenzer (1991) advances a class of probabilistic mental models (PMM) to model choice under uncertainty.

Gigerenzer (1991) illustrates the working of such models by how we might consider a question such as "Which City has more inhabitants? (a) Heidelberg, (b) Bonn?". Unless you happen to know the answer (I have no idea) you need to make an informed guess. Gigererzer suggests doing so by invoking a few cues that might indicate the relative size of these two cities.

Gigerenzer (1991) suggests two such possible cues that might indicate size. Is the City in the Budesliga? Great cities have great teams, Chelsea, Paris St Germain, LA Galaxy; so hosting a Bundesliga teams means you are most probably a major German city. Is the City a Capital? London, Abuja, Tehran are capital cities and so likely to be big ones. It's true Lagos may be larger still, but being Nigeria's capital, makes Abuja a very significant place and certainly likely bigger than other Nigerian Cities you have never heard of.

To implement a PMM model of choice I need to settle on a reference class, that might suggest cues for choice, so all German cities, all Bavarian cities, or all US equities. Bounding a reference group is part of defining context, financial stocks and manufacturing stocks are different and might need separate consideration in the same way as Brandenberg–Berliners may require separate consideration to Bavarians.

Once we have our cues we order them hierarchically. So in our city size problem we might simply ask which city is the capital? Answer Bonn. So we infer Bonn is the bigger city. On this basis we infer Bonn is the bigger city, without considering if either is in the Bundesliga. Bonner SC, the Bonn football team, is not in the Bundesliga, but neither is Heidelberg FC. So this cue is not that helpful in deciding which city is larger.

Crucially PMM resolve the choice between unique, or just very rare, events. So leaving the EU might be a unique event for Britain, but if we put it in reference class of leaving multilateral agreements we can pool it with the decision by the US to quit the Paris accord on Climate Change,

NAFTA and the Iran nuclear arms containment deal. If we regard these as sufficiently similar events we can speak about their frequency of occurrence.

5.6.4 PMM: a new lens on decision-making under uncertainty

If Gigerenzer is a rebel "who says No and then says Yes" his yes comes in the form of a new structure for making decisions. These are PMMs. Gigerenzer et al. (1991) outline both the PMM itself and some of the advantages it offers. We follow them by illustrating this by returning to the "Which is the bigger city Heidelberg or Bonn?" question. We might have a good guess of roughly how many people live in Heidelburg, say 150,000 to 250,000. If we know Bonn has at least 250,000 inhabitants the choice is made in Bonn's favour.

Let us return to the "Chose the biggest City?" task. The task compares two alternatives cities a and b, on the basis of a target t, here the number of people living in that city. If the person asked knows the answer from memory we simply assume he has full, 100%, confidence in the answer supplied. Here personal recall of the two cities properties is enough to complete the task with no invocation of probabilistic reasoning.

Such a local mental model, LMM, is schematically represented in Fig. 5.2. It begins with a detailed understanding of the local environment of the decision-task being faced. Personal experience of visiting the cities a and b allow the decision-maker to answer the question, directly without recourse to any cue variable information. Here being a native, with long experience of German civic life, is essential to resolving the question accurately.

A probabilistic mental model is invoked when the subject's memory fails them, or it is just a difficult task, like will stock returns on the Frankfurt market rise or fall next year? A PMM tries to match the given decision-making task to its environment's simple decision-making cues.

To be an effective, have high validity, a cue must covary closely with the target variable. So capital cities must be big ones, like Paris, London, etc. Or major football clubs must be located in large cities, Manchester United, or Barcelona FC, etc.

Outlines of a simple PMM

A central element in the construction of a predictive PMM is the clarity of construction of a clearly delineated *reference class*, so German cities, or Bavarian cities. Ambiguity about the reference class will tend to undermine

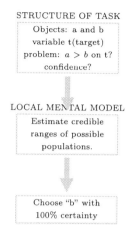

STRUCTURE OF TASK

> Objects: a and b
> variable t(target)
> problem: $a > b$ on t?
> confidence?

LOCAL MENTAL MODEL

> Estimate credible
> ranges of possible
> populations.

> Choose "b" with
> 100% certainty

Figure 5.2 A local mental model of deciding which German City is most populous. *Note*: Source: is Figure 2, p. 508 Gigerenzer et al. (1991).

the predictive value if any PMM model. It is the reference class which will largely determine relevant and feasible cues.

So a PMM model brings together four elements

1. a *reference class* of objects,
2. a *target variable* of that class, size, rate of return, probability of surviving/growing as a constituent element of that reference class,
3. *probability cues*, C_i, indicating likely size, prospective rate of return, etc., for items contained in the reference class,
4. *cue validities*, indicating the ability of a cue to predict the target variable, t.

Gigerenzer et al. (1991) define a confidence cue, C_i, for a target variable t and a target level of confidence, as arising when the probability that answer a to the question asked is correct, p(a), differs from the conditional probability a is the right answer, given that answer a and b differ in their recorded values of that cue variable C_i.

Or formally

$$p(a) \neq p(a \mid aC_ib; R) \tag{5.4}$$

where the term aC_ib captures the relation between answers a and b on the cue variable C_i, for example that city a has a team in the Bundesliga, while city b does not. Thus $p(a \mid aC_ib; R)$ is the cue validity of C for reference class R.

One intuitive way to think about such conditional probability cues, C_i is as statistical correlations, but they need not be symmetric as such correlations are. So while the cue, C_i, may predict the number of people living in a city well, t, despite the fact the number of people living in a city, a continuous variable, is poorly correlated with the binary choice variable a/b?

Here cue validity mirrors the concept of *ecological validity* in the environment studied. So the validity of the soccer cue in Germany, one of the best football nations in the world, is different from what it would be in the United States, where soccer takes second/third place to football and basketball. The choice and measurement of cues reflects an intensely observed knowledge of the decision-making environment and how it is changing.

A PMM's decision-making scheme is represented in Fig. 5.3. This figure shows how a good mental model of the task reflects its structure, on left–hand–side of Fig. 5.3, and the environment into which it is to be deployed, on the right–hand side of Fig. 5.3.

Models of classical rationality do capture the task structure they address, yet they still typically ignore the decision-making environment in favour of fostering a generality of application. PMM redress this imbalance, focusing on relevant, easily observed, predictive decision-making cues, enabling swift decision-making on the basis of very limited information.

Choices within PMMs are made on the basis of confidence cues, C_i, applying the rule:
Choose a if

$$p(a \mid aC_ib; R) > p(b \mid aC_ib; R) \tag{5.5}$$

So when the alternative a is chosen, the confidence it is the correct answer is given by its cue validity.

$$p(a \mid aC_ib; R) \tag{5.6}$$

and since cues are ranked by a single, highest rated, target variable we often can decide an issue by invocation of the "just one reason" heuristic.

So good PMMs invoke the cues with the greatest cue validity for the relevant decision-making context. So Heidelberg and Bonn are quite big cities.[2] It is quite likely the bigger one has a football club.

---

[2] Heidelburg has 143,345 inhabitants, Bonn 313,125. See http://worldpopulationreview.com/countries/germany-population/cities/.

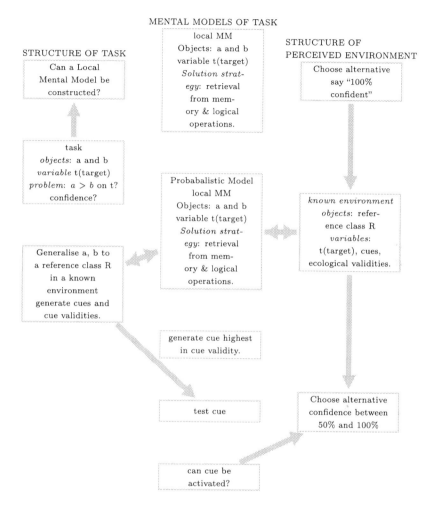

MENTAL MODELS OF TASK

Figure 5.3 A probabilistic mental model (PMM) of solving a two-alternative general knowledge task. *Note:* Source: is Figure 1, p. 508 Gigerenzer et al. (1991).

But what about the question "Which place has the larger population Singen or Gotha?". Both these places are tiny.[3] Neither is likely to be either the German capital or have a football team. Here we might look for other cues, such as does it have a designated representative on the regional Lutheran/Catholic Church Lander/regional council, or a regional Hospital?

---

[3] Singen has 45,696 inhabitants, Gotha 46,615. See http://worldpopulationreview.com/countries/germany-population/cities/.

Decisions are made reflecting an *ecological*, not, *classical* rationality, focusing closely on the structure and decision-making environment of the task. Expertise is defined locally and no heroic attempt at global application is made. When the environment changes, so does the applicable decision-making routine, sacrificing generality of application in favour of local decision-making accuracy.

5.7 Conclusion

When should we go fast-and-frugal and when should we keep our behavioural hat on? One way of answering this is simply to say always go fast-and-frugal. As Knight argues life is fundamentally uncertain and in truth we most likely like it that way.

We idolise Gugielmo Marconi, Howard Hughes, and Steve Jobs precisely because they leaped into a void in electronics, aviation, computing and brought us products we now rely upon; often showing suitable arrogance along the way. Further, we must ask how behavioural is behavioural finance? Stripping away all the redescription and broad labelling how much is there to truly explain observed investor/trader behaviour?

In some, perhaps not frequent, setting we may be able to define reference classes pretty well, say a futures contract for three month delivery of Brent Crude oil to the Hook of Holland. All such futures contracts may seem the same, although petrologists maybe argue about details. But often this will be harder. Tesla and GM are both car manufacturers, but is pooling them a good idea? When shaping a reference class is hard then fast-and-frugal reasoning becomes attractive as a *predictive* device.

But fast-and-frugal models may seem attractive as *explanatory* devices when they capture essential investment/manufacturing routines. Often the utility functions embedded in currently popular behavioural models offer so many degrees of freedom in estimation that "anything goes".

The reformulation of prospect theory (Kahneman and Tversky, 1979) as cumulative prospect theory (Tversky and Kahneman, 1992) illustrates this danger. It enhances that theory's meaning, but also gives additional opportunities to "tweek" the model avoiding refutation of its premise. Enough tweeks of a model can render it almost vacuous in its content. Since nothing can come from everything we might feel the need for "behavioural" finance researchers to speak again.

Fast-and-frugal trees and PMM models can add much needed structure to how financial decisions are made and how that decision-making mechanics might change with the decision-making environment into which its deployed. Further, fast-and-frugal modelling can capture a powerful ecological rationality in decision-making choices under uncertainty.

The fast-and-frugal approach has advanced an attractive alternative to standard statistical decision-making models in the form of PMMs. But it remains largely untested upon financial decision-making questions. This means there is a rich harvest ahead of fast-and-frugal reasoners working to solve standard problems in financial decision-making. We hope this book can begin the process of reaping these rewards.

PART 2

Applications of
fast-and-frugal finance

CHAPTER 6

Fast-and-frugal asset pricing

Asset pricing constitutes the jewell in the crown of financial economics. If asset value is taken to be the discounted value of future cash-flows, then having a decent model of the appropriate discount rate to use in such valuation exercises is pretty central. An examination of the pantheon of the greats of finance scholarship, Samuelson, Markowitz, Sharpe, Jensen, Fama, and Shiller confirm the centrality of this asset pricing. A great finance scholar will certainly often contribute widely, but influencing asset pricing theory seems to be a qualifying characteristic of intellectual leaders in our field.

Despite all this, even here, where the greatest effort has been made, a coherent, universally accepted, asset pricing model is not yet in sight. Campbell (2000) in a generally upbeat review of the field states

"it is unrealistic to hope for a fully rational, risk-based, explanation of all the empirical patterns that have been discovered in stock returns. A more reasonable view is that rational models of risk and return describe a long-run equilibrium towards which financial markets gradually evolve."

Campbell (2000), pp. 1557–58.

Such advice which seems unlikely to imbue a client with confidence about the value of the investment guidance being given.

In this Chapter we compare a fast-and-frugal model of asset pricing with one of the leading models in the asset field, the Fama-French 5-factor model (Fama and French (2015)), henceforth FF5. This application of fast-and-frugal reasoning should only be regarded as illustrative, as other popular models of asset pricing are available, not least the Fama-French 3 factor model (Fama and French (1993)), henceforth FF3.

Berg and Gigerenzer (2010) point out in all three cases the standard behavioural approach works in a very similar way. First the model, FF3 or FF5, proposes a change to the investor/agent's utility function to account for the fact that standard theory does not explain observed data/practice that well. Second both models adopt the benchmark of classical rationality for how an investor/agent should behave.

The estimation and inference from such asset pricing models has proved rather fraught (Harvey et al. (2016)). So here we explore the possibility that

A Fast and Frugal Finance
https://doi.org/10.1016/B978-0-12-812495-6.00014-8

"less is more" and adopt a fast-and-frugal modelling technique based on Gigerenzer and Goldstein (1996) and Goldstein and Gigerenzer (2009).

As we shall see evidence that very simple models beat regression analysis in particular has existed for a very long time (Dawes and Corrigan (1974), Einhorn and Hogarth (1975)) yet the ability of finance researchers, in common with most of their social science colleagues, to ignore this fact has been impressive. One reason for doing so is that such models do not work/predict so well in the context of fast–moving, contextually rich, financial markets and this would certainly be one legitimate conclusion from the study conducted here.

But the dismissive attitude of finance scholarship to fast-and-frugal reasoning is striking, implying the best estimates/predictors are those that use the widest range of information and not to do so is just bad practice. Here we simply ask is this true, or could fast-and-frugal, biased, predictive methods; that consciously ignore valuable information, have something to commend them after all?

6.0.1 The current stare of empirical asset price modelling

Most of what we know about asset pricing is drawn from, largely US based, publications in the main academic journals which serve as the gatekeepers of received truth for such knowledge claims. Harvey et al. (2016) point out such Finance journals have a bias towards publishing results that are statistically significant rather than those that confirm the null of no effect. So a paper reporting I looked for the impact of football results on asset pricing and found none is unlikely to be published, but a paper finding the reverse is (see Ashton et al. (2003)).

So for every x factors, 3 or 5, reported in the literature to determine stock market movements we might imagine a multiple of x has been tried by academics/practitioners, as possible explanations of stock price movements, and failed. So the evidence we study in Business School finance classes is a selection of all there is.

Some academic fields, like Medicine, publish replication studies to check, and hopefully build confidence in, existing knowledge. But economics and finance journals, for the most part, do not. So a claim, once accepted, becomes hard to refute in asset pricing.

6.0.2 The fraught process of asset–pricing factor discovery

Harvey et al. (2016) adopt a standard representation of hypothesis testing in statistics, see Table 6.1. Empirical work throws up two types of errors (see

Table 6.1 Contingency table in testing M hypothesis.

	H_0 not rejected	H_0 rejected	Total
H_0 true	$N_{0|a}$	$N_{0|r}$	M_0
H_0 false	$N_{1|a}$	$N_{1|r}$	M_1
Total	M-R	R	M
	Unpublished	**Published**	**Total**
Truly insignificant	500	50	550
Truly significant	100	50	150
Total	600	100(R)	700 (M)

Source: Based on Table 2 Harvey et al. (2016), p. 12.

Harvey et al. (2016), p. 12). In the upper panel of Table 6.1, $N_{0|r}$ records instances of Type I errors; when the null, while true, is nonetheless rejected. Similarly, in the upper panel of Table 6.1 $N_{1|a}$ captures Type II errors, when H_1 is rejected, or H_0 accepted, despite the fact the alternative hypothesis, H_1 is true.

Harvey et al. (2016) illustrate the problem that arises by considering a case where 100 asset–pricing "factors" are published in academic Journals. So these R "factors" reflect some that are correctly statistically identified, by valid refutations of the null H_0, and some that are not. Suppose half of these factor discoveries are truly driving returns and half just derive from statistical noise, so $N_{0|r} = N_{1|r} = 50$. Assume researchers have tried another 600 factors that were found to be insignificant in the search for the 100 found to be significant.

So they are two type statistical errors made in this factor–discovery process. Firstly, 50 factors are falsely found to be driving stock returns, a false positive, Type I, error. Secondly, factors which truly influence stock returns, but lie buried under rejection letters from journals or somewhere in abandoned projects, these are false negative, Type II, errors. Let us assume Type I errors occur with a frequency α, which is often called the "level of significance".

Assume that the second type of statistical inference error, Type II errors, occur with frequency β. Harvey et al. (2016) explore a form of "multiple–testing" that aims to lower the ratio of false positives to false negatives, $\frac{\alpha}{\beta}$, here $\frac{50}{100} = \frac{1}{2}$.

Of course such "testing" is strained as it requires invoking the influence of "unobserved factors", such as the influence of research that was abandoned when no correlation between the proposed factor and asset returns

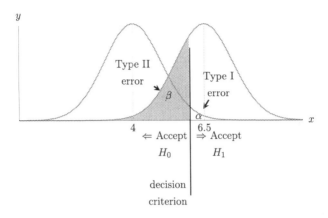

Figure 6.1 Testing the null, H_0, versus the alternative, H_1. *Note*: Based on Figure 1.2 (Gigerenzer and Murray, 1987), p. 13.

could be found. Fig. 6.1 gives a schematic representation of the hypothesis testing process.

In this example suppose the distribution of returns under the null has a mean of 4 (%) and under the alternative of 6.5 (%). Since the two distributions overlap we need to impose a cut-off point when we will reject the null H_0 in favour of the alternative H_1. We accept a probability α of drawing from the overlap of the distributions of stock returns under the null, H_0, of no effect and the alternative H_1. So standard hypothesis testing simply accepts that one might be sampling the extreme right–hand–side of the distribution under the null, where asset returns are lower, when one believes one is sampling the distribution of returns under the valid alternative.

The area β represents the proportion of the distribution of returns under the alternative which we discount/ignore in confirming the truth of that alternative hypothesis. So the area β shows how often we reject the alternative, H_1, when it is true. Hence one can see why the "power" of a statistical test is given by $1 - \beta$, because this is the proportion of cases when we reject a false alternative.

Why does this matter anyway? The power of a statistical test tells us how likely our test is to detect a real effect in our sample data. Or conversely how likely we are to miss a real asset–pricing factor that is lying in our data awaiting discovery. So a test with a 90% power means that in 10% of samples of returns, which are randomly drawn, we will not detect the effect of a factor which truly drives asset returns.

The power of a test determines its replicability, a test with a power of 90% has a 81% (0.9^2) chance of being replicated by subsequent authors if the subsequent sample is drawn independently of the first (which is extremely unlikely in finance scholarship). As we shall see replicability is now a major issue both in social science and science itself.

6.0.3 The weakness of measures of statistical power in finance research

Karolyi (2011) in a study that contains much encouragement about the healthy state of empirical work in finance comments upon the disparity between the strength of the treatment of issues concerning statistical significance compared to discussion of, and corrections for, the low power of the statistical tests employed in published finance research.

Karolyi studies all the empirical papers published in the *Journal of Finance*, *Journal of Financial Economics* and *Review of Financial Studies*, three of best, most influential, academic finance journals in the world for the years 1989, 1999, and 2009, to get a feel of how best empirical practice is evolving. This yields a crop of some 457 individual papers eligible papers. Karolyi then answers 10 yes/no questions about each of the 457 papers he examines.

Here we just focus on the questions on which the answers reflected worst on empirical finance research, largely ignoring Karolyi's basic conclusion that there is much good news about how empirical work in finance is going. But to offset any feeling of a counsel of despair it is wise to recall Karolyi's conclusion (Karolyi (2011), p. 508)

> *"Published papers in top–tier Journals these days are meticulous in distinguishing between statistical and economic significance and in quantifying and interpreting the economic magnitude of the statistical relationships they measure. More than 80% of published papers appear to understand these distinctions, which is a pretty good success rate."*

But this silver lining belies the cloud of ignorance finance researchers display with respect to the statistical power of the tests they undertake. Karolyi's first three, power related, questions in his 10 question survey are

1. Does the paper mention the power of the tests?
2. If the paper does mention power, does it do anything about it?
3. Does the paper use any type of simulations; such as Monte Carlo simulations and bootstrap methods?

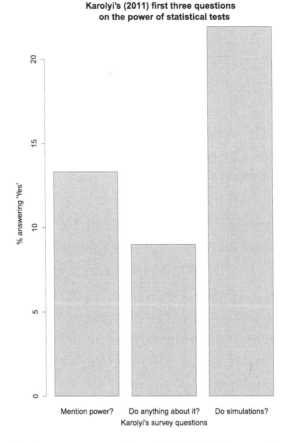

Figure 6.2 The first three survey questions of Karolyi (2011) concerning the power of statistical tests in published finance work. *Note*: Source: Table 1, (Karolyi (2011), p. 491).

The results over the whole sample, of 457 published papers, make grim reading, as Fig. 6.2 shows. Only 13.3% of the sample papers even mention power at all. Of those that do, even fewer, only 9% do anything about it. The use of simulation experiments, bootstrap methods, randomisation techniques (Noreen (1989)) is more widespread, appearing in 25.2% of sample papers in 2009, the final year sampled.

Overall an impression of lack of interest, or care about, the power of the statistical tests used remains. Nor is interest in statistical power increasing, as Table 6.2 shows. There has been a marked and steady increase in the use of simulation methods, but this may be more to address issues of

Table 6.2 How attention to power issues in statistical inference is progressing/regressing in three premier finance Journals published work 1989–2009.

Question in survey (% attracting answer "Yes")	1989	1999	2009
Power of test mentioned?	18.9%	11.2%	12.8%
Anything done about power?	6.8%	8%	10.1%
Simulations performed?	14.9%	19.2%	25.2%

Note: Based on answer to first 3 question in Karolyi (2011) survey. See Table 2, p. 493.

non-normality in the distribution of asset–returns than to address issues of statistical power directly.

Explicit discussion of statistical power is falling steadily over the sample period. This is very odd, given the general improvement in the quality and robustness of empirical work in finance Karolyi's survey overall records.

When a finance researcher looks for asset pricing factors they confront the data with a possible factor, attempting to correlate its movements with returns, to see if the null hypothesis of no effect, H_0 is true. So in the upper panel of Table 6.1 a "0" denotes the null hypothesis and a "1" its alternative. Here an "r" denotes rejection of the null/alternative, while an "a" denotes its acceptance.

So $N_{0|r}$ captures the number of false factor discoveries, Type I errors, while $N_{1|a}$ represents the number of missed factor discoveries, which further research could affirm. In any single hypothesis test, the level of significance, α, is used to guard the researcher against a Type I/false positive, error.

Only if the factor has a significance above the α threshold, say only a 5% probability of such a correlation occurring by chance, is it regarded as a candidate for being a legitimate driver of asset–returns. But since the same factors are often tested for significance by many finance researchers, using broadly similar datasets, we may need to raise α, to reflect the fact that any given researcher is revisiting a possible asset–pricing factor, and often a data set, examined by a researcher before them.

Repeated testing and false discoveries

The more possible asset–pricing factors that are tested the more likely it becomes one is confirmed as a significant driver of asset–returns by pure chance, yielding a false positive, Type I, error. So the chances of empirical finance researchers discovering something "by chance" is higher given they were told where to look for the factor. Any statistical test of a multifactor asset–pricing model must incorporate the possibility of such multiple false–discoveries.

A satisfactory measure of overall statistical error combines both false discoveries and true factors which are missed, $N_{0|r} + N_{1|a}$. Harvey et al. then define the false discovery rate, for asset–pricing factors, as follows

$$FDP = \begin{cases} \frac{N_{0|r}}{R}, & \text{if } R > 0. \\ 0, & R = 0. \end{cases} \quad (6.1)$$

So the false discovery proportion, FDP, is defined over those research contributions which claim to reject the null; capturing that proportion which makes a false, by chance, claim of statistical significance. FDP thus captures the proportion of false asset–pricing factor discoveries in all recorded asset–pricing factor discoveries.

One easy way to reduce FDP is simply to raise the required level of significance which is used to make a factor discovery credible, say by raising the requisite level of significance from 95% to 99%; so that the results could only be obtained by chance in 1 in 100 replications, rather than the more conventional 1 in 20.

But this type of statistical adjustment will only exacerbate Type II errors of missed discoveries. Type II errors of missed discovery can be measured in the upper-panel of Table 6.1 framework by the ratio $\frac{N_{1|a}}{(M-R)}$. Any credible estimator must focus on minimising the sum of Type I and II errors, balancing them effectively. Harvey et al. explore a number of such adjustment methods.

6.0.4 Balancing Type I and II errors in finance research

Harvey et al. examine a sample of 313 articles of which 250 are published in leading Finance Journals. They divide their factor discovery into two; those investigating two risk types,

those studying "common" risk-factors expected to influence all stocks, like interest rates or the business cycle (Fama and MacBeth (1973), Fama (1990)), and

those studying particular "characteristics" that might only effect some stocks, such as dividend omissions or high R&D expenditure (Michaely et al. (1995), Al-Horani et al. (2003)).

Within these broad groupings they consider a range of risk categories as follows:

accounting

behavioural

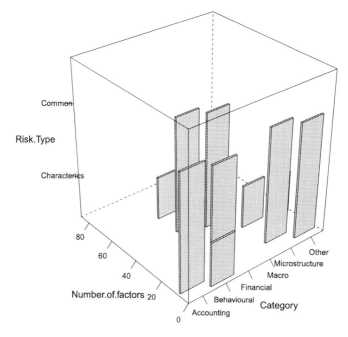

Figure 6.3 The type of factors identified by Harvey et al. (2016). *Note*: Source: Figure 1, Harvey et al. (2016), p. 10.

financial macroeconomic
market microstructure
other

where macroeconomic factors are only considered amongst the common factors, as characteristic risk factors are stock/sector specific by design. Akerlof and Shiller (2009), following Keynes (1936), emphasise the importance of the State as a lender of last resort, especially in times of crisis. This reminds us of the importance of macro/sentiment factors in driving individual stock's returns.

Fig. 6.3 shows the distribution of factors discovered across their sample of 313 asset–pricing factor studies (based on Table 1 of Harvey et al., p. 10). The authors sample incorporates investigations of 113 common factors and 202 characteristic types of risk. Amongst common factors the authors found financial (46 factors), macroeconomic (40 factors) and market microstructure (11 factors) predominate as established explanations for changes in asset returns. Amongst characteristic types of risk accounting (87 factors), financial (61 factors) and market microstructure (28 factors) surface as the primary drivers of asset–returns in the sample of empirical papers studied by the authors.

Examining the evolution of the literature from 1962 to 2012 Harvey et al. find that the rate of, alleged, factor discovery grows with the scale of academic interest in an area, with very few factors being found until the late 1980's when a rapid accumulation of factors begins and continues until the end of the sample.

In the late 1980's about one asset–pricing factor a year was discovered, by the early 1990's this had grown to five factors a year. After 2003, until 2012, the rate of factor discovery swelled to eighteen factors a year.

Never has the "less is more" principle in statistical modelling been more needed it seems. This might bring much needed order to the "zoo of new factors" John Cochrane describes in his Presidential address to the American Finance Association (Cochrane (2011)).

6.0.5 The research reproducibility crisis in science as a whole

Given the focus of this book it is appropriate for us to focus on research in finance Journals on finance topics. But the extent of doubts about empirical work in finance cannot be separated from doubts about the value/reliability of empirical studies in general, including those in Economics and Science. While it is certainly true claims for spurious asset pricing factors never killed anyone, the same cannot be said for medical studies.

For that reason is troubling to come across a study in a leading medical journal entitled "Why most published research findings are false" (Ioannides (2005)). Summarising the prevailing wisdom in medical research Ioannides states (Ioannides (2005), p. 696)

"Simulations show that for most study designs and settings, it is more likely for a research claim to be false than true. Moreover for many current research scientific fields, claimed research findings may often simply be accurate measures of prevailing bias."

In this regard it is interesting to note the reasons given by Ioannides (2005) for such spurious results production these include
1. when there is a financial or status reward to finding a particular result,
2. when research teams compete for publishable results,
3. when the precise research method to replicate prior results is flexible.

These seem like an almost perfect description of the conditions prevailing in finance research regarding asset–pricing factors currently. Careers are launched on the discovery of new factors and consulting opportunities, in investment banks, arise from those keen to exploit the newly minted factor.

While it is certainly inspiring that valid discoveries are rewarded by the market, such discoveries can also incentivise bad practice. For this reason academic Journals are increasingly asking authors to surrender their data and the computer code they used to generate their reported results before final acceptance of their paper for publication.

Within Economics there is increasing interest in Metadata studies, which examine studies testing the same hypothesis on a similar data set, to confirm that they find comparable results (Maniadis and Tufano (2017)). Ioannidis et al. (2017) examine the results of 159 metadata studies undertaken in the economics field which themselves review some 6,730 underlying primary empirical studies.

To be included in the Ioannidis et al. study metastudy authors needed to be contactable by Iionnidis and his co-authors and enter into a dialogue about their study; this favoured recent studies, with more confident authors who were open to discussion about their published findings. After reviewing the wealth and variety of evidence contained in the 159 metadata studies of empirical work in economics Ioannidis et al. (2017, p. F253) conclude

"Regardless of how [the] "true" effect is estimated typical statistical power is no more than 18% and nearly half of the areas surveyed have 90% or more of their reported results stemming from underpowered studies... The majority of the average effects in the empirical economics literature are exaggerated at least by a factor of 2 and at least one–third are exaggerated by a factor of 4 or more."

This suggests our reading of the empirical finance literature should always be sceptical and alert to the possibilities of a false discovery.

6.1 The Fama-French asset pricing models

Over a period about 25 years (from Fama and French (1992) onwards) Eugene Fama and Kenneth French have been developing asset–pricing models that have now, for better of worse, become the benchmark for "event-day"/information content studies in finance. Certainly they must have been doing something right as Eugene Fama received the Nobel Prize for Economics in 2013, twenty years after the FF3 model appeared (Fama and

French (1993)), although this was certainly not Fama's only contribution to our subject (see (Fama et al., 1969), (Fama, 1970), (Fama, 1991)).

Recently Fama and French have extended their FF3 model to incorporate five factors, extending the number of asset–pricing factors in the hope of getting a better representation of what drives asset prices. This led them to the FF5 model we study in this Chapter, (Fama and French (2015), Fama and French (2016)). Fast-and-frugal reasoning was not their primary concern it would appear.

So since we have two versions of the model, FF3 and FF5 it seems a perfect opportunity to ask is complicated better, or is keeping it simple (stupid) still good advice? Fama himself seems pragmatic in his attitude to empirical asset price stating in an interview after receiving the Prize (Fama and Stern (2016), p. 10)

> "we use models only as a way of organising our thinking... we shouldn't take the model itself seriously."

So if the particular model is not too important should we just go for the simplest, most frugal, model possible?

6.1.1 The motivation for the FF3/FF5 models

Fama and French ground their models in the idea that a stock's value, and hence price in an efficient market, which reflects the discounted value of the future dividend stream its owners can expect from holding the stock forever

$$m_t = \sum_{\tau=1}^{\infty} \frac{E(d_{t+\tau})}{(1+r)^\tau} \qquad (6.2)$$

where m is market value–per-share, or price, E(d) are expected dividends–per-share and finally, r is the appropriate, risk-adjusted market–rate of interest applicable to the future dividends stream, $d_{t+\tau}$.

So since investors get future dividends as a reward to holding stocks, a higher discount rate, r, implies a lower stock price, m_t. A higher discount rate applicable to those stocks implies a lower price, so more company specific risk implies a lower price and therefore a higher return, recall $r_t = \frac{(d_t+(p_t-p_{t-1})}{p_{t-1}}$.

The Fama-French model relies on a convention of accounting practice which states that successive book–values, or the "bottom line" of the balance sheet, should reflect past earnings, as netted–off against dividends/Owner's contributions. So book value this accounting period, B_t equals that last year, B_{t-1} period plus last year's earnings, Y_{t-1} minus dividends paid out last year, d_{t-1}. So

$$B_t = B_{t-1} + Y_{t-1} - d_{t-1} \qquad (6.3)$$

under such "clean-surplus" accounting; that ensures all changes in value are fully represented in successive corporate balance–sheets.

So we can restate Eq. (6.2) to read

$$M_t = \sum_{\tau=1}^{\infty} \frac{Y_{t+\tau} - \Delta B_{t+\tau}}{(1+r)^\tau} \qquad (6.4)$$

where the numerator now reflects how changes in shareholder capital, ΔB_t, as well as impact reported earnings in the future, $Y_{t+\tau}$. Dividing both sides by book–value gives

$$\frac{M_t}{B_t} = \frac{\sum_{\tau=1}^{\infty} \frac{E(Y_{t+\tau} - \Delta B_{t+\tau})}{(1+r)^\tau}}{B_t} \qquad (6.5)$$

Fama-French consider three comparative static exercises to indicate how returns might move in response to expected changes (where investors' expectations are captured by the expectations operator E() in Eq. (6.5)) in market values, M_t, book–values, B_t and earnings, Y_t. These are

1. a lower market value, M_t, or alternatively a higher book–value, B_t, implies a lower expected future rate of return, $(1+r)^\tau$, all else being equal. The former being directly implied by the definition of return itself, $\frac{(d_t + (p_t - p_{t-1}))}{p_{t-1}}$.

2. the higher are expected earnings, $Y_{t+\tau}$, the higher current returns, all else being equal.

3. more investment, or a growth in book value, $\Delta B_{t+\tau}$, implies a lower return, all else being equal. This makes intuitive sense, as increased investments will reduce profits, out of which all dividends are paid. And incremental investments may be expected to move further down a company's NPV schedule, as the most profitable investments are those made first.

So overall Eq. (6.5) implies the book to market ratio, $\frac{B}{M}$ is a noisy indicator of future movements in earnings and investment.

The rationale of the FF3/FF5 models

Fama and French (2015) ground of their FF3/FF5 models in earlier work by Campbell and Shiller (1988). Campbell (1991) suggests a decomposition of excess stock returns into three elements as follows

$$R_{t+1} - E_t R_{t+1} = E_{t-1}[R_{t-1}] + (E_t - E_{t-1}) \left[\sum_{j=0}^{\infty} \rho^j d_{t+1+j} \right] \tag{6.6}$$

$$-(E_t - E_{t-1}) \left[\sum_{j=1}^{\infty} \rho^{j-1} R_{t+1+j} \right]$$

which sees the trajectory of future excess stock returns as separating into three elements
1. expectations of current excess returns formed last year, R_{t-1},
2. changes in expectations, $(E_t - E_{t-1})$, about future/dividends cash-flows into the infinite future,
3. changes in expectations about future excess returns, R_{t+1+j}, into the infinite future, which will determine discount rates used on future cash flows.

Note higher expected future discount rates lower current excess returns because they imply a lower net present value to assets held in the investor's portfolio. Hecht and Vuolteenaho (2006) point out the relation between observed returns and changes in fundamental earnings must reflect all three of these elements (see Sadka and Sadka (2009)).

Hence to decompose the covariance of earnings changes and returns appropriately we form the expression

$$Cov(R_t, \Delta Y_t) = cov(E_{t-1}[R_t], \Delta Y_t) + cov(N_{cf}, \Delta Y_t) - cov(N_R, \Delta Y_t) \tag{6.7}$$

where again the last term captures how expected future increases in discount rates will lower current returns by reducing the present value of the future earnings derived from holding shareholders' equity.

Kothari et al. (2006) report that for a wide group of US companies in the years 1970–2000 aggregate current earnings changes and aggregate returns are negatively correlated. This implies that the third term in Eq. (6.7) above might predominate in observed empirical samples which aggregate over many firms. Further, Kothari et al. (2006) report that changes in current shareholder returns are negatively correlated with changes in the US T-bill interest-rate and the default spread (the difference between the yield on low and highly rated bonds) two commonly used proxies for time-varying discount rates.

Hence current returns cannot be explained by how current earnings differ from their expectation. The effect of this is to set the third term in the decomposition in Eq. (6.7) above to zero. Current returns cannot reflect an adjustment to changes in earnings, as investors know those earnings at the start of the year, hence they are imbued with "the mind of God"/perfect foresight.

This means any returns a contrarian profit generates reflects the trade-off between a positive covariance of current returns with cash-flow innovations, signalled by changes in dividends, embedded in the second term of Eq. (6.7) above, and the negative covariance between current returns and future expected earnings realisations, embedded in the first term in Eq. (6.7) above.

6.1.2 Empirical specification of the FF5/FF3 models

Fama French implement their models, FF5 and FF3, via cross-section, (Fama and MacBeth, 1973) regressions of excess returns on 5/3 indicators of future value, taking the form

$$R_{i,t} - R_{F,t} = a + b(R_{M,t} - R_{F,t}) + sSMB_t + hHML_t$$
$$+ rRMW_t + cCMA_t + e_{i,t} \qquad \text{FF5} \qquad (6.8)$$
$$R_{i,t} - R_{F,t} = a + b(R_{M,t} - R_{F,t}) + sSMB_t + hHML_t + e_{i,t} \quad \text{FF3}$$

where FF3 is embedded within FF5, allowing it to be compared by a simple F-test of the linear restriction, r=c=0 in Eq. (6.8). Here $R_{i,t} - R_{F,t}$ captures excess stock return on the market/index portfolio over the risk–free rate of return, $R_{F,t}$, for the relevant time period, here a month, t, a is a measure of excess returns, performance, or α, exceeding the FF5/FF3 benchmark. SMB is a measure of the difference in the return on smaller, more risky, stocks and bigger, less risky ones. HML is a measure of the difference in return between a portfolio of high book to market, $\frac{B}{M}$, stocks, which are high risk being at, or below, their liquidation value, and a portfolio of low book to market which substantially exceed their liquidation valuations. CMA is the difference between average returns on a portfolio of stocks with a conservative/low investment profile and one with a high/aggressive investment profile, which surrenders current dividends in the hope of earning higher dividends/cash-flows in the future. I plot the Fama-French five factors in Fig. 6.4. Finally, e_i

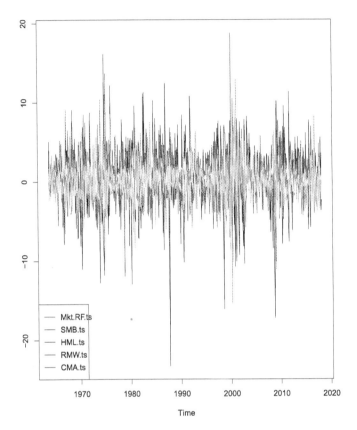

Figure 6.4 Plot of the five Fama-French factors. *Note*: Source: Ken French's personal website in Data Library section. http://mba.tuck.dartmouth.edu/pages/faculty/ken.french/data_library.html

is some error in the estimation of the true underlying asset-generating model. If the true model of asset–returns is FF5/FF3 and that model accounts for all variation in asset returns, for company i, then $\alpha_i = 0$ (see Eq. (6.8)).

Rejections of the restriction a=0, across all sample companies, could mean inefficiency in pricing with respect of these three/five risk-factors or could mean that some other group of "true" return generating factors lead to investors earning risk-premia on these observed factors, which may, or may not, be the true factor generating variables. This reminds us all asset pricing tests are tests of the joint hypothesis of (a) market efficiency and (b) the particular asset price model considered. The difference in returns to stocks of different sizes, value, profitability, investment intensity and can

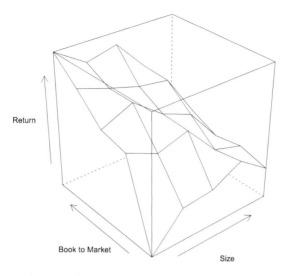

Return

Book to Market

Size

Figure 6.5 Size/Market Capitalisation to Book to Market/"Value" shareholder return profile. *Note*: Source: Table 1 of Fama and French (2015), p. 3.

be shown by examining their returns once ordered in quintile portfolios according to each of these four characteristics, plus overall stock market movements embedded in the market risk–premium, $R_{M,t} - R_{F,t}$.

6.1.3 Difference in shareholder returns across size, value, profitability, and investment portfolios

The difference in returns for value, profitability, and investment intensity is shown within size quintiles in Figs. 6.5 to 6.6. Looking along the size axis of Fig. 6.5 the premium paid to small, low market–capitalisation companies, regardless of their value/glamour, implied by their book–to–market ratio, is clear.

The peak of the surface of portfolio returns at the intersection of high book–to–market and small size; which indicates that "value" stock companies, which cannot command even their book value in the stock market, earn a premium over "glamour" stocks, which trade at some multiple of their book–value. This relationship is monotonic, with value enhancing shareholder returns regardless of company size and at a pretty even cumulative rate.

A fairly similar relationship emerges when we look at the relationship between shareholder returns and operating profit, conditional on company size. But the relationship between returns and operating profitability is

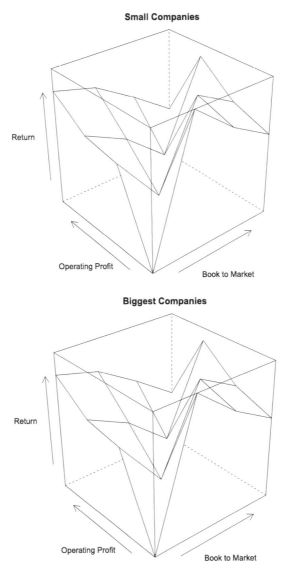

Figure 6.6 The distribution of shareholder returns across book–to–market/operating profitability quintiles for smallest (upper figure) biggest (lower figure) quintile of firms. *Note*: Source: Table 2 of Fama and French (2015), p. 4.

somewhat uneven, with returns rising in tandem with operating profitability until we get to the smallest companies where a modest fall in shareholder returns emerges. So for the smallest quintile of firms it appears increasing operating profitability is of declining value to investors.

When we look a how shareholder returns vary with investment intensity across size quintiles, in unshown calculations, the very poor performance of small/aggressively investing companies is obvious. But this fall in investor returns is really restricted to the most aggressively investing quintile of companies. Prior to that investor returns rise across all size quintiles, as investment intensity increases.

6.1.4 An analysis of extrema portfolios

Since trading strategies almost inevitably buy/sell at the extremes of any chosen risk characteristic Fama and French (2015) examine the response of share returns to changes in value, profit, and investment intensity portfolios for the smallest and biggest companies in their sample; that is those in the first and last market–capitalisation quintile portfolio.

Ideally we would simply examine returns sorted by size, value, profitability, and investment intensity. But this would require breaking the sample into 81 (3^4) portfolios and this would almost certainly yield some very sparsely populated sub-portfolios.

Examining the relation between value and (operating) profitability for both the smallest quintile of companies and for the largest quintile of companies in both these extrema size portfolios high value, or high book–to–market, stocks, which also have low operating profitability, deliver the worst stock market performance of all. But nonetheless shareholder returns rise steadily in profits.

Stocks with minimal investment, defined here as the change in book value, and a low level of book value perform worst of all, regardless of firm size. This makes sense as a stock that investors regard as glamorous, despite having almost no investment for the future in place, seem likely to be heading for a fall. Once again investor returns peak before the lowest quintile of book–to–market, where perhaps a "glamour discount" emerges for those companies which are most overvalued relative to their book value of equity.

When we look at the difference between returns to stocks split into different profitability/investment intensity portfolios, low investment value firms, that are near liquidation/break up value, but have no investment in place to turn the company around, fare especially badly. Once again a sharp decline in the returns to the most glamorous of stocks, in the lowest book–to–market portfolio, is clear.

Thus overall Fama and French (2015) report

"the size factor is roughly neutral with respect to value, profitability, and investment... Likewise HML is roughly neutral with respect to size, operating profit and investment and similar comments apply to RMW [the operating profitability pricing factor] and CMA [the investment intensity pricing factor]."

In later analysis Fama and French (2015), (p. 8) report on the relatively high correlation between the HML and CMA factors included in FF5 asset–pricing model in estimation equation (6.8) of 0.7. As they state it is perhaps not surprising that companies trading at, or near, their break up value; when their market value is at, or below, the recorded book value of their assets in the balance sheet, do not invest much.

More difficult to rationalise is the high correlation of 0.63 between the HML and RMW factors once we control for size, operating profitability, and investment intensity. This suggests that in the full five–factor model, FF5, one of these three variables is likely to be redundant, with its impact on returns being captured by the other two.

6.1.5 Is value/HML a redundant asset–pricing factor?

This leads us to the most striking claim of Fama and French (2015) (p. 12) that the HML/"value", $\frac{B}{M}$ factor is redundant once the other four variables in the FF5 model are accounted for. They note

"controlling for other factors, value stocks behave like stocks with robust profitability, even though unconditionally, value stocks tend to be less profitable."

Fama and French (2015) present evidence on the comparative performance of FF5 and FF3, using their sample of U.S. stocks over the period 1963–2013. They report FF5 gives a better explanation of investor returns in all but one sub-portfolio of U.S. investor returns, this is when FF5 and a four factor model, excluding HML, are compared. It appears in this case we can say "less is more" in asset price modelling.

The FF3 model performs especially badly, relative to FF5, for those companies with very high operating profitability and aggressively high investment. For small firms that invest a lot, despite low profitability, the factor loadings on the RWW and CMA pricing factors turn negative and this induces under–performance relative to the benchmark, $R_m - R_f$, market portfolio, so now $\alpha < 0$ in FF5.

In concluding their paper (p. 19) Fama and French (2015) argue that the performance of small firms with negative factor loadings on operating profitability/RWA and investment intensity/CMA factors should form a focus for continued evaluation of FF5 as a potential asset–pricing model.

Fama and French (2016) examine the ability of the FF5 asset–pricing model to explain asset–pricing anomalies that defeated the FF3 model. These include those surrounding

1. net shares traded,
2. volatility,
3. accounting accruals,
4. momentum.

Stracca (2004) gives a five–fold typology of recorded asset–pricing anomalies of the form: **a)** decision heuristics, **b)** emotional and visceral factors, **c)** choice bracketing, **d)** stochastic and context dependent preferences, and **e)** reference dependence. Thus a successful alternative to standard asset–pricing theories must shed light on how these "anomalies" arise and how their presence might be resolved. Fast-and-frugal models of financial decision-making seem well placed to achieve this objective.

Fama and French (2016) find FF5 makes progress in resolving each of these anomalies apart from that associated with accounting accruals. Further Fama and French (2016) accept that Cahart's momentum factor, MOM, (see Cahart (1997)) has an important role to play in explaining away remaining asset–pricing anomalies.

6.2 The robust beauty of a simple linear model of asset–pricing

A striking feature of the development of the FF3/FF5 is the tangled relationship between the weights on the various factors employed to price stocks. Factors that were deemed central to asset pricing, like value, becomes less so as the number factors expand. Hence the choice of potential factors, included in asset–pricing models, can be driven by remaining asset–pricing anomalies to be "ticked off list".

One response to all this is to simply to abandon estimation of specific weights in estimating linear asset–pricing models. This is certainly one way to stop worrying about trading off Type I and II statistical errors. Just stop estimating and this problem is solved, even if other problems are now created.

While this may seem an extreme step, there is evidence that the simple imposition of equal weights can be a very effective predictor of performance (Dawes and Corrigan (1974), Dawes (1979)). Could it be in asset–pricing

"The whole thing is to decide what variables to look at and then know how to add."

Dawes and Corrigan (1974), p. 105.

6.2.1 A fast-and-frugal asset pricing model

Thus we could devise simpler alternatives to the FF5 model. The first is FF3 and the second is a version of the FF5 model that, rather than estimating factor weights, simply imposes equal weights on each of the five factors, which we henceforth denote FF5=. So the three models we compare in the exercise below are

$$
\begin{aligned}
R_{i,t} - R_{F,t} &= a + b_i(R_{M,t} - R_{F,t}) + s_i SMB_t + h_i HML_t \\
&\quad + r_i RMW_t + c_i CMA_t + e_{i,t} \qquad\qquad\quad FF5 \\
R_{i,t} - R_{F,t} &= a + b_i(R_{M,t} - R_{F,t}) + s_i SMB_t + h_i HML_t + e_{i,t} \quad FF3 \\
R_{i,t} - R_{F,t} \\
&= a + \frac{(R_{M,t} - R_{F,t}) + SMB_t + HML_t + RMW_t + CMA_t}{5} \qquad FF5 =
\end{aligned}
$$

$$(6.9)$$

Where the third model of the alternative listed in Eq. (6.9) is a "fast-and-frugal" asset pricing model that simply uses a weighted average of the five factors suggested by Fama and French (2015). The FF5= model is certainly biased, as it does not even attempt to extricate the relative contribution of the five factors to the movement of prices. In this sense it is an ignorant, biased, model turning its back on easily available information. But every act of estimation is also a source of estimation error.

This leads to the bias variance trade-off embedded in the forecast error decomposition of any good statistical text (Geman et al. (1992)) and often invoked to construct fast-and-frugal models in managerial decision-making contexts, see (Artinger et al., 2014)

$$\text{Total error} = (\text{bias}^2) + \text{variance} + \text{noise}$$

Once we accept that there is little a forecaster can do to predict un-forecastable noise, we simply seek forecasting methods that best trade off bias and forecast variance. This opens up the possibility of a fast-and-frugal asset–pricing model which simply devotes equal weights to each asset pricing factor.

6.3 Conclusion

This Chapter introduced a classic asset pricing, model, the FF3/FF5 model, and compares it to a simple alternative, the FF5=, that uses a simple weighted–average of the five factors employed in the FF5 regression model to predict stocks. So the FF5= model does not even try to estimate the sensitivity of stock prices to the various asset–pricing factors used to describe their likely trajectory in terms of current and future returns.

In explaining current returns the FF5 and FF3 are fairly close substitutes, producing very similar forecasts, including hugely underestimating the performance of the best performing stocks in the sample. Indeed upon the inclusion of the additional two factors of the FF5 the value/HML factor of the original FF3 model begins to look redundant. This suggests we need to focus on including the right group of asset pricing factors and not just constantly adding in additional factors.

While there has been a huge amount of empirical testing of asset–pricing models, generating a seeming "zoo" of asset pricing factors, the power of these tests, their capacity to reject false alternatives is very low. Indeed, few academics seem interested in discussing the low power of asset price modelling as currently performed. This may reflect the career advantages offered to new asset price factor discovery and the indifference of Finance Journals to publishing replication studies.

In this context we suggest fast-and-frugal asset pricing models, such as FF5= discussed here, have something to commend them. This may be especially true when one recognises the difference between in–sample and out–of–sample model performance. As has often been pointed out asset price models are developed to explain expected returns.

Asset price modelling which implements tests of proposed asset price models invariably model actual, not expected, returns. This is fine when returns follow a random walk and no consistent trend in asset returns is present. But much evidence recording the presence of short-run momentum in asset returns suggest this random–walk assumption is invalid. If this is the case substituting current for future expected returns, when conducting tests of models of expected returns, is problematic. So modelling the evolution of future returns maybe be both sensible and favour far more frugal asset–price models than those currently being advanced.

CHAPTER 7

Fast-and-frugal portfolio theory

In a previous chapter we considered models to price individual assets, often with respect to various proposed pricing factors. But if Finance theory has taught us anything it has taught us the importance of diversifying investment portfolios both across individual assets and asset classes (equity, bonds, cash). Indeed perhaps the clearest implication of the EMH is to buy and hold the "market portfolio", without even attempting to stock pick based upon individual asset characteristics.

The CAPM, perhaps the single most used "product" of finance theory, selects this market portfolio for investors to buy and hold. This portfolio is the mean-variance efficient portfolio in that its offers the greatest return for minimum risk and its identification was in many ways the foundation of all subsequent asset price theory (Markowitz (1952), Markowitz (1959)).

Despite the huge influence of mean-variance efficient portfolio (MVP) mechanics in promoting index–tracker funds and passive investment more generally, a number of well established principles of investment practice seem irreconcilable with that model. Take for example the advice that the young, with a lifetime ahead of them, should invest in equities more than the old; who have only the grave awaiting them.

This reminds us that the representative investor is more of a simplificatory modelling device than a practical guide to portfolio construction. Indeed the huge calculative demands of mean-variance efficient portfolio construction suggest many investors will not follow that model in practice. This is especially true if those investors regard the environment into which they invest as being uncertain, rather than risky.

Consider the plight of investors concerned about Brexit, a (so far) unique re-arrangement of the international order. Or more recently investors concerned with Italy's flirtation with leaving the Eurozone. Neither of these hugely importance events can really have a frequency distribution, based on past outcomes, placed over them.

Knight (1921) introduced a three-fold categorisation of uncertain outcomes ((Mousavi and Gigerenzer, 2017), see Table 1, p. 1673)

those invoking probability to measure the likely nature of a future prospective world,

A Fast and Frugal Finance
https://doi.org/10.1016/B978-0-12-812495-6.00015-X
157

those using statistics   to estimate probabilities of future events, correlations between prospective events, etc.,

truly uncertain events   where such quantification cannot reasonably be applied.

In the third case of uncertain events heuristic tools, matched to the decision-making environment, become most attractive. Hudson et al. (1999) argue

> *"individuals may conclude that the subjective expected utility framework is not going to be a helpful method for enabling them to make decisions. Instead they may adopt heuristics... and other rules to cope with the difficulties of making decisions in the context of highly uncertain environments."*
>
> *Hudson et al. (1999), p. 511.*

In this chapter we examine such heuristics and how they might be used to construct a faster, more frugal, and more profitable guide to portfolio construction.

7.1 Portfolio construction: elegant theories and a messier practice

7.1.1 Markowvitian portfolio theory

Markowvitz (Markowitz (1952), Markowitz (1959)) built his pioneering theory of portfolio choice on the simple insight that investors like to have a good expected return on their investment, but fear risk; especially the prospect of taking a loss. This fairly normal form of utility function can be depicted as indifference curves in Fig. 7.1.

Competitive security markets throw up investment portfolios offering different combinations of risk and expected return, $E(R_p)$, where the risk of that portfolio is captured by its standard deviation, σ_p. Tracing the best combinations of expected return and risk in $\frac{E(R_p)}{\sigma_p}$ space draws out the "efficient frontier" of possible investments to indicate a mean-variance (efficient) portfolio, or MVP, at the tangent point to the investor's budget–line.

Choosing the MVP requires choosing weights for assets included in the portfolio, w_i, to ensure the investor is located on the highest possible indifference curve accessible by them; while still buying a portfolio within the market determined efficient frontier.

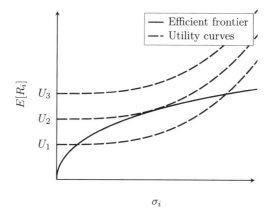

Figure 7.1 Choosing a mean-variance efficient portfolio (MVP). *Source:* https://tex. stackexchange.com/questions/417939/ticks-at-end-of-axis

This can be set up as a simple constrained maximisation problem of the form (see Ang (2014), p. 89)

$$\max_{w_i} E(r_p) - \frac{\gamma}{2} var(r_p) \tag{7.1}$$

subject to any constraints.

This invokes a standard assumption that investor that well-being, utility, is a function of their level, not changes in, wealth. So an investor's utility for takes the form

$$U(W) = \frac{W^{1-\gamma}}{1-\gamma} \tag{7.2}$$

where γ is a measure of the investor's risk aversion. Fig. 7.2 gives a plot of a constant relative risk–aversion, CRRA, utility function for the cases γ equals a quarter and a half. The plot of the CRRA utility function for a $\gamma = \frac{1}{4}$ is plotted in straight blue line, that for $\gamma = \frac{1}{2}$ in red line broken by square dots along it. As can be seen more risk averse investors gain more utility from gambles of smaller size than their more risk–tolerant peers, for whom $\gamma = \frac{1}{4}$.

Eventually for higher stakes gambles, in which more of their wealth is put at risk, at a value of $\gamma = \frac{1}{2}$ an investor gains less utility than his less risk adverse peer investor, for whom $\gamma = \frac{1}{4}$. This implies higher risk aversion investors will be keener to undertake low stake gambles than low risk-aversion investors, because the contracted denominator of Eq. (7.2) dominates the effect from the similarly contracted numerator.

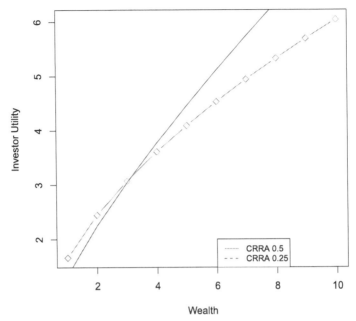

CRRA utility function for Gamma equals 0.25 or 0.5.

Figure 7.2 Plot of CRRA Investor utility function with increasing investor risk-aversion.

The CAPM model of Sharpe (1964), Lintner (1965b) then results from allowing the investor to lend/borrow at a fixed, "risk–free" rate, so as to locate themselves on any point on the security market line (SML), as shown in Fig. 7.3 below.

7.1.2 A folk law based, but profitable, tradition of investment advice

Keasey and Hudson (2007) discuss the theory and practice of investment advice and especially asset allocation. They make clear investment advisors do not use mean–variance optimisation in advising clients because of perceived problems in its structure which include the fact(s):

1. often choices faced by clients seem more uncertain than risky.
2. clients may be worried about liquidity of an asset class, a topic not addressed by the MVP analysis.
3. correlation between assets are unlikely to be constant and may "all go to one" in a moment of crisis, like that of September 2008.

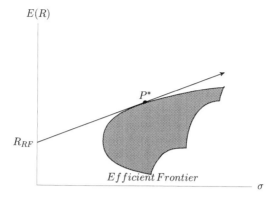

Figure 7.3 The Markowitz mean-variance diagram. *Source:* https://sites.google.com/site/kochiuyu/Tikz

4. clients are very sensitive to how much they might lose; their downside risk. Even Marowvitz himself, who might be expected to know about the MVP, seemed to regard the semi-variance, calculated on the basis of potential losses, as the appropriate risk–metric for giving investment advice (Keasey and Hudson (2007), p. 943).

Investment advisors seem to prefer to largely adopt, or "mirror", their clients view of the world. They adopt a "safety first approach". First they ask the client whether they are a "Conservative"/Not liking risk, "Moderate", or "Aggressive"/Liking risk. Fidelity advises conservative investors keep 50% of their wealth in cash, 20% in equity, and 30% of bonds in their portfolio.

Advisors attempt to fit the investment advice to a client's context, their age, level of wealth, need to provide for dependents, etc., rather than simply recommending a "one size fits all" market portfolio. Cash as an asset class is simply never mentioned in the MVP analysis, but cash-holdings feature heavily in practical investment advice.

This might seem to produce an "anomaly", since we would ask why those paid to advise make such a bad job of it, despite the easy availability of the basics of MVP construction in textbooks taught in most business schools. But the truth is the investment advice given by the advisors Keasey and Hudson (2007) studied seemed to beat that offered by constructing an MVP portfolio, although the advisor's dominance is much less clear in the case of advise given to "aggressive" investors.

So the anomaly is really only apparent to those who cleave to standard theory almost regardless of the evidence before us. It seems those who spend their lives in investment management do not pay much heed to even the basics of investment management as formulated by standard finance theory.

7.1.3 A behavioural model of asset allocation

Siebenmogen and Weber (2003) advance a behavioural model of investor asset allocation, the division of client wealth between stocks, bonds, etc. They incorporate into their model three elements

expected return

pure risk   where covariance between asset returns are ignored,

naive diversification   by not "holding your eggs in one basket".

This framework shares the first two elements with the MVP approach, but ignores the covariance/correlation terms in the "law of covariance" equation usually invoked to calculate the portfolio variance, σ_p. They advance an alternative model of asset allocation, to describe the sort of investment management we observe in practice, noting that their practitioners

> *"do something "wrong" with respect to traditional portfolio theory, which however, is quite appealing to the way their clients think intuitively and the loss of efficiency due to following this behavioural theory is not so large."*
>
> **(Siebenmogen and Weber (2003), p. 16.)**

The Siebenmogen and Weber model of asset allocation

So Siebenmogen and Weber (2003) define portfolio return as simply the weighted average of individual asset returns in the portfolio, so

$$E(R_p) = \sum_{i=1}^{n} \alpha_i \mu_i \Rightarrow \max \tag{7.3}$$

As in the normal MVP framework expected return is maximised subject now to "pure risk", which ignores the covariance between asset returns, meaning pure risk is simply a weighted average of the standard deviation of the individual assets included in the portfolio, $\sum_{1}^{n} \alpha_i \sigma_i$.

Further, Siebenmogen and Weber (2003) assume investors engage in a form of "naive diversification" that gives them a marked preference for investing an equal amount of their wealth in each asset class, with deviations from this equality damaging the investor's utility. Thus (naive) diversification is captured by individual assets' portfolio weights' deviation from their average value. So Siebenmogen and Weber (2003) define *pure risk* as being the standard deviation of asset portfolio weights (i=1,...n) from their average value $\bar{\alpha}$.

Siebenmogen and Weber (2003) compare the performance of two simple, stylised, models characterised by two alternative utility functions, both of which are weighted averages of key elements of the investor's supposed utility function; these are

$$\text{Min}_\alpha \beta \times \text{Diversification} + (1 - \beta) \times \text{Pure risk} \quad \mathbf{M1} \quad (7.4)$$

$$s.t. \quad \text{Expected Return} = \hat{e}$$

$$\sum_{i=1}^{n} \alpha_i = 1 \quad and \ 0 \geq \alpha_i \leq 1 \forall i = 1, ...n.$$

$$Max_\alpha \times \gamma \times \text{Expected Return} - (1 - \gamma)\text{Diversification} \quad \mathbf{M2}$$

$$s.t. \quad \text{Pure risk} = \hat{r}$$

$$\sum_{i=1}^{n} \alpha_i = 1 \text{ and } 0 \geq \alpha_i \leq 1 \forall i = 1, ...n. \quad (7.5)$$

In the first model of portfolio construction, given in Eq. (7.4), investors are hypothesised to minimise the degree of diversification from that implied by equal weights on all assets, subject to the investor's desire to minimise the pure risk of their portfolio and obtain some benchmark level of return on their portfolio, $\hat{e}$. While in the second model of portfolio construction, described by Eq. (7.5), the investor is hypothesised to maximise their return, subject to their desire to avoid deviations from equal weights on assets held in the portfolio and some benchmark level of risk, $\hat{r}$.

Note that neither of these models bother with calculating covariances, multiplying out portfolio matrices with their portfolio weights, etc. As such they constitute fast-and-frugal alternatives to the standard MVP mechanics. How well do they serve investors who adopt them as a guide to asset allocation?

Siebenmogen and Weber (2003) report that the two alternative behavioural models, M1 and M2, described in Eqs. (7.4) and (7.5) above, describe the investment practice of the sample of south German bank advisors far better than the MVP can.

Further, they find when they use historic returns to proxy for expected returns, so assuming expectations are on average correct the loss of efficiency, in the risk/return trade-off, to following the advice from the

M1/M2 models is minimal. This implies this path to a fast-and-frugal asset-allocation model may have some promise.

7.2 Heuristics for portfolio management

The MVP model of portfolio management assumes asset return distributions are normal, investors have the calculative power of a "Laplacian demon" and the availability of a risk–free asset. The defence of these assumptions is often that what matters to investors is a model's predictions, not the realism of its assumptions. Newton's law of gravity ignores frictions, but it still gives me a good guide to what might happen if I throw a heavy object off the roof of skyscraper.

For *ecological rationality*, as opposed to *economic rationality*, good heuristic tools develop from our experience of their use. Mousavi and Gigerenzer (2017) describe the value of heuristic tools as follows

> *"Heuristics are tools that are developed by direct learning over the course of evolution... a complex uncertain problem often calls for a simple rules of thumb that solve complex uncertain situations, precisely because of their simplicity not despite it... More calculation time and information is not always better. Less can be more."*
>
> **Mousavi and Gigerenzer (2017), p. 1672.**

Thus in uncertain investment environments, such as the UK exiting the European Union, or Italy possibly leaving the Eurozone, heuristics may work best. Here frequency distributions, of such unique events are useless and investors may need to rely on intuitive priors, based on analogies with other acts of international discord; such as derogations from EU wide legislation or Hungary's refusal to admit its quota of refugees/migrants entering Europe.

But such intuitive estimates can sound like little more than "gut feelings" (Gigerenzer (2007)) and a large part of the fast-and-frugal reasoning approach is an attempt to systematise the evolution and deployment of such intuitive rules. For those who would dismiss gut–feelings as mere prattle, without substance, it is worthwhile to note about half of the 1000+ CEOs surveyed reported in Graham et al. (2013) reported gut feel, regarding a proposed project, as either important or very important in deciding upon whether to undertake it (see Figure 1, p. 1674, Mousavi and Gigerenzer (2017)).

7.2.1 Using recognition is stock picking

Associative matching is a commonly observed trait both in nature and in life. Many of us have married good Christian/Muslim boys/girls for that reason. We associate, trade, form relationships with, those we know, being wary of outsiders with strange languages/social practices. So we often invest in what we know, or at least recognise.

Huberman (2001) examining the pattern of investment in the various regional companies that making up the Bell telephone corporation in the US concludes

> *"The geographic bias of... investors is related to the general tendency of household's portfolios to be concentrated, of employees' tendency to own their own employers' stocks in their retirement accounts, and to the home country bias in the international arena. Together, these phenomena provide compelling evidence that people invest in the familiar while often ignoring the principles of portfolio theory."*
>
> *(Huberman (2001), p. 659)*

This form of reasoning motivates one of the most extensively investigated heuristics in Gigerenzer's adaptive-toolbox; the recognition heuristic. This can be stated as requiring that

> *"When choosing a subset from a larger set, choose those things in the larger set that are highly recognised."*
>
> *(Ortmann et al. (2008)).*

Before we become familiar with a people/culture/product we must first recognise it. Goldstein and Gigerenzer (2002) use this fact to develop the idea of a recognition heuristic. For example if I am asked, as an Englishman, to choose which is the bigger city Bremen, or some place I have never heard of, I would say Bremen. I would do so just because I know about Bremen, even though I have no idea how many people live there, never mind the relative population of Bremen compared to some other place in Germany I do not know.

Another cue I might use to decide if Bremen is bigger than another unheard of German town/city is whether it has a football team in the Bundesliga. Great cities have great teams, like Manchester United, Chelsea, or Glasgow Rangers in Britain. So SV Werder Bremen is currently ranked 11th in the Bundesliga.

Table 7.1 Are you better off getting stock market advice from a park bench or a University?

	German companies/subjects	US companies/subjects
Lay people (in park)	8 German	8 US
Experts (in economics/ finance class)	14 German (2 US)	20 US (1 German)

Note Source: Table 3.1, p. 63, (Borges et al., 1999).

So surely Bremen must be a great place, with many inhabitants. Of course this sort of reasoning is useless if the unknown place also has a Bundesliga team. So FC Ausburg also has a Bundesliga team, ranked twelfth in the Bundesliga currently. So when comparing Bremen and Ausburg the Bundesliga cue is not helpful. So here knowing less is literally more here.

For this reason Ortmann et al. (2008) speak of a "beneficial degree of ignorance"; which is somewhere between being a complete know nothing and a know all. When I know Bremen is in the Bundesliga, but another place is not, I can infer Bremen has a bigger population. But for the comparison of Bremen and Ausburg the Bundesliga cue is of no help, because both are in the Bundesliga and exhibiting similar performance. So in many contexts (beneficial) ignorance may be bliss.

7.2.2 Are recognisable stocks a better buy?

Borges et al. (1999) apply the recognition heuristic to a stock picking exercise. Business School teachers know many of their best students will eagerly enter investment banks, where many of the finest minds already reside. So Borges et al. (1999) ask can (literally) the man on the street beat the refined minds of finance professionals in the making?

To do so they went into public parks in Munich and Chicago to see what stocks in Germany and America 360 sound citizens of those cities recognised from the S&P 500 and DAX 30 lists respectively. They also asked 120 graduate finance and economics students, studying at the Universities of Chicago and Munich respectively, the "experts", to do the same.

Table 7.1 gives the results of asking people in the park, laypeople, about what stocks they recognise versus asking, "experts", graduate students in class (Warren Buffett was not available to participate it seems). Folk in the park were just asked about their own country's stocks.

Experts, in the form of the 120 economics and finance students from Chicago and Munich University respectively, know more companies than the 360 lay folk from the park. Students, the experts, were also asked about which stock they recognised in the other country's list. Amongst American students only Luthansa was a company recognised by all the students. But all German students recognised both Microsoft and American Express.

American students knew more companies than their German peers; but then there are so many more companies to be recognised. So experts know more about the stock market, recognising more companies. But does that help the "experts" make more money than their lay folk peers?

Borges et al. examine the relative performance of the four stock picking groups. These four groups are US/German lay folk and US/German experts. They ask if investment managers which held a portfolio of stocks recognised by at least 90% of subjects in the park, or classroom, when they were asked which stocks they knew, did well relative to four alternative investment strategies? These are:

1. a portfolio of unrecognised stocks,
2. investing in a stock market index,
3. holding a mutual fund, here Fidelity,
4. a portfolio drawn at random from US/German stocks, maybe by throwing darts at a list of stocks.

They find when German lay people, in the park, buy a portfolio of stocks they know they earned higher returns than all of these benchmarks considered. Here recognised stocks are those known to 90%, not all, subjects in each group.

Overall Borges et al. (1999) conclude

"The striking returns generated by recognition-based portfolios substantiate evidence... that the recognition heuristic can make accurate inferences in real-world domains... The stock market might be a real world environment in which lack of recognition is not completely random, but rather systematic and informative. In investments there may be wisdom in ignorance."

The average return to the portfolio of recognised stocks was three times that of a portfolio of unrecognised ones. A related test that simply compared the performance of the 20 or 30 most/least recognised stocks yielded a very similar result, suggesting that the recognition heuristic is robust to reasonable changes in the research method followed to confirm/reject its presence.

Borges et al. (1999) distinguish between stocks attracting "domestic recognition", by being known to those who are citizens of their own land,

Table 7.2 The recognition heuristic in a down market.

Grouped by major	Non-finance student	Finance students	Non-business students	All participants	Market portfolio
Number of participants	90	14	80	184	0
Number of stocks	22	28	24	23	111
3-month return	−7.16%	−10.88%	−9.06%	−9.06	1.65%
σ return	18.18%	19.01%	19.95%	19.95%	24.96%
6-month return	−13.54%	−17.68%	−14.75%	−14.75%	−4.54%
σ return	29.13%	27.45%	29.05%	29.05%	37.38%

Note Source: Table 5, p. 155, of Boyd (2001).

and "international recognition"; when a US stock is recognised by German citizens or vice–versa. The authors found that international recognition, by those who presumably know far less about the relevant market than natives, brought particularly high returns. So holding a portfolio of the four stocks that were recognised by 90% of laypeople abroad was particularly profitable relative to the four benchmarks employed to capture normal/acceptable performance.

7.2.3 Can the recognition heuristic for stock–picking survive a market downturn?

A central theme of the fast-and-frugal reasoning approach is that the value of any cognitive evaluation is closely linked to the context into which it is deployed. While during booms the general public have a huge interest in, and enthusiasm for, the stock market. In the downturn, shame, and even revulsion, can set it in. For this reason the recognition heuristic may not be robust to the wax and wane of the business cycle. Boyd (2001) explores this idea in a follow up study to the original Borges et al. (1999) one.

Boyd (2001) in June 2000, just after the "rude awakening" implosion of the Internet bubble in April 2000 (Demers and Lev, 2000), revisited the efficacy of the recognition heuristic as a tool for portfolio construction. He asked a group of business (experts) and non-business (lay folk), to choose from a list of stocks the ones they recognised.

Subjects were given a list of 111 US companies and asked which ones they recognised. From their selected stock list they were then asked to select up to eight stocks they thought would outperform the market in the near future.

Boyd (2001) also told his subjects that in a market downturn a well-performing stock could just be one that lost the least amount of investor's wealth. On the basis of the 184 participants responses Boyd (2001) formed a portfolio of twenty-three stocks recognised by 90% of all participants, experts (business students) or not (other majors). The subsequent stock market performance of this "recognised", twenty-three stocks, portfolio was then measured over the period June 15th to September 15th. The performance of the "recognised" portfolio, which 90% of students recognised, was compared to that of the market, as captured by all 111 stocks originally presented to student experimental subjects.

The results for each of Boyd's sub-groups is given in Table 7.2. It is clear Finance students recognise the most stocks, which is re-assuring.

But it is also clear recognising a stock does not help choose stocks that perform well in this sample. The portfolio of "recognised" stocks perform much worse, over both a three month and six month investment horizon, than the "market portfolio" of the 111 stocks subjects had originally chosen their "recognised" stocks from.

Experts, in the form of finance students, choose stocks that did even worse than those chosen by lay folk, as represented by either non-business or non-finance students. So it appears the recognition heuristic may only work in bull markets when lay-folk feel interested in, and sympathetic too, stock market speculation. In market downturns the recognition heuristic seems to lose its glitter for investors.

Ayton et al. (2011) explore how the decision-making context impacts upon the power of the recognition heuristic by examining how well English and Turkish students can predict the fortunes of the other nation's soccer teams. In their experiment Ayton et al. (2011) allow their Turkish students to choose whether they are also told the half-time score of the matches they are asked to predict, as an additional source of decision-making information.

They found students were more likely to invoke the recognition heuristic when the half-time score information confirmed its predictions, rather than refuting them. This reminds us that the recognition heuristic forms part of an adaptive toolbox which is deployed strategically by its users to best exploit the information environment they find themselves choosing in.

7.2.4 Can the recognition heuristic work in both bull and bear markets? Further evidence

But before we conclude that the recognition heuristic can only perform well in bull marks it is worth revisiting another follow up study to the Borges et al. (1999) study. Ortmann et al. (2008) study the efficacy of the recognition heuristic in predicting stock market values using two successive stock–picking competitions offered by two German magazines targeted at the investing public.

The first competition was offered to readers of *Capital* magazine running from February 28th to April 7th 2000, almost entirely before the "rude awaking" (Demers and Lev, 2000) of the implosion of the Internet bubble and the second offered by *Stern-Bourse Online* magazine, which ran in successive issues of the magazine from May 29th to July 21st 2000; well after the bubble has burst. Thus these magazine competitions offered a sort of platform for a natural experiment of whether the recognition heuristic for the selection of a profitable trading strategy is robust to dramatic changes in stock market fortunes.

To choose which stocks to enter into the magazine competitions Ortmann et al. (2008) turn to our usual oracle 50 male and 50 female pedestrians on the streets of Berlin. The pedestrians stopped were asked to state which stocks they recognised from lists they were presented with. This exercise allowed the Ortmann et al. to construct a portfolio of well and poorly recognised stocks which were entered separately into the magazine competitions.

In the *Capital* magazine competition Ortmann et al. entered their 10 most/least recognised stocks as separate entries. For the subsequent *Stern Bourse Online* competition the portfolio of stocks entered were those recognised by 90% of the group of 50 male/female strangers stopped in Berlin's streets. This method produced a portfolio of 14 stocks recognised by 90% of men and 7 stocks recognised by 90% of women. Clearly, following the stock market is a manly pursuit amongst Berliners.

The results in both competitions confirmed the power of the recognition heuristic in guiding the formation of profitable portfolios in boom and bust markets. In the earlier *Capital* magazine competition, conducted before the Internet bubble imploded, the ten stocks in the high recognition portfolio earned a return of 2.53% in the ensuing stock market meltdown. The portfolio of unrecognised stocks declined in value 16.97%.

In the subsequent *Stern Bourse Online* competition, held after the Internet bubble had imploded, all portfolios of recognised stocks outdid their unrecognised competitor portfolios, produced positive returns and beat the performance of the median portfolio submitted by subscribers.

In a victory for their sex, the portfolio of just seven stocks known to 90% of the Berliner women stopped in the street beat the portfolio of fourteen stocks known their male peers. Perhaps boys do not just trade too much (Barber and Odean (2001)) but also know too much.

Overall Ortmann et al. declare victory for the recognition heuristic as a fast-and-frugal guide to the selection of profitable portfolios, stating

"The results reported here provide evidence for the surprising viability of the recognition heuristic in the notoriously difficult environment of financial markets...and down markets for that matter. Once again, high recognition portfolios outperformed both low recognition portfolios and various reasonable benchmarks."

(Ortmann et al. (2008), pp. 1002–1003.)

7.2.5 The $\frac{1}{N}$ heuristic

Markovitzian portfolio theory guidance to buy and hold the MVP is finance scholarship's usual advice to investors. But "naive diversification", just holding an equal share of each asset in the portfolio, represents an intuitive and very simple alternative. Is the extra work, in data collection, estimation, to implement the Markowvitzian portfolio choice technique justified by the risk-adjusted returns it offers?

DeMiguel et al. (2009) present extensive evidence it is not. Examining a range of data sets, both archival and simulated, over long and short horizons, they find almost no model based on standard finance theory can beat naive diversification, or the $\frac{1}{N}$ heuristic. The reason for this is simple; the whole mechanics of constructing MVP is estimation intensive. Recall the basic law of covariance underlying the MVP

$$\sigma_p^2 = \sum_{i=1}^{n} w_i^2 \sigma_i^2 + 2\sum_{i=1}^{n-1}\sum_{i=1}^{n} w_i w_j \rho_{ij} \sigma_i \sigma_j \tag{7.6}$$

With every estimate comes an estimation error and these can multiply to overwhelm any improvement in shareholder's returns MVP modelling can in theory offer investors.

7.2.6 Can the $\frac{1}{N}$ beat other portfolio choice models?

DeMiguel et al. (2009) examine the attractions of the $\frac{1}{N}$ as a portfolio management tool by comparing it to other models that are already used in the finance industry and academe. The first of these alternatives is the MVP. DiMiguel et al. consider models that use bayesian inference models to construct the weights, w_i and others that place some restrictions on the portfolio weights, for example not allowing short–selling of stocks.

DiMiguel et al. estimate the vector of N expected excess returns, $R_i - R_f$, of a portfolio under the MVP, by explaining a vector of excess returns over the sample period, R_t, and Σ, an $N \times N$ covariance matrix capturing the correlations between the N stocks in the investor's portfolio, $\mathbf{1}_N$ is an identity vector of ones, where $\mathbf{I}_N$ is an identity matrix and, finally, w_t is the vector of portfolio weights used to construct the (MVP or alternative) model portfolio; with any remaining part of the investor's wealth, a proportion $1 - \mathbf{I}$, being invested in the risk–free asset.

This allows us to construct a vector of *relative* weights, w_t, in the portfolio with only-risky assets.

$$w_t = \frac{w_t}{|\, \mathbf{1}_N^T w_t \,|} \tag{7.7}$$

where the denominator normalises the sum of portfolio weights to be positive in the cases where this may not already to be true.

As is usual in the MVP analysis we assume investors' utility is derived from drawing returns from a normal distribution entirely described by its mean, abnormal, return μ and its variance Σ.

So the MVP investor maximises their utility by selecting, w_t to maximise expected utility

$$\max_{w_{it}} w_t^T \mu_t - \frac{\gamma}{2} w_t^T \Sigma_t w_t \tag{7.8}$$

where γ in Eq. (7.8) captures the investor's coefficient of risk aversion and the solution to the optimisation problem of Eq. (7.8) is simply $w_t = (\frac{1}{\gamma}) \Sigma_t^{-1} \mu$. Scaling to obtain the vector of relative weights we obtain

$$w_t = \frac{\Sigma_t^{-1} \mu_t}{\mathbf{1}_N \Sigma_t^{-1} \mu_t} \tag{7.9}$$

where all the alternative models to the MVP and equal weights model considered by DiMiguel et al., in their comparison of the explanatory/predictive power of alternative models for portfolio management, can be expressed as a variation of Eq. (7.9).

Different models of portfolio construction primarily differ on how μ and Σ are estimated. Of course the MVP is theoretically formed by some "true" mean and variance, but in reality we can only use sample estimates for these unknown true characteristics, $\hat{\mu}$ and $\hat{\Sigma}$.

Using these estimates simply assumes away the problem of estimation error. However since sample characteristics are estimated it is clear that MVP portfolio construction and its derivatives are estimation intensive and one may wonder if all this effort is worthwhile for investors?

Some of the alternatives to the standard MVP model try to address the problem of sample estimates of μ and Σ changing each time period by allowing for reasonable (bayesian) priors about what the future might be, for example, in May 2000 investors may reasonably believe that the good times are gone for a good while.

Another alternative "shrinks" the estimation space searched for the vector of weights, $\mathbf{w}$, to an area which has an intuitive appeal (Neyman (1955)). The form of Bayes-Stein estimator employed by Dimiguel et al. constrains the weights vector used, $\mathbf{w}$, to lie somewhere on the efficient frontier of Fig. 7.3.

Such a "shrinkage" estimator uses the fact we expect rational investors not to choose an inefficient portfolio, but we cannot be, a priori, be sure which of the efficients ones they will choose. The prior that an investor will choose an efficient portfolio is embedded in the bayesian prior, leaving the likelihood, to be inferred from the data.

Another fast-and-frugal way of estimating portfolio weights is to impose sensible restrictions on the type of portfolio the investor can choose. Note this is a somewhat stronger condition than simply having a prior. A prior can be refuted by new evidence. Placing a restriction on the portfolio the investor chooses forestalls such learning occurring.

While Green and Hollified (1992) argue that in the presence of a single dominant factor in the pricing of asset portfolios it is likely some assets will have extreme weightings both positive and negative. Jagannathan and Ma (2003) show that even in those cases where this is the case ignoring negative weights, by ruling out the possibility of short–selling a stock, leads to a reduction of the risk of the estimated investment portfolio. Surely an attractive characteristic from a client's perspective.

7.2.7 Three criteria for evaluating different investor portfolio construction methods

DiMiguel et al. compare the performance of an equal weight, $\frac{1}{N}$, portfolio and competing models of portfolio construction in choosing wealth–maximising portfolios on the basis of three criteria. These are

Table 7.3 Which portfolio performs best $\frac{1}{N}$ or its alternative?

Measures of portfolio performance Method of portfolio construction	Sharpe ratio	Certainty equivalent	Turnover
Equally weighted	0.187	0.069	0.03
MVP (in sample weights)	0.385	0.048	0
MVP (pre-estimated weights)	0.079	0.003	38.99
Bayes-Stein	0.081	0.003	22.41
MVP (no short-sales)	0.083	0.004	4.53

1. the Sharpe ratio, $\frac{R_p-R_t}{\sigma_{RM}}$,
2. the investor's certainty equivalent, or the amount they would be willing to accept as cash to pass up the opportunity to take the gamble of choosing the selected portfolio,
3. the turnover in assets required to hold a position in the portfolio over the specified investment period.

DeMiguel et al. consider the comparative performance of fourteen models, relative to the $\frac{1}{N}$ heuristic, in their paper, testing their models upon six indices. Here we only report the results of five models implemented on the "S&P Sectors" data. The equal weight, $\frac{1}{N}$ model, the "shrinkage" Bayes–Stein estimator and, finally, the MVP portfolio.

Di Miguel et al. consider three portfolio weight estimation regimes; (a) when weights are estimated in sample, (b) when portfolio weights are pre-estimated, (c) the constrained MVP model that does not allow for short–selling of, or negative weights, upon stocks in the MVP portfolio.

The difference between the first two forms of the MVP model is that if weights are estimated in sample no estimation error is present. But if the weights of the MVP model are pre-estimated, on an earlier sample, this introduces estimation error and a decline in the relative performance of the MVP model.

The results of the portfolio construction method comparison across the three criteria considered for the S & P Sectors data set are summarised, for the specified subset of DiMiguel et al.'s results, in Table 7.3. It is clear if we consider *in sample* performance, when we require no estimation of portfolio weights by either the MVP or $\frac{1}{N}$ model, the MVP portfolio weights construction method wins hands down, yielding higher risk adjusted returns, as measured by the Sharpe ratio and certainty equivalent measures, generating no transaction costs during the sample period, as the MVP is a buy and hold portfolio.

The *out of sample performance* of the MVP model shows it offers lower risk–adjusted returns and hugely higher trading costs, as stocks are bought/sold to reflect changing portfolio weights. So *out of sample* the MVP method of constructing investor portfolio is plagued by large estimation error, but it remains an attractive method of portfolio choice when used with *in sample* portfolio estimated weights.

This may seem enough of an achievement in itself, making some content to endorse the MVP as the theoretically justified model. But to do this would be to ignore one of the central tenets of *positive*, as opposed to *normative*, economics/finance. That is that a theory must be evaluated by the quality of its predictions, not its assumptions.

It is true that the $\frac{1}{N}$ heuristic of portfolio construction is biased. But to reject it on that basis alone is to indulge the "bias bias". Brighton and Gigerenzer (2015) define the bias bias as follows:

"to develop, deploy or prefer models that are likely to achieve low bias, while simultaneously paying little or no attention to models with low variance."

Brighton and Gigerenzer (2015), p. 1772.

7.2.8 Optimally combining low bias and low forecast variance portfolio construction method

Clearly a good estimator optimally trades–off low bias and forecast error variance in the reduction if overall forecast error, accepting noisy estimates are always with us. Tu and Zhou (2011) suggest one way to do this is to simply combine the prediction of portfolio construction models with low bias, like the MVP, with models with low, or no, forecast error variance, like the $\frac{1}{N}$ rule.

Tu and Zhou (2011) consider such a portfolio construction model with weights, w_c, which are some weighted average of two models selected to optimally trade-off bias and forecast error and so minimise overall forecast error. So we have

$$\hat{w}_c = (1 - \delta)w_= + \delta\tilde{w} \qquad (7.10)$$

where $w_=$ are simply equal weights/$\frac{1}{N}$, and $\tilde{w}$ are the estimated weights from an estimated portfolio construction model, like the MVP, or a Bayes-Stein estimator.

Invoking a standard assumption in finance that the returns on the N stocks in the investor's chosen portfolio are identically and independently distributed, with mean μ and variance/covariance matrix Σ, holding such a combined weight portfolio yields investor utility of the form

$$U(\tilde{w}_c) = r_{fT+1} + \mu'\tilde{w}_c - \frac{\gamma}{2}\tilde{w}_c'\Sigma\tilde{w}_c \qquad (7.11)$$

where the γ is the MVP investor's coefficient of risk–version and first term in Eq. (7.11) captures the risk free rate of return in the next time period, the second the weighted average investor return and, finally, the last term reflects the weighted disutility of the risk associated with holding the combined weights portfolio.

So the model weighting scheme, δ, must be chosen to optimally trade-off bias and forecast variance in the selection of a combined weighted prediction made up of two, or more, models. We can regard model selection as minimising losses due to errors in forecasting returns due to both bias and forecast error variance, choosing δ, to minimise a loss function stated as follows

$$L(w^*, \hat{w}_c) = U(w^*) - E[U\hat{w}^c] \qquad (7.12)$$

where $U(w^*)$ denotes the utility offered by the optimal portfolio rule, for which $w^* = \Sigma^{-1}\frac{\mu}{\gamma}$ and $E[U\hat{w}^c]$ denotes the utility associated with the equal weights/estimated asset weights mixed portfolio, of Eq. (7.10) above. One way to interpret such a weighted average of alternative predictions is as a shrinkage estimator with equal weights as the chosen focal point of convergence.

Combining the MVP and $\frac{1}{N}$ to form an optimal investment portfolio

Perhaps the most intuitive application of such a combined weighted prediction model is to find the optimal weighting on the MVP model of standard theory and our trusty $\frac{1}{N}$ heuristic. Here the MVP's portfolio weights are chosen to maximise the risk-adjusted returns on assets within it, to yield

$$\bar{w} = \frac{1}{\gamma}\tilde{\Sigma}^{-1}\hat{\mu} \qquad (7.13)$$

where $\bar{w}$ is the vector of weights on assets in MVP portfolio, $\hat{\mu}$ is the estimated portfolio mean, $\hat{\Sigma}$ the estimated portfolio variance and $\tilde{\Sigma} = \frac{T}{(T-N-2)}\hat{\Sigma}$.

Using Eq. (7.10) we calculate the optimal MVP/$\frac{1}{N}$ combined weighted portfolio weights as

$$\tilde{w}_c = (1-\delta)w_= + \delta\bar{w} \qquad (7.14)$$

and the resulting loss function, associated with the combined MVP/$\frac{1}{N}$ combined weight portfolio is

$$L(w^*, \hat{w}_c) = \frac{\gamma}{2}[(1-\delta)^2\pi_1 + \delta^2\pi_2] \qquad (7.15)$$

and

$$\pi_1 = (w_= - w^*)'\Sigma(w_= - w^*)$$
$$\pi_2 = E[(\bar{w} - w^*)'\Sigma(\bar{w} - w^*)]$$

so that π_1 reflects the bias which the equal weight/$\frac{1}{N}$ induces and π_2 captures the forecast error variance present in the MVP's portfolio weight estimates.

Given the objective is to choose δ to optimally trade off bias and forecast error variance, by using a combination of the portfolio weights; suggested by the MVP model and the equal weight/$\frac{1}{N}$ heuristic, this suggests an optimal value of value of δ, δ^*, where

$$\delta^* = \frac{\pi_1}{\pi_1 + \pi_2} \qquad (7.16)$$

So that weight placed on the equal weight/$\frac{1}{N}$ heuristic grows in the amount of bias present in the MVP's estimates of realised shareholder returns.

Can a weighted average of MVP and $\frac{1}{N}$ portfolio weights beat the $\frac{1}{N}$ heuristic?

Tu and Zhou (2011) present evidence that giving some weight to the MVP in the construction of the investor's optimal portfolio, so $\delta < 1$ in Eq. (7.14), raises portfolio returns for investors. Allowing a deviation from the $\frac{1}{N}$ heuristic to reflect the weights suggested by MVP, reduces overall forecast error in estimating optimal investment portfolio weights.

Reviewing their empirical evidence (Tu and Zhou (2011), p. 214) conclude

"some of the combination rules can perform consistently well and outperform the $\frac{1}{N}$ rule significantly. Overall our study reaffirms the usefulness of the investment theory and shows that combining portfolio rules can potentially add significant value in portfolio management under estimation errors."

7.3 Conclusions

This chapter explored the value of heuristics in investor portfolio management. While the recognition and $\frac{1}{N}$ heuristic were shown to have some potential uncertainty remains regarding the range of their application in developing an adaptive toolbox for portfolio management. The distinction between boom and bust markets seems to be important for the application of the recognition heuristic; although the jury is still out on this issue. Any one heuristic forms only one part of an "adaptive toolbox" an investor uses to navigate an ever changing landscape of investment opportunities.

The $\frac{1}{N}$ rule for portfolio construction erases any forecast error variance encountered in predicting future investor portfolio weights. By invoking the $\frac{1}{N}$ heuristic a portfolio manager goes large on bias, as a source of forecast error, in the hope of more than recovering the loss by a diminution in forecast error variance. But if this gamble does not work out it might be wise to combine the $\frac{1}{N}$ heuristic with insights from the more traditional, estimated model, like the MVP.

The relative weightings on equal weights, $\frac{1}{N}$, and estimated weights might reasonably vary by time/industry, trading costs, etc. This is all part of the ecological evolution of a reliable adaptive toolbox for portfolio management which we hope to see emerging in the near future.

CHAPTER 8

Fast-and-frugal financial analysis

It is rare for the conditions of the Savage axioms underpinning expected utility theory to be met for those trading in financial markets. In the analysis of a particular company's prospects conjecture, based on little evidence, seems to play a prominent role.

Keynes in his General Theory states (Keynes (1936), p. 98)

"The outstanding fact is the extreme precariousness of the basis of knowledge on which our estimates of prospective yield have been made. Our knowledge of the factors that will govern the yield of an investment some years hence is usually very slight and often negligible. If we are to speak frankly, we have to admit our basis knowledge for predicting the yield ten years hence of a railway, a copper mine, [or other concern] amounts to little and sometimes nothing."

Indeed there is often confusion over what exactly financial expertise consists of. Barker (1998) in a study of the market for information, regarding companies in the UK, found the tasks his sample analysts ranked as having the highest importance for their reputation with fund-managers were analysis of particular companies and "value-added" research.

In truth the function of analysts may be both as an "engine" constructing investors' perception reality, as well as being a camera/telescope, looking forward into what the prospective returns on stock purchases will be (MacKenzie, 2008). In this view an analyst has a "feel for the game"; which allows them to frame the process of investment and the advice they give regarding it (Imam and Spence, 2016). In developing this gamesmanship analysts rely both on their *technical* capital for forecasts, via formal financial analysis and chartist methods, and their *social capital* in the network of contacts they keep to gather information, compare viewpoints.

8.1 What financial analysts do

Barker (1998) reports analysts focus on providing good "stories of corporate value creation/destruction". Issuing profitable recommendations and accurate earnings forecasts were considered important, but less so than the broader corporate valuation story they fitted into.

A Fast and Frugal Finance
https://doi.org/10.1016/B978-0-12-812495-6.00016-1

As such analysts provide ways of seeing market plays, as opposed to direct, quantifiable, guidance to fund-managers. Here we focus upon "sell–side" analysts, associated with investment banks, marketing stocks to clients, rather than the "buy–side" analysts assisting/guiding fund managers in the process of allocating capital. Buy–side analysts often purchase Sell–side analyst's reports to help structure the advice they give to fund-managers.

Nor is any one mode of analysis universally accepted as the right, or "rational", way to infer company value. Rather what is rational depends on the industrial and competitive context the company inhabits.

Demirakos et al. (2004) in their study of the contents of 104 analysts' reports, produced by 26 major investment banks, for companies in the beverages, electronics, and pharmaceuticals sectors, uncover substantial variation in the valuation model used, depending on the context in which it is to be applied. In their conclusion they state

"Analysts appear to vary the choice of valuation methodology in understandable ways with the context in which the valuation is made, but analyst familiarity with a valuation model and its acceptability to clients is a strong driving force."

(Demirakos et al. (2004), p. 237)

Imam et al. (2008) in their survey of valuation methods, employed by 35 UK sell–side analysts, 7 buy–side analysts, and 10 UK investment banks report that, while cash-valuation is the primary valuation tool, professionals still employ earnings based models in some industries.

They summarise the interaction of how the cognitive process of valuation is performed and the context within it is performed thus.

"analysts' preferences are multi-dimensional, reflecting both technical and contextual considerations... analyst's preferences are client driven [and] the recent popularity of DCF is also significantly related to fund managers' preferences."

(Imam et al. (2008) p. 531)

Thus in the profession of financial analysis, as opposed to its academic study, context and cognition are interwoven. This suggests there is scope for academic studies which embed this reality.

Imam and Spence (2016) study 49 financial analysts, where the 31 sell–side, and 18 buy–side, analysts were drawn from ten major firms, and conclude (p. 227) *"sell–side analysts' main role is not to accurately forecast earnings or recommend a stock but to provide rich contextual information on companies and industries. Overall we conclude that although sell–side analysts have cognitive limitations and incentives to generate trading volume, their work needs to be understood in terms of the context of the field in which they operate."*

8.1.1 Forecasting uncertain corporate prospects

A major theme of the interviews conducted with buy–side analysts by Imam and Spence (2016) and many earlier studies (Holland, 1998) is the importance of meetings with management and personal contact, rapport. This reminds us of the importance of *social*, as opposed to *technical* capital, in shaping analysts' perception of a company's prospects, investment value.

Thus the social capital of analysts complements their technical capital, directing its focus, suggesting key information sources/metrics, etc. In interrogating company management analysts want to see a clear articulation of the company's unfolding strategy, rather than a litany of accounting metrics achieved or promised.

The focus is on intuitive feel, rather than applying some proscribed external calculus (Imam and Spence (2016), p. 234)

"The buy–side showed a propensity for 'heuristics' and 'rules of thumb to simplify a complex world.'"

8.2 Accounting evolving, or irrelevant, accounting regime?

Lev and Gu (2016) in their book *The End of Accounting* (henceforth EoA) critique the value of current financial reporting practices for investors and advance a reform agenda to regain the lost relevance of financial reports for valuation. The book thus doubles as a polemic and a manifesto. In this chapter we use this Lev and Gu's book to understand how accounting needs, and thus the framework in which financial analysis occurs, have been evolving over a long period.

8.2.1 Corporate reporting then and now: a century of progress

To judge the value-added from accounting reform/regulation Lev and Gu (2016) compare the insights produced by the 40 page long 1902 accounts for US Steel and its 172 page 2012 counter-part. US Steel is an interesting case for such a comparison because, while production methods and uses of steel undoubtedly changed in 110 years, the basic objective of selling steel at a profit has not really changed in that period.

While some differences in the accounts have emerged on the 110 years the structure of the income statement and balance sheet remains the same. Lev and Gu state

> "Imagine if the report that people today get following a comprehensive physical check up were the same as what patients received from their doctors a 110 years ago. Yet the corporate annual check-up report is fixed in time."
>
> **EoA, p. 2.**

Where differences do exist they do not always show an improvement. One of example of this is the twelve pages of "risk factors" US Steel faces in its 2012 accounts, this includes such gems of wisdom as the steel industry being cyclical and facing risks of failing to comply with environmental regulations. Lev and Gu state

> "we have not met a single analyst or investor who learned anything valuable from, or based a decision on, the risk factors boilerplate or glossy graphs in financial reports. These are widely ignored as are the smiling pictures".
>
> **EofA, p. 5**

The great length of the 2012 report, compared to its 1902 counterpart, largely reflects the burden of financial regulation by the US Financial Accounting Standards Board (FASB). Lev and Gu conclude

> "Overall, it's doubtful that the 174-page 2012 report provides substantially more relevant information than the 40 pages released in 1902... the profound changes in financial information over the past 110 years have not been met with a commensurate improvement in the financial reports released by public companies to their shareholders."
>
> **EoA, pp. 6–7**

Here "less is more" and such profuse disclosure simply serves to bury any useful disclosures the accounts may contain.

This stability of financial reports does not reflect its establishment as the most efficient system after decades of trial and error. Indeed, Lev and Gu

(2016) argue, even perfectly reasonable suggestions for possible improvements were never seriously considered for adoption by the Profession.

So while the structure/format of financial accounts have remained unchanged for a Century, or more, the relevance to investors has declined over that period. Hence there seems some blockage on beneficial adaption of the structure of published financial accounts. This is all the more amazing given the role social developments, fashion, and shared frameworks of reference have in shaping heuristic tools ((Pachur et al., 2004), (Hertwig et al., 2013b), (Hertwig et al., 2013a)). Throughout all the vicissitudes of changed business models and regulatory fads the essentials of our financial reporting technology has remained unchanged.

Buy versus sell–side analysts

So if published accounts are the imperfect input into the market for financial information who receives those inputs? The buy–side analysts interviewed by Imam and Spence (2016) took the view that sell–side analysts covered any accounting issues that did arise, leaving them free to focus on the articulation of a clear and consistent corporate strategy. This leaves buy–side analysts very reliant upon the technical capital of sell–side analysts. Since buy–side analysts typically cover a much broader portfolio of stocks they delegate the detailed work of unravelling published financial accounts to their sell–side peers.

Buy–side analysts see sell–side analysts as offering competing business models for the interpretation of a company's performance. Imam and Spence (2016) (p. 236) report one buy–side analyst, following retail and industrial companies, as commenting

> *"I try to understand who has the best understanding of the business model. I tend to use his model as the starting point."*

In this narrative, good stories are key, rather than numerical forecasts, a buy–side technology analyst told Imam and Spence (2016) (p. 236)

> *"They need to convince me with stories. If they cannot I look somewhere else."*

8.2.2 What makes analysts advice attractive to investors?

When Imam and Spence (2016) asked their buy–side sample how they chose the sell–side analyst to follow. Buy–side analysts mentioned a number of motives, these were

1. those that offered convincing business models to interpret the company's performance,
2. those offering convincing insights into the company's future performance,
3. those with better access to information, perhaps reflecting their higher *social capital*,
4. those with better understanding of, insight into, relevant accounting issues (that buy–side analysts rarely bother with).

Here we can see the evolutionary adoption, adaption, and disposal of valuation models/mental frames by buy–side analysts, according to the shifting market context.

Forecasting accuracy is not the primary criteria for evaluating a sell–side analyst's ability

One startling omission from this list of favoured characteristics of sell–side analysts is their accuracy. Imam and Spence (2016) report buy–side analysts seem unconcerned with forecast/recommendation accuracy, as they simply assume it is poor in general, and prefer to focus merely on the direction of change, up/down, a sell–side analyst is indicating. The real value added of the sell–side is thus located in the contextual background they provide for buy–side analysts in coming to an investment decision.

Barker (2000) in a participative observation study of UK analysts finds that analysts themselves do not see forecasting earnings as their primary duty. Indeed, unless announced earnings markedly deviate from the consensus forecast of them, analysts see little "news" value in their announcement.

For sell–side analysts themselves forecasting accurately is not their primary concern. Partly this is because they recognise that forecasting a company's stock price requires predicting the confluence of two outcomes, **a)** the company's performance, and, **b)** the stock market's reaction to that predicted performance.

Barker (2000) (p. 102) states

"forecast accuracy is not itself a unique selling point for analysts because it does not differentiate between them in the eyes of fund manager clients. Indeed, a

more general statement is that the usefulness of the analyst's service to fund manager clients is not closely correlated with forecast accuracy per se."

The processing of earnings announcements by financial analysts

Barker (2000) provides a flow–chart description of how analysts in his sample processed earnings as they arrived. This describes how the analysts in his participative observation study typically responded to earnings announcements.

Once earnings are announced they are compared to the outstanding consensus forecast. A large deviation triggers a search for some reason for the difference observed. One reason for this may lie in one of the information disclosures made alongside the earnings announcement.

One of these is embedded in the UK's Financial Reporting Standard 3, issued by the UK's Accounting Standard Board in 1992, and concerns the need to publish an "all-inclusive" measure of earnings-per-share; which includes the effects of write-offs to accounting reserves and plant rationalisations/closures. Such additional information might form part of a "story" helping to rationalise the "news" contained in the earnings announcement.

Once a financial analyst has their own story about the earnings announcement they disseminate it, within their, sell–side, brokerage firm. Via traders, within the analyst's brokerage house, the analyst's view is communicated to individual clients. After these analysts collectively pool their knowledge in joint meetings, designed to brief fund-managers and buy–side analysts.

This dialogue may give rise to further quizzing of the company's management. If it does this give rise to the question whether this investigation should be done in public, alerting others' to one's concern, or in private? Finally, analysts prepare a written report for brokers which feeds into their trades, forming a revised stock price. This ends the price revision cycle until more, value-relevant, information arrives in the market.

The Barker (2000) flow–chart (presented here in Fig. 8.1) is of interest in the close resemblance it bears to the fast-and-frugal tree representation so beloved of Gigerenzer and the ABC research group (Martignon et al., 2011). As in the fast-and-frugal tree the Barker (2000) flow–chart looks for "one good reason" to decide if an earnings–announcement is newsworthy.

Analysts use substantial deviations from the consensus forecast to trigger further investigation/discussion of recently announced earnings. Similarly,

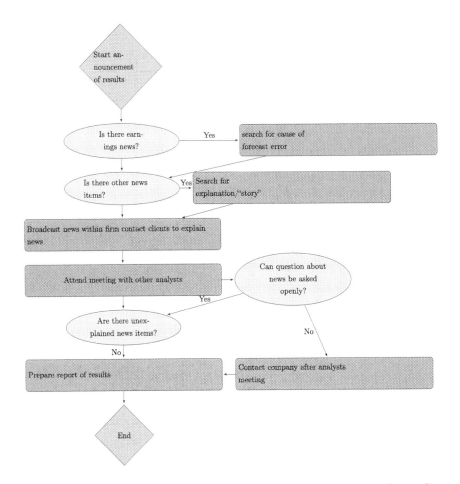

Figure 8.1 Flow chart of analysts' response at earnings announcement. *Note* Source: Figure 1, p. 101, Barker (2000).

discussion at meetings with analysts dictates if earnings "news" is discussed publicly at the analysts' meeting, or in a subsequent conference call, or via private contact with that company's management.

Martignon et al. (2011, p. 142) describe the essence of a fast-and-frugal–tree as follows

> "A fast-and-frugal binary decision tree is a decision tree with a least one exit leaf at every level. That is for every checked cue, at least one of its checked cues can lead to a decision."

A fast-and-frugal representation of the forecast revision cycle?

The Barker (2000) flow–chart representation of an analyst's response to an earnings announcement shares some, but not all of these features. A crucial node/juncture for the analyst's response derives from whether the earnings announcement disturbs the consensus forecast of what it would be. If it does not move the consensus the analyst simply confirms the expected nature of that company's earning profile. But if announced earnings do contradict the consensus forecast markedly, a wider search for a "story" of why the disturbance to expectations has arose occurs. This initiates a reconsideration through discussion with other, peer group, analysts.

So if earnings number announced is roughly in line with its forecast the analyst essentially just reports earnings without further ado. This part of the story accords with a fast-and-frugal representation. If earnings substantially deviate from the consensus forecast the analyst can develop a "story" of why this occurs, using other company disclosures, whether from the published accounts or not. If clients accept this rationalisation discussion ends there.

If the proposed story for the unexpected earning announcement does not satisfy their clients the analyst has two further routes/nodes for resolving the problem. One is via public discussion with other analysts. The other is through private discussions with the company's management. So once a story aiming to explain a difference between actual and forecast earnings fails it is not clear the analyst's further efforts to interpret earnings are re-solved at either of the two subsequent unique nodes; as a fast-and-frugal tree representation would require.

8.2.3 Earnings versus cash-flow as valuation metrics for investors

Lev and Gu (2016) find that for the period 1989–1997 earnings easily dominated cash-flows as an indicator of future returns. But it appears things changed at around the end of the last millennium. The authors conclude

> *"Over recent decades there has been a continuous erosion in the usefulness of reported earnings, relative to other information, a symptom of the decline of much of the usefulness of accounting information."*

EoA, p. 19.

Overall the authors conclude

"the relevance of reported earnings to investors faded. In generating investor returns, earnings are surpassed by cash-flows, and in assessing corporate performance investors feeble reaction to earnings surprises casts serious doubt on the economic meaning of reported earnings."

EoA, p. 21.

8.2.4 The widening chasm between financial information and stock prices

Lev and Gu (2016) document the declining investment value of data taken from published accounts by looking at simple regressions of corporate market values, (market value=price × # of shares issued), observed three months after the fiscal-year end, to allow for publication and discussion of the results, on earnings and book value for each year in the years 1950–2013.

So their focus is very much long-run trends in the explanatory power (or R^2 from the linear regression) of accounting characteristics for stock prices. Following the "market-based"/capital markets tradition of scholarship (very much the dominant one in US business schools) the authors suggest useful published financial accounts, from an equity-investor standpoint, move a company's stock price when the financial report is published.

Lev and Gu (2016) state

"Stock prices thus reflect the aggregate reaction of investors to the information conveyed to them... [this] allows the ranking of alternative information sources.... The indicator that triggers the strongest possible reaction, measured either by stock price change (stock return), or by trading volume change, or is more consistently reflected in stock prices, and therefore is more useful to investors, simply because it is used more effectively by them."

EoA, p. 30

The ability of earnings and book value to explain the market capitalisation of companies has been in sharp decline, from a high of 80–90% in the 1950's, down to 70–80% in the 1960's and 70's, to less than 50% now (with an R^2 of more like 35% for the regression final annual regression reported by Lev and Gu (2016) of company market values on earnings and book value in 2013).

Lev and Gu (2016) describe this finding thus

"The steady decline of the graph [of correlations of stock price on earnings and book value] from about 90% in the 1950's to around 50% currently, a fall of almost a half, tells vividly the decline in the relevance of corporate financial information to investors. That's quite a fall from grace for the ubiquitous investor's information source accounting and financial reporting."

EoA, pp. 31–32

So one might ask "What did it? Earning or book-values?" It turns out the answer is both. Lev and Gu (2016) report the R^2/explanatory power of univariate regressions of market values (measured 3 months after fiscal year end) on earnings alone and book values alone. The decline in explanatory power looks exactly the same as that of earnings and book value together. Suggesting both earnings and book values are of declining relevance to investors.

8.2.5 The growing importance of intangibles

The increased appearance of managerial guesstimates in published accounts, as opposed to relatively grounded figures, like revenues, plant, and machinery, etc., is part of an advancing tide in accounting practice. This has been exacerbated by the increasing adoption of "fair value" accounting with resulting market revaluations.

A rise in the importance attached to discrete business events, IPOs, acquisitions, product launches, regulatory approvals, etc.; often unrelated to the financial reporting cycle, has diminished the role of published accounting data. Since the FASB has earnestly been "improving" the value of accounting disclosures, with a view to helping investors, this decline in published financial reports use to investors seems odd.

Much of the drop in earnings and book values ability to explain corporate valuations seems to have coincided with the birth major technology-driven companies such as AOL, Cisco, National (previously Fairchild) Semiconductor, emerging in the dot com boom of the late 90s. These concept companies, often lost money, reporting accounting losses, had negative book-value and just made no sense to invest in from a normal "Graham and Dodd" investment perspective (Graham and Dodd (1934), Graham (1949)).

Entire industries based on such intangibles rich, earnings poor, companies arose over time, software, biotech, internet companies with Google, Amazon, and Tesla Cars being exemplars of the field (Hand, 2001). A further decline in earnings value relevance has occurred because of the increased reliance on guesstimates in valuation.

Lev and Gu (2016) comment

"Successive accounting regulations have increased the role of managerial sub-jective estimation and forecasting in the calculation of financial items (asset write-offs, fair valuing of assets and liabilities) further diminishing the integrity and reliability of financial information and distancing it from reality. Warren Buffett famously quipped of the requirement to mark to market non-traded assets/liabilities: 'This is not mark to market, but rather marked to myth.'"

EoA, p. 37.

Overall the Lev and Gu (2016) conclude the value of financial reporting, as currently constituted, has been, and is being, eroded at its foundations. One industry where the rise of intangible value, and its disorientating effect, has been particularly marked has been banking, the preferred target of all those who fear the operation of free–markets.

Chen et al. (2014) study of intangible valuation and the UK banking crisis

Chen et al. (2014) study the impact of the rise of intangible assets in UK banks and how that fed into the swelling financial crisis from 2003 onwards. Increasingly the deposit–taking function of banks became less important and algorithmic trading, proprietary trading rules and star, big whale, traders more important. Increasingly this made, banks value more reliant on obtaining, retaining, and enhancing intellectual capital.

Intellectual capital has at least three elements. These are (Meritum, 2002):

1. *human* capital, embedded in company founders' and workers' minds,
2. *structural* capital, organisational routines, procedures, and systems, which characterise an evolutionary theory of economic change (Nelson and Winter, 1982),
3. and, finally, *relational* capital; derived via alliances formed with those outside the company, customer lists, friendly relations with regulators, competitors, etc.

Chen et al. interview senior managers in UK banks during the period June 2008 to September 2009, when the global financial crisis was plaguing them and they were trying to save their corporate life. Obtaining access at this time was quite a coup, allowing them to hear the reflections of bank board members currently wracked by an unfolding global financial crisis.

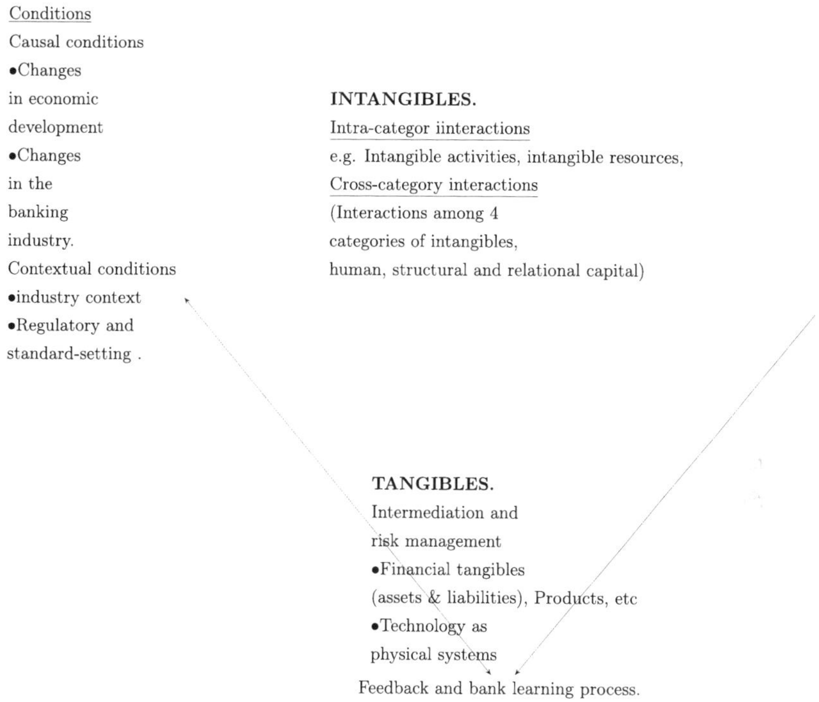

Conditions
Causal conditions
•Changes
in economic   **INTANGIBLES.**
development   Intra-categor iinteractions
•Changes   e.g. Intangible activities, intangible resources,
in the   Cross-category interactions
banking   (Interactions among 4
industry.   categories of intangibles,
Contextual conditions   human, structural and relational capital)
•industry context
•Regulatory and
standard-setting .

                               TANGIBLES.
                               Intermediation and
                               risk management
                               •Financial tangibles
                               (assets & liabilities), Products, etc
                               •Technology as
                               physical systems
                               Feedback and bank learning process.

Figure 8.2 A Grounded theory of bank intangibles. *Note* Source: Figure 1, p. 570 Chen et al. (2014).

Focusing upon the role of intangibles in valuation Chen et al. canvassed the views of 11 senior bank managers and 12 bank analysts. This uncovered an intricate network between a bank's tangible and intangible assets' development.

Chen et al. (2014) depict the evolution of intangible assets with their UK bank sample, as shown in the flow–chart given in Fig. 8.2. This (reading from left to right) shows how the asset base of the bank reflects the market conditions into which it is placed. This includes both the broader economic terrain in which the bank is embedded and the banking regulatory regime. One of the key elements of the bank's relational capital, is the financial trading networks, with other counter-parties, it must grow and maintain.

Such networks assume, and draw upon a tangible asset-base of large capital resources and effective, computer–based, trade execution systems. The outcomes of such an interaction of bank tangible and intangible assets for a bank's performance, and hence market value, require unravelling.

Such outcomes feed into the learning process of bank management; launching the next iteration of the bank's trading/operations strategy. This learning feedback process, captured at the base of Fig. 8.2, is then reflected in financial disclosures made by the firm and embedded into analysts' own reflection on their own forecasting, recommendation, practice.

A central intangible, that came to the fore during the global financial crisis, is good customer relations. Chen et al. (2014, pp. 14, 572) quote one of their analyst respondents thus

"[N]ow when all the consumers and general public are very anxious about their bank, I think it becomes far more important than ever that you have a strong customer franchise."

Another change in context in which bank valuation occurs has been the rise of digital banking and with it the decline, hollowing out, of the local branch; with the importance of service quality rising in private banking, for the very wealthy, but levelling out for retail customers. Within retail banking the focus was increasingly upon strong and consistent branding, designed to attract and retain customers.

Both analyst and management felt a bank's performance reflected the interaction of a wide variety of intangibles, including, customer relations, and the human capital embedded in the bank's employees, who are trained in their products, telesales and, appropriate product targeting.

In this Chen et al. (2014, p. 576) find different forms of intangible capital are complementary, with one management respondent stating

I think its a combination of all three [human capital, strategic capital and relational capital]... I don't believe in those companies that will focus on relational capital, because its all very nice to have very loyal customers, but if your business model is too expensive, you can't make money."

Analysts were very much focussed upon the quality of management, as a source of competitive advantage, during a period of intense market turmoil. But in general they find it hard to quantify, benchmark, intangibles, and find managers evasive/vague on the topic. Both managers and analysts expressed a need to develop credible intangible value metrics, capable of being reported on a consistent basis.

Some of Chen et al.'s sample banks had indeed begun to develop intangible value metrics for internal usage, but others had merely discussed the importance of intangibles, without any attempt being made to quantify them. So while intangibles are clearly an essential element of contemporary banks' business model reporting practice is yet to reflect this, although some, unpublished, experimentation is now beginning.

This matters because new business models of bank value–creation are "performative" in the sense of supporting the launch of new financial products and investment strategies. Thus a new "way of seeing" value–creation creates new sources of value to be seen/measured, traded upon, as intangible value metrics/indicators become heuristic tools for driving price towards "true value".

8.2.6 Other causes of the decreased predictability of reported earnings

Lev and Gu (2016) examine the ability of losses to predict future losses. Are companies currently reporting current losses, "losers", really heading for liquidation or just experiencing a minor lull. So they look at which companies are ranked in the bottom 10% of earnings performance each year, the "loser" group. Investors, like any economic agent, really hate losses; being "loss-averse" (Kahneman and Tversky (1979), Barberis et al. (2001b)).

Part of the reason for this is they just see things getting worse. The authors report a declining recurrence of reported accounting losses sufficient to enter the bottom 10% loser group. So in the 1950's if you had losses this year there was a 60% probability you would also report losses next year. By the 1970's losses recurred 50% of the time. Today if you are in the bottom 10% of earnings performance there is only a 40% chance you will be in that group next year.

Lev and Gu suggest about 60% of companies currently reporting losses, aren't in fact real losers, because they recover and report a smaller loss, or even a profit, in the subsequent year. Accordingly, before you panic and dump a stock; when a company you are invested in reports a loss, check carefully the reasons for the loss. It is likely that the losses are temporary: a write off, effect of an accounting change, or simply bad luck. EofA, p. 58.

8.2.7 Chartism and the practitioner rebellion against the efficient market hypothesis

Preda (2007) chronicles the emergence in the early 20th century of a group of analysts committed to finding patterns in the daily chaos of stock returns. Normally the search for such time–series patterns in consumer purchases, strikes, crimes, or many other social phenomena, is both normal and thought of as good practice.

It is only since the wide–spread acceptance of the efficient market hypothesis, EMH, or that stock's price=a stock's value, with some un-predictable error, that looking for time–series patterns in stock prices has become regarded as the first sign one is an untutored buffoon by academic colleagues.

But before the enthronement of the EMH such time–series modelling of stock price patterns were enthusiastically pursued by academic colleagues and professionals alike. As we write the Chartered Market Technicians society boasts 49 chapters around the World with 35,000 enrollees in its educational programs. If Chartism is dying its death lies some years ahead.

Preda (2007) focuses upon the evolution of the key tool of Chartism; the Chart of recent prices. This has four important elements

1. they are *minute*, to capture short–term price fluctuations before they disappear,
2. they are *accurate*, to prevent the dissemination of false leads,
3. they are *fresh*, to focus action on current, not past, dissipated, market trends,
4. they are *standardised*, so repeated trends are repeated when the same measure of what a stock price, or stock price return, are used.

From the late 1860's in New York and the early 1870's in London a stock market ticker system facilitated the almost continuous recording of stock prices, a pre-condition of a Chartist strategy. Almost immediately ticker "tape readers" providing real–time, accurate, prices to traders to in-form their trades emerged as a service to stock markets.

Pioneers of Chartism

A central concern of early tape–readers was correcting errors in published market prices. But soon the earliest Chartist manual of sorts, "Studies in Tape Reading" (1910) by Richard Wyckoff was published to widespread market interest.

Wyckoff's *The Ticker* magazine become the publication of choice amongst embryonic Chartists. Such data compilation exercises were re-garded as drudgery, suitable merely for drones, motivating the more able Chartists to seek employment elsewhere.

Roger Ward Babson was one of the leading Chartist theorists to develop the tradition, within the pages of *The Ticker*, who later formed the Moody Manual Company, from his friend John Moody, giving birth to the first investor focused news service. From 1907 onwards Babson published his *Babson Reports*, that plotted stocks' trajectories relative to what he termed "the normal line", or what is often now called the "trend line".

The emergence of the trend-line

Preda (2007) (p. 50) quotes Babson as stating that his

> *"contribution to the analysis of and forecasting of business conditions was in connection with the study of areas above and below this Normal [trend] line. Other systems of forecasting only considered the high and low of the charts, while our system considered the areas of the charts."*

Another leading light in this early group of Chartists was Charles Dow; whose "Dow Rule" has remained a focus for tests of the credibility of Chartism ((Brown et al., 1998), (Zhu and Zhou, 2009)). By 1920 Babson, via the Babson Statistical Company, and others sold Chartist advice to investors. A movement was launched and during the 1930's a burgeoning Chartist literature emerged.

Dow, now crowned as the father of Chartist advice, developed no such advisory service himself. But Dow did introduce a key distinction between three types of market fluctuations. These were:
1. daily fluctuations,
2. a short–term market swing, of a fortnight to a month in duration,
3. longer–term market swings, of five years or more.

Chartist trading typically relied on regularity of these cycles, both individually and in tandem with each other. So daily cycles were predicted to accumulate/end when certain trigger characteristics emerged.

Thus like the Adaptive Market Hypothesis of Andrew Lo, discussed in Chapter 3, Chartists emphasised the natural cycles, dynamics, we observe in Nature. Thus Babson represented his "normal"/trend line as analogous to Newton's "law of action and reaction" (Preda (2007), p. 54).

Chartism exploited the common belief that "there is a tide in the affairs of men" and applied it to stock–market trading. In a profound sense Chartism regards the market, and price especially, as an all–seeing, prophetic eye. Preda (2007) (p. 59) cites Wyckoff/Tape's view of 1910 in *Studies in Tape Reading* in stating that

> *"The tape tells the news minutes, hours and days before the news tickers, or newspapers, and before it can become current gossip. Everything from a foreign*

war to the passing of a dividend; from a Supreme Court decision to the ravages of the boll–weevil is reflected primarily on the tape."

Sadly for Chartism practitioners early evidence on the efficacy of their advice was not encouraging, with Cowles (1933) (pp. 323–324) report on the performance of forecasting agencies concluding

"A review of the various statistical tests, applied to the record of this period, of these 24 forecasters, indicates that the most successful records are little, or any better than, what we might expect to result from pure chance."

And the bad news just kept coming for Chartists until the 1970's and its disappearance from enlightened discussion.

8.2.8 Should we care about the decline in the value relevance of published financial accounts?

Lev and Gu (2016) ask should business folk and business academics (outside the accounting group in the Business School) care about the decline in the investor value relevance of accounting? After all fund managers, and even business school undergrads, have Bloomberg screens and Reuters tickers to keep them informed. Isn't all this accounting guff a bit old school and it is time to cheer up and move on?

As the authors point out the sad news is the parlous state of financial reporting really does matter and is about time we got cracking on reforms to sort these problems out. The authors outline a reform manifesto.

Do good shareholder returns now foretell good company performance later?

Putting our Finance, Efficient Market Hypothesis, hat on we might think we are looking at the wrong variable here? Maybe stock prices are the best predictor of future earnings since prices reflect (at least) all publicly available information (plus anything exposed by the trades of naughty insider traders). In this view as Lev and Gu (2016) put it

"well informed share prices are good predictors of companies' performance. In contrast poorly informed share prices will inaccurately predict companies' performance."

EofA, p. 69.

A recent study by Bai et al. (2016) examined the relationship between share price returns and future company performance for about 400 non-financial firms in the S&P 500 over the years 1960 to 2014. In this select group, about 10% of all traded equity in the US, the informativeness of share price regarding future corporate performance increased.

What was a bit more worrying was what happened to share price informativeness with respect to future corporate performance for the remaining 90% of traded equity. This markedly declined; suggesting that outside the charmed circle of major US corporations investors are increasingly clueless about the fortunes of the stocks they invest in, making equity portfolio more of a gamble than a reasoned investment.

As Lev and Gu (2016) interpret Bai et al.'s results

"This suggests for the vast majority of public companies, the alternative (to accounting) information sources are unable to compensate for the deteriorating informativeness of corporate financial reports that we have documented above."

EofA, p. 69.

8.3 Accounting valuation metrics in explanation and prediction of stock returns. Can fast-and-frugal models win out?

Accounting is clearly struggling as an information source for valuation, but is the problem the model used to map accounting value into investor returns or the information provided in the first place? Since Graham (1949) investors have been seen as "buying earnings" when they acquire stocks. Often stocks are just valued by earnings multiples, or as a simple perpetuity in earnings implying the company's price equals $\frac{\text{Earnings}}{r}$.

Others have advanced more complete/complex models of stock value, including book-value as a measure of the "stock of value" embedded in tangible company assets, like plant and machinery, and inventory ((Ohlson, 1995), (Ohlson and Juettner-Nauroth, 2000)). In this final section we content ourselves to examining the ability of announced actual earning-per-share annual, or forecast earnings-per-share for one year ahead, or, finally, the fitted values of a regression of current returns on book-value per-share plus the forecast of earnings-per-share one year ahead, to explain current/future shareholder's returns.

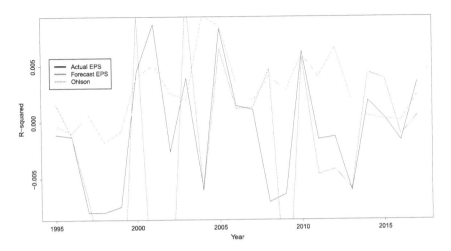

Figure 8.3 Explanatory value of three accounting valuation metrics for current shareholder returns.

So our three measures of financial accounting's value relevance are

1. the Spearman rank correlation of actual annual reported earnings with the company's current stock return,
2. the Spearman rank correlation of the consensus/mean forecast of earnings one year–ahead with the company's current stock return,
3. the Spearman rank correlation between the fitted values of a regression of the current stock return on the company's book-value-per-share plus the consensus/mean forecast of earning-per-share one year ahead on the company's current stock return.

We compare these three valuation metrics ability to explain and predict shareholders' returns. So we examine Spearman rank correlations of the three valuation metrics in explaining current shareholder returns in Fig. 8.3 and predicting next year's returns in Fig. 8.4.

Examining the ability of the three accounting performance to explain current returns, in Fig. 8.3, the very low and highly volatile Spearman-Rank Correlations are obvious. Lev and Gu (2016) (in Chapter 3, Figures 3.1 to 3.3) examine the ability of earnings and book value to explain annual company value, or the company's share price, in their sample.

The exercise reported here examines the ability of actual earnings per–share, forecasted earning per-share, and book value per-share plus forecasted earnings per-share to explain current and future monthly shareholder returns. This is of course a far more demanding task than that considered

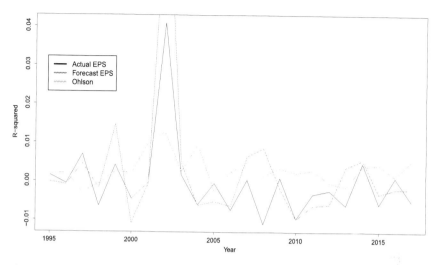

Figure 8.4 Explanatory value of three accounting valuation metrics for returns one-year ahead.

by Lev and Gu (2016), although a task likely to be of central interest to investors.

We note both actual and forecasted (for one year–ahead) earnings-per-share are often negatively (perversely?) related to returns, implying an increase in earnings reduces share–holder returns, but this is less common once book value per-share is introduced as an "anchor of value". Certainly after the "rude awaking" of the Internet bubble implosion (Demers and Lev, 2000) the Ohlson inspired valuation model (Easton and Harris, 1991) seems to explain current shareholder returns best, at least yielding consistently positive, if very low, Spearman rank correlations between accounting measures of value and shareholder returns.

Earnings, whether of actual or forecast earning–per–share, produced negative correlations with current returns throughout the period studied, 1995–2017, although far from consistently. So for explaining current returns rooting valuation in book value seems worthwhile, with the regression based model producing solidly positive correlations with shareholder returns after 2000.

So a relatively complicated, two variable regression model, seems best at *explaining* current returns. But will complex, or fast-and-frugal models, win out in *predicting* next year's returns (or returns 12 months ahead for our monthly data)? Fig. 8.4 shows the relative performance of our three alternative valuation metrics in explaining next year's returns. Now the dominance of the Olhson inspired/complex model is far less clear and very much reversed in the years 2003/4, as the overvaluations of the Internet boom period unwound themselves.

The recorded Spearman rank correlations for all three metrics are higher and are generally more positive. This accords with our intuition that stock markets are forward–looking in their valuation of companies using accounting data.

But the relative improvement in the Ohlson inspired/complex, regression based, model is not enough to give it the clear dominance it had in explaining current returns. So in predicting next year's shareholder returns simple, fast-and-frugal, models seem very comparable to, if not better than, more complex ones, that may simply overfit themselves to current data, drawn from volatile markets.

8.4 Conclusion

Financial analysis, the prediction of one company's fortunes from its history of accounting performance, is truly a high-wire act of financial decision-making. Here the risks of the future recede in the face of a truly uncertain future. If Keynes and Frank Knight (Knight, 1921) diagnosed the condition of the businessman/entrepreneur fast-and-frugal models give us some tools for managing that uncertainty. This aid is most welcome in an age in which the rise of intangible values are rendering published accounts increasingly useless for valuation, or stock–picking, purposes.

While the context of managers' stewardship has dramatically changed in the last one hundred and fifty years often its appears the accounting has struggled to respond. Many have just given up on accrual accounting and reverted to cash-flow metrics of value, or even more dramatically, adopted Chartist methods in contradiction of notions of efficient markets. As we have seen already in Chapter 3 this, while heretical, may reflect a superior *ecological* rationality.

If we cannot take earning forecasts, or perhaps financial analysis itself "too seriously", then the simple, fast-and-frugal, models of value are an attractive way forward. Our, admittedly crude, tests of the relative value of simple and more complex models suggests for predictive, if not explanatory, purposes this might indeed by the case. But most qualitative evidence of what analysts actually do suggests such quantitative prediction tasks are neither what others look to them to do, or what they aspire to.

Fund managers and buy–side analysts, the primary users of sell–side analysts' reports, use their work as inputs to a broader judgement about how the competitive market, regulatory and technological landscape around an individual firm is changing. Accurate forecasts of future earnings, or investor returns, are not regarded as a characteristic capable of elevating a (sell–side) analysts above the crowd of their peers.

Fund managers simply accept that predictions of the extent of future earnings, price changes is so fraught as to be almost useless and prefer to concentrate on forecasts of the direction, if not degree, of change. So good analysts sense shifts in the market, regulatory, technological context, and the need for evolution in the valuation frame used in response to such changes.

CHAPTER 9

Inference under the law of small numbers: Earnings streaks rather than earnings numbers*

9.1 Introduction

Humans have always faced the choice between alternatives from what to eat for breakfast to what to wear to the office. As pupils, at some point in our lives, we are confronted with the need to choose which degree pro-gramme from many alternatives to study at university. We approach this choice problem by taking into account the things we enjoy doing as well as the things we are capable of doing. So, our individual preferences and capabilities are key to whatever choice we make. This need to make deci-sions extends even to economic activities such as a need to choose between alternative investments. Irrespective of the task at hand, the need to collate relevant information is common to every decision-making process.

The information set has to be relevant to the decision that we wish to make. Consider a seventeen-year-old school pupil who wants to study medicine at university. To decide which medical school to attend from the 33 in the UK, the first step is to gather relevant information about these schools. This includes information about the entry requirements, fees, cost of living, national student survey ranking, distance from home, availability of sports facilities, availability of part-time jobs, and the duration of the study, among others. Theoretically, relevant information that can be in-cluded in this information set is infinite. On the other hand, the amount of information that the pupil is able to include in his set ultimately depends on a number of factors. First, is the amount of time he has at his disposal before the application deadline. Second, his capacity to collate these pieces of information and to fully and correctly analyse them is most likely to be limited. Third, his knowledge of the UK universities and their medical schools will most likely be limited. And finally, at this point, there is also the uncertainty regarding whether this pupil will make good grades in his

* This chapter is written by Aloysius Igboekwu.

A Fast and Frugal Finance
https://doi.org/10.1016/B978-0-12-812495-6.00017-3
203

future GCSE A-level examinations to be eligible for admission to a medical school.

The availability of the information that will affect our hypothetical pupil's choice is limited in supply. In addition, the pupil faces uncertainty as to achieving eligibility for admission into his degree programme of choice. So, this pupil is simply facing a situation of choice under uncertainty. Considering these limitations the pupil is likely to resort to using shortcuts (or heuristics) to arrive at a decision. For example, he might simply choose to apply to the schools he already knows about–an example of decision-making using the availability heuristic. He might also resort to asking his classmates and tutors which medical schools they think are good, seek the opinion of his family members or friends who have gone through medical school education in the past or even seek the opinion of a family doctor. These are all examples of advice-taking, which can be viewed as employing heuristics in decision-making. This pupil's choice, whatever it ends up to be, has uncertain future outcomes.

Modern economics and finance theory postulates that rational individuals facing choice decisions under uncertainty must apply the axioms of rational choice of mathematician John von Neumann and economist Oskar Morgenstern (Von Neumann and Morgenstern, 1944). By correctly applying axioms of rational choice, the standard models see economic agents as utility maximisers.

In this chapter, we will use alternative concepts of rationality; namely ecological and bounded rationality, to explain how investors can use the information contained in streaks of quarterly earnings-per-share changes to predict future stock market returns. In the last few decades, economists have referred to the standardised unexpected earnings (SUE) as the innovation in earnings news. This implies that besides SUE, there is no other source of relevant information in earnings news which investors can use in stock valuation. This chapter turns the focus to earnings streaks instead and addresses this topic from the viewpoint of the law of small numbers (Rabin, 2002). Also, it addresses the issue of investor rationality from the bounded and ecological rationality viewpoints.

9.2 The law of small numbers, gambler's fallacy, and overinference

The law of small numbers is a parody of the well-known law of large numbers. This concept was first mentioned in Tversky and Kahneman's

1971 paper in the *Psychological Bulletin*. The authors found that individuals tend to see patterns in randomly drawn samples. They reported that individuals erroneously believe that such randomly drawn samples are representative of their parent populations, and termed this erroneous belief "belief in the law of small numbers". The Gambler's fallacy and representativeness heuristic are two major heuristics emanating from the law of small numbers which influence investors' decision-making processes ((Barberis et al., 1998), (Rabin, 2002)), which are labelled as "irrational" behaviour. These heuristics can be alternatively explained through the bounded rationality concept first postulated by the late Herbert Simon, and ecological rationality propounded by economist Vernon Smith, and more recently by psychologist Gerd Gigerenzer.

9.2.1 Rabin (2002) formulation of the law of small numbers

In his 2002 paper entitled "Inference by believers in the law of small numbers" published in the *Quarterly Journal of Economics*, Matthew Rabin presents a model which postulates that when individuals observe short streaks of independent and identically distributed (*i.i.d.*) random signals, they tend to exaggerate the extent to which they resemble the long-run sequence which generates them. For example, observing a streak of heads in a sequence of coin flips leads to the belief in a diminished probability of the next coin flip turning out a *head*. This erroneous belief is a result of the individual believing that a short-run of finite N flips of a coin should produce a sequence of heads and tails that resembles a long-run normal distribution of heads and tails; that is, N times coin flips must produce a sequence with a balanced number of heads and tails. For such an individual, the sample must have the same statistical properties as the population.

An individual who behaves in this manner believes in the gambler's fallacy. Gambler's fallacy is a phenomenon observed in gambling where a gambler believes that an early draw of heads diminishes the chances of drawing a *head* next time around and expects a reversal to occur. Rabin (2002) develops a model that describes instances of this phenomenon in economics, finance, and other disciplines. He uses an example of a representative investor whom he calls Freddy to illustrate how this model applies to an investor's decision-making process.

Rabin's model shows that Freddy begins his decision-making process with correct prior beliefs about the probability distribution of the signals he is observing. So, he can be said to be fully Bayesian at this stage. Thus, according to standard theory, Freddy's beliefs are fully rational. However,

Freddy has a fundamental flaw in updating his prior beliefs at the arrival of new information. He always fails to recognise that his data-generating process is *i.i.d.* When he observes a finite number of binary signals (say, a and b) drawn from a non-replacing "*urn*" (population), he believes that each time the "*urn*" is sampled, drawing signal 'a' diminishes the chances of drawing another signal 'a' in the next sampling period. On the arrival of a new signal, a Bayesian believes the signal is drawn from an *urn* (containing binary signals) with replacement, while in contrast, Freddy believes the urn is sampled without replacement, or at least that replacement does not occur at every sampling period. Since Freddy's belief-building process resembles that of a gambler, he is a believer in the gambler's fallacy.

In his model, Rabin demonstrates that if individuals (investors) are uncertain about the rate generating a particular signal (e.g., an earnings-generating process), they overinfer from short streaks of its signals in a manner that suggests that the rate is more extreme than it actually is. Rabin posits that when Freddy observes longer sequences, he believes the streaks of the signals are sub-sequences embedded within the longer sequences of signals. This shows that even though Freddy started off fully Bayesian and rational, he turns "irrational" or at best a quasi-Bayesian in the end. To illustrate this behaviour, Rabin's model shows that both a Bayesian and Freddy possess the same initial posterior probabilities when they observe a streak of *i.i.d.* signals. However, as the streak continues to grow, Freddy's posterior probabilities become too extreme and diverge from that of a true Bayesian. In this way, the model is able to capture two different but related phenomena – the gambler's fallacy and overinference.

9.2.2 An illustration of the structure of Rabin (2002) model of the law of small numbers

To illustrate overinference in the model, Rabin demonstrates how a Bayesian and Freddy revise their beliefs at the arrival of some new firm value changing fundamental signals such as earning news. At earnings announcements, there are three possible earnings outcomes: a rise, a fall, or a no-change with respect to earnings in the most recent preceding quarter. Rabin shows that a Bayesian believes that in the next earnings announcement, each of the three possible outcomes is equally likely to occur and has the same posterior probabilities given the earnings outcome last quarter. In other words, the probability (*Pr*) of a:

$$Pr_{rise} = Pr_{fall} = Pr_{no-change} = \tfrac{1}{3}.$$

Let us consider an example. Assuming an observer believes that a certain company with a fall in earnings last quarter has a 25% probability of a rise in earnings next quarter, a company with no-change in earnings last quarter has a 50% probability of a rise next quarter, and a company with a rise in earnings last quarter has a 75% probability of a rise next quarter. Applying the Bayesian revision rule, for the company with a fall in earnings last quarter, there is an inferred posterior probability of a sixth of observing a rise next quarter, i.e.

$$Pr_{(rise|fall)} = \frac{\frac{1}{4}}{\frac{1}{4} + \frac{1}{2} + \frac{3}{4}} = \frac{\frac{1}{4}}{1.5} = \frac{1}{6} \tag{9.1}$$

Similarly, for a company with a no-change in earnings last quarter, the posterior probability of a rise next quarter is a third, i.e.

$$Pr_{(rise|no-change)} = \frac{1}{3} \quad \text{or} \quad \frac{\frac{1}{2}}{1.5} \tag{9.2}$$

And finally for a company with a rise in earnings last quarter, the posterior probability of a rise next quarter is one-half, i.e.

$$Pr_{(rise|rise)} = \frac{\frac{3}{4}}{1.5} = 0.5 \tag{9.3}$$

9.2.3 Inference of probabilities of alternative earnings streaks

If a Bayesian and Freddy observe two consecutive earning outcomes for the companies presented in section 9.2.2 above, their inference could differ quite significantly depending on which earnings outcome was realised last quarter. If Freddy observes two consecutive quarterly earning rises, his inference differs from that of a Bayesian. In particular, Freddy's inferred posterior probability of earnings rise next quarter given a fall last quarter is less than a Bayesian's:

$$Pr_{(rise|fall)} = \frac{\frac{1-1}{4-1}}{\frac{1-1}{4-1} + \frac{2-1}{4-1} + \frac{3-1}{4-1}} \quad \text{Or} \quad \frac{0}{\frac{0}{3} + \frac{1}{3} + \frac{2}{3}} = \frac{0}{1} = 0 \tag{9.4}$$

For a rise next quarter given a no change last quarter, Freddy's posterior probability is the same as the Bayesian:

$$Pr_{(rise|no-change)} = \frac{\frac{2-1}{4-1}}{\frac{1-1}{4-1} + \frac{2-1}{4-1} + \frac{4-1}{6-1}} \quad \text{or} \quad \frac{\frac{1}{3}}{\frac{0}{3} + \frac{1}{3} + \frac{2}{3}} = \frac{1}{3} \tag{9.5}$$

For a successive rise in earnings next quarter given a rise in the last quarter; for Freddy, there is an increase in posterior probability compared to the Bayesian:

$$Pr_{(rise|rise)} = \frac{\frac{3-1}{4-1}}{\frac{1-1}{4-1} + \frac{2-1}{4-1} + \frac{3-1}{4-1}} \quad \text{or} \quad \frac{\frac{2}{3}}{\frac{0}{3} + \frac{1}{3} + \frac{2}{3}} = \frac{2}{3} \tag{9.6}$$

From the above, we can see that while a Bayesian believes there is a one-half probability of a rise next quarter for a company with a rise last quarter, Freddy believes it is two-thirds. So, when Freddy observes two consecutive earning rises (unexpectedly), he overinfers from the short streak of earning rises and his forecast is skewed towards a rise next quarter. This is the overinference bias in Rabin's model.

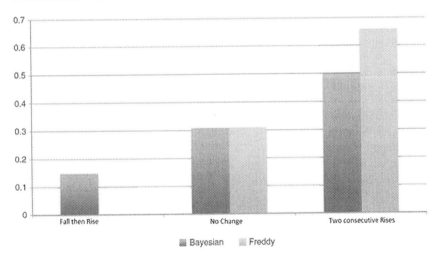

Figure 9.1 Distribution of Bayesian and Freddy's posterior priors (adapted from (Forbes and Igboekwu, 2015)).

The differences in beliefs between a Bayesian and Freddy when they observe repetitions of random signals is shown in Fig. 9.1 above. So Rabin's model can predict both the gambler's fallacy and the overinference bias which are the two key attributes of the law of small numbers. Gambler's fallacy occurs when investors underpredict short-run repetition of streaks of signals such as quarterly earning outcomes. This leads to a short–term underreaction to companies quarterly earnings announcements or other similar corporate performance announcements. Similarly, overinference is predicted in the model when investors overpredict the repetition of a longer streak of signals; this can lead to medium-term overreaction to corporate performance announcements.

9.3 Bounded rationality and the limits of arbitrage

In Rabin's model examined in section 9.2 above, the question that needs to be asked is whether Freddy is irrational or he is simply applying his decision-making ability in the best possible way he can, given the limitations and constraints he faces in collecting, updating and processing all 'relevant' information to enable him to make the best choice. The standard theory will categorise Freddy as irrational since he fails to apply the Bayes' rule fully in updating his prior beliefs in the presence of new information. However, contrasting theories, and concepts have emerged mainly through psychology experiments, showing how human beings actually make decisions under uncertainty. These alternative views would argue that even though Freddy's predictions may be less than accurate, he is unlikely to be unreasonable or irrational. Behavioural finance researchers argue that due to the impact of bounded rationality, Freddy cannot possibly be rational in the von Neumann, and Morgenstern sense. Bounded rationality ((Simon, 1955), (Simon, 1956)) posits that human beings make decisions under the constraints of limited resources such as time, knowledge, money, information, computational capacity, and so forth. In contrast to the rational choice theory, Simon postulates that human beings, unlike supercomputers are not capable of correctly analysing huge amounts of information speedily or knowing the probabilistic distributions of uncertain future outcomes from such analysis. Alternatively, he believes that humans make choices that satisfice their needs rather than optimise their choices as rational choice theory postulates. Simon argues that human beings would choose the first outcome which satisfies their ambition instead of repeatedly surveying alternative possible outcomes, determining their probabilities and expected utilities, before choosing the outcome that ranks first.

Human rationality is bounded in that humans cannot be rational in the way of the super "economic man" as the standard theory suggests. For Simon, the concept of bounded rationality can be viewed from two main aspects – the cognitive aspect and the ecological, or environmental aspect. The cognitive aspect highlights the limitations of the human mind as lacking the capacity to behave like the superfast computer, mimicking the Laplacean demon (Gigerenzer and Goldstein, 1996). In addition, Simon emphasises that the human mind adapts to the real-world environment where decisions and choices are made. So, to arrive at a decision, the human mind and the environment have to work in harmony with each other.

The limits of arbitrage theory ((Shleifer and Vishny, 1997), (Gromb and Vayanos, 2010)) postulates that informed investors cannot always use arbitrage to eliminate inefficiencies in the prices of securities and, therefore, prices may not achieve equilibrium for long periods. This is contrary to the efficient market hypothesis claims. The reason for this is partly because arbitrage opportunities can be expensive to execute and at the same time risky. Even though informed and smart investors may spot arbitrage opportunities in the market, they may not always be willing or motivated to take on those opportunities. One corroborating fact is that most investors and fund managers use borrowed funds to trade and are likely to be more risk-averse when they are not convinced of the true risk–return distribution of an arbitrage opportunity.

9.4 Ecological rationality and real-world financial market decision-making

Simon A. Herbert was among the first to propose that the environment influences the way the human mind make decisions. This is what other academics such as Vernon Smith refer to as ecological rationality. In his Nobel Prize lecture, Smith (2003) posits that there are two types of economic rationality: the constructivist and ecological forms of rationality.

The constructivist approach deals with the sort of rationality propounded by Bayes' rule and the expected utility theory. It requires that any rational decision-making process be based on a set of optimal principles which must be duly observed in arriving at a decision. If this normative rule is not fulfilled, any choice made from the process will be construed as irrational. In contrast, ecological rationality is derived from learning over time through interaction between agents in the environment (Smith, 2003), (Smith, 2008). Thus good rules and practices emerge through the interactions and superior practices are selected thereafter. So, while the constructivist approach to rationality presupposes a set of a priori rules to be followed to arrive at an ideal and generalised form of decision-making, ecological rationality does not require any such set of rules and does not generalise. Ecological rationality recognises the differences in various environments in which decisions are made. Different environments will influence agents in different ways – therefore, for ecological rationality, decision-making is local to the environment. This line of reasoning supposes that the human brain has not evolved the capacity to process huge amounts of information at the speed that the logic-based constructivist approach seems to require.

Evidence from economics and psychology experiments shows that people in the markets are able to find price equilibrium through a surprisingly small number of repeated interactions over time (Smith, 2008). So, in the real world, equilibrium is not established through the intense gathering and processing of information as suggested by the standard theory. This is more so because people appear to discover equilibrium in markets despite the fact that information is private and information asymmetry plays an active role in the markets. Two core assumptions of the standard theory are that information is free and homogeneous in the markets and that these help to establish price equilibrium. However, we know that information is not free in the financial markets. Additionally, information asymmetry and insider trading exist and these cause distortions to the price discovery process.

Efficient market anomalies exist partly because of the disparity between standard models of asset pricing and the manner asset pricing is done in practice. Just as in everyday life, investors do not consistently apply the von Newman and Morgenstern principles of rationality when revising their asset pricing models. Even though one can argue that the standard theory is a good place to start, certainly, it does not tell the full story. With all the empirical evidence showing that the theory is imprecise in its assumptions and outcomes, it is therefore crucial that a new theory is developed which can complement it. Such a theory must take into account the shortcomings of the standard theory and reflect the exact way people make decisions in various situations.

A theory of ecological rationality may be the right model to fill in the gap left by the standard theory. However, ecological rationality and other concepts from psychology theory and experiments will have to be practical and applicable rather than being just another set of theories with an unending list of impractical assumptions.

9.4.1 Fast-and-frugal reasoning in financial markets

Gigerenzer and Goldstein (1996) propose the use of simple cognitive algorithms for decision-making under uncertainty. These algorithms are modelled based on inferences from memory, which Gigerenzer and Goldstein call the probabilistic mental model (PMM) (Gigerenzer et al., 1991). The PMM model assumes that the probability of an outcome in an uncertain state of the world can be inferred from probabilistic cues and cue values of an object. Generally, the probabilistic cues are part of knowledge reference pool which is used when the need for decision-making arises.

PMMs are built based on the insights from Brunswik (1955) and Simon ((Simon, 1955), (Simon, 1956)), and have three fundamental pillars:

1. The inductive inference must be studied taking the natural environment into account.
2. The inductive inference should be made using the satisficing (rather than the utilitarian) algorithm and
3. The inductive inference can be derived from frequencies of events in a reference group as proposed by the frequentist statisticians.

The key argument of the PMMs is that simple and plausible psychological mechanisms should be applied in decision-making processes rather than some complex principles such as those of the rational choice models. So, whereas rational choice models propose optimisation based on all relevant information, PMMs search the memory for information within the constraints of limited knowledge, time, computational capacity, and the need for other necessary resources. Hence, the search for information in PMMs is reduced to the barest minimum. During the search process, probability cues can be substituted with one another. Gigerenzer and Goldstein (1996) demonstrate through computer simulations that PMMs either outperform or match rational choice models in speed and accuracy.

Thus a PMM can be described as an inductive tool that makes fast inference using a limited knowledge reference pool which consists of a set of cues sometimes with missing values. To make a choice between two alternatives, a set of probability cue and cue values are selected from the knowledge reference pool. Usually, two alternative objects are assessed by assigning a probability cue with potential binary outcomes to each of the objects. The alternative that scores the highest cue value is chosen as the best among the alternatives. An unknown cue value is assigned a question mark. In the PMM framework, a choice forecast is made based on the individual's knowledge of the issue at hand.

Will a PMM be beneficial to investors rather than the standard asset pricing models such as the capital asset pricing model (CAPM) and its variants? Given that investors have to make decisions in a very fast–moving environment such as the financial market, using models with minimal information and knowledge requirements seem appealing. Standard asset pricing models are based on conditions that are almost impracticable in the financial markets. For example, to construct a portfolio of securities, investors first have to build an infinite number of portfolios by combining different weights of the constituent securities each time and comparing the portfolios' means and variance to determine the efficient frontier. In addition, the investor needs to understand the variance-covariance matrix of the portfolio; for multi-asset portfolios, this task requires huge computational power. So, it is not surprising that return anomalies persist in the stock markets and their persisitence seems to be a testimony that the standard asset pricing models are flawed.

The study of bounded rationality from the cognitive and emotional perspective will not be complete without the understanding of the environment within which decisions are made. Ecological rationality models combine those cues which have been identified and learned from the environment and match them with the structure of heuristics (Gigerenzer and Selten, 2001b). Therefore, ecological rationality models demand analysis and understanding of the environment within which a choice is to be made over a period of time. In addition, the models require that there is an understanding of the structure of heuristics at work in that environment. A choice decision is then made by matching the outcomes from the analysis of the environment with the structures of the heuristics. Here, the environment does not refer to the totality of the physical or biological environment, but to that part that pertains to the person's needs and goals. In a number of articles, Gigerenzer and his co-authors show that some heuristics can be adaptive within certain environmental structures and can be used to make quick, accurate, and frugal inferences that are sometimes better than those made using the rational choice models.

9.4.2 Stock market valuation models: change in quarterly earnings as the innovation in earnings outcomes

Investors, financial analysts, and other market participants use the information contained in reported company earnings to predict the future value of those companies' common shares. Usually, companies report periodic earning figures at different time horizons depending on the requirements of the law in their countries. For example, publicly listed companies in the US and China are required by law to publish their financial standing every quarter. In the UK and other countries in Europe, the law requires companies to publish their earning biannually. In both cases, earnings data are publicly made available for investors, market participants, and other end users. They use the earnings figures to predict the future market values of these companies' common shares.

Over the years, a number of models have emerged which are used to forecast earnings figures. Two of those models are the most widely used in research and practice. One model uses a company's historical earnings figures to forecast future earnings. The other model is based on analysts' forecast of earnings. Therefore, the fundamental difference between the two models is the variable used in forecasting earnings numbers.

In both models, the standardised unexpected earnings (otherwise known as SUE) is the innovation in earnings news. The SUE is simply the difference between the reported actual earnings and the earnings forecast number over a period. Investors look at SUE as the carrier of true information in earnings news. So, the earnings figures do not matter so much to them. This assertion is well-documented in the literature. Investors focus on the sign as well as the magnitude of SUE as a predictor of the sign and magnitude of future stock returns. If SUE is large and positive, which implies that the company has outperformed market expectations, evidence suggests that there is an initial market underreaction to the earnings news. Conversely, if SUE is large and negative, it implies that the company's earnings have not met market expectations, and the market reacts accordingly.

9.4.3 Earnings surprise measures

Foster et al. (1984) provide methods for constructing different types of SUE metrics along with their scaling formats. Evidence in the literature shows that the magnitude and sign of SUE capture the investor's (market) response to the difference between the expected earnings and actual earnings realisations (Bernard and Thomas, 1989), (Bernard and Thomas, 1990), (Abarbanell and Bernard, 1992), (Brown et al., 1987a), (Brown and Zmijewski, 1987). Thus, SUE captures investors' sentiment (in stock prices) as they underreact to the new information captured in the most recent quarterly earnings surprise.

Researchers and practitioners use different earnings forecast measures to compute the SUE (SUE is the earnings surprise metric). In the early literature, researchers used the quarterly earnings first-order autoregressive data-generating model of the type shown in Eq. (9.7) to compute SUE:

$$E[Q_{it}] = \delta_i + Q_{it-4} + \Theta_i(Q_{it-1} - Q_{it-5}) + \Theta\varepsilon_{it-4} + \varepsilon_{it} \qquad (9.7)$$

where Q_{it} is company i's quarterly earnings-per-share in quarter t and δ_i is the drift term, while Q_{it-1} to Q_{it-5} represent the prior earnings-per-share value from period t-1 to t-5. Bernard and Thomas (1989; 1990) document that while Eq. (9.7) is the true data-generating process, investors when forecasting earnings omit the first order autoregressive term $[\Theta(Q_{it-1} - Q_{it-5})]$ from their model and think that quarterly earnings are generated by $[E[Q_{it}] = \delta_i + Q_{it-4}]$ instead. Liu et al. (2003) observe that Eq. (9.7) contains a seasonal random walk, with or without a drift, as seen in a special case where $\Theta_i = 0$ or $\delta_i = 0$. Their model defines SUE as the unexpected earnings deflated by the standard error of unexpected earnings. The model computes earnings surprise based on the time series of historical earnings. Some of the early works to adopt this model include (Latané and Jones, 1977), (Latané and Jones, 1979), (Foster, 1977), (Foster et al., 1984), (Barov, 1992), and (Brown, 1993). These models define SUE as:

$$SUE_{it} = \frac{UE_{it}}{\sigma UE_i} \qquad (9.8)$$

where $UE_{it} = Q_{it} - E[Q_{it}]$, $E[Q_{it}]$ is the expected earnings from the univariate time series model, Q_{it} is company i's actual earnings in time t, whereas σUE_i is the standard error from the time series regression equation.

However, evidence (Livnat and Medenhall, 2006) shows that SUE computed from the consensus analyst forecast of earnings explains stock returns better than those from historical earnings. The method involves the use of the most recent consensus monthly analyst forecast to proxy investors' expectation of future earnings. SUE is then computed using the consensus monthly analyst forecast and actual quarterly earnings-per-share in the most recent quarter. This is shown in the model below in Eq. (9.9).

$$SUE_{it} = \frac{A_{it} - F_{it}}{P_{it-4}} \qquad (9.9)$$

In Eq. (9.9) above, F_{it} represents the consensus monthly analysts' forecast for company i in the most recent month before the earnings announcement in time t. A_{it} is company i's actual quarterly earnings-per-share in time t whereas P_{it-4} is the prior year end stock price of company i's common share.

Brown and Zmijewski (1987) observe that analysts' forecasts of earnings are better in capturing earnings expectation than earnings forecasts from time series models. The authors posit that the reason is that analysts recognise and distinguish between permanent, transitory and irrelevant earnings shocks and can adjust their forecasts more accurately. Furthermore, analysts have more information about the political, regulatory, and technology risks that companies face. In addition, (Brown et al., 1985), (Fried and Givoly, 1982), (Elton et al., 1984) document that analysts' consensus forecasts capture the market's expectation of future earnings better than time series models. Brown et al. (1987b) show that the reason for the superiority of the consensus analysts' forecasts over forecasts from univariate time series models is not certain. However, the authors in their study found that earnings surprise from the consensus analyst forecast model explains the association between earnings expectation and stock returns better than time series models.

In more recent literature, Livnat and Medenhall (2006) document that consensus analysts' forecasts of earnings provide better forecasts than those of time series models in measuring SUE. Other authors confirm the Livnat and Medenhall (2006) model suggesting that consensus analysts' forecasts provide a better explanation of post-earnings announcement drift than forecasts derived from time series models. However, it is good to note that although time series forecasts might be less accurate, they might also be less biased, as analysts can become swayed by "bubble psychology".

So, the magnitude and sign of SUE have been used to explain the post-earnings announcement drift (PEAD) in stock returns following earnings announcements. And as seen above, the model which is used in determining SUE does matter in explaining the relation between stock returns and the unexpected earnings. Stock trading strategies based on SUE have been shown to be profitable.

9.5 Streaks of quarterly earning changes: better cues to future stock returns than earnings figures?

Evidence from recent research shows that streaks of earnings possess more explanatory power than the magnitude and sign of SUE. We define a streak in earnings changes as a consecutive trend of two or more earnings changes of the same sign. This is either a consistent rise or fall in earnings changes for two or more consecutive periods. In most empirical works, the period is usually a quarter. A termination of streaks occurs when a change in earnings of a different sign arrives at the most recent earnings announcement. Both negative and positive streaks in earnings changes are better indicators for the future stock market returns than negative and positive SUE. Streaks of both negative and positive earnings changes explain post-earnings announcement drift anomaly better than the SUE metric. Loh and Warachka (2012) and (Forbes and Igboekwu, 2015) show that different lengths of streaks of earnings changes explain the persistence of stock returns over a considerable period of time following the most recent earnings announcement.

Most researchers believe that the gambler's fallacy is the phenomenon driving the explanatory power of earnings streaks. In stock valuation, this finding suggests that investors do not only take into account the difference between earnings in the same quarter in two adjacent years but also the streaks in earnings over multiple time periods. At the arrival of earnings news, this behaviour cause investors to underreact to streaks in earnings changes of the same sign. This underreaction implies that investors fail to adjust their expectations fully for future earnings outcomes.

A growing streak of negative earnings changes might be a cue to the fact that the company is in troubled waters while growing positive streaks in earnings over a number of quarters might be an indication that a company has good prospects. In the most recent announcement, growth in a streak implies a stronger post-earnings announcement drift. However, if a growing streak is terminated at the arrival of the most current earnings news, the post-earnings announcement drift is weak and insignificant (Loh and Warachka, 2012).

So, considering the above evidence that streaks in earnings can explain stock returns; can investors incorporate earnings streaks in their asset pricing models? Stock trading strategies based on post-earnings announcement drift have been known to be profitable both in the US and international markets. Could the introduction of streaks in earnings into asset pricing models improve these models? These questions can only be answered correctly when we examine various pieces of empirical evidence which seem to affirm them. Various lengths of streaks in earnings possess different explanatory powers. So, the investor draws different inferences depending on the "streakiness" of earnings changes. The investor's inference will partly depend on whether he is observing negative or positive streaks. In addition, his inference will depend on the length of the streaks. For example, the investor draws a different inference from a positive streak of two earnings changes to that of a negative streak of four.

So let us go back to the empirical evidence in the finance literature to see if there is any tangible support for streaks in earnings changes as explanatory variables for stock market returns. Loh and Warachka (2012) report that a trading strategy that buys stocks with positive streaks in earnings and sells stocks with negative streaks yields a four-factor positive monthly abnormal returns of 0.603% over a six-month holding period. A very interesting finding of this research is that even when the strategy is based on very liquid and large stocks with huge analyst following, it is still economically and statistically significant. Ordinarily, one would expect that such liquid, popular, and highly traded stocks would not be profitable using this strategy, as price discovery for such stocks happens much quicker. The profitability of this strategy seems to support the gambler's fallacy hypothesis, as investors seem to underreact to streaks in earnings changes. Loh and Warachka report that another strategy based on the most recent SUE conditioned on streaks in earnings generates an even higher positive monthly stock return of 0.882% than the previous strategy. In a third strategy, the authors conditioned streaks in earnings on the magnitude of earnings changes. The results of this strategy show that the positive and significant PEAD returns are concentrated around streaks rather than the magnitude of earnings changes.

To confirm whether the sign (negative and positive) of the streak plays any important role in its explanatory power, the authors use another strategy which simply buys all stocks with positive earnings changes in the most recent quarter and sells all stocks with negative earnings changes in the most recent quarter. Their result shows that this strategy has similar explanatory power to the streaks and explains similar sizes of PEAD returns. So the relation between the sign of the most recent earnings changes and the PEAD is only significant if that sign is associated with a growing streak in earnings changes. Loh and Warachka report that trading strategies with streaks in earnings changes lengths of 2 to 3, 4 to 5, 6 to 9, 9 yield monthly portfolio abnormal returns of 0.78%, 0.92%, 1.19%, and 1.12% respectively. These results show that streaks induce stronger underreaction as the streaks grow longer. The authors find that similar trading strategies using earnings reversal yields insignificant results.

Forbes and Igboekwu (2015) working with S&P 500 constituent companies report similar findings to Loh and Warachka (2012). In their sample frame, the authors find that there is a marked market response to streaks of quarterly earnings change rises and falls. The response is even more pronounced as the streaks of earnings change rise and falls lengthen. The authors report that while the market response to lengthening streaks of different earnings rises is quite stable, the response to sequences of earnings falls and declines becomes more erratic as the streak lengthens. This market behaviour is consistent with the gambler's fallacy described in Rabin (2002). Investors first underreact to a growing streak of a particular sign, as ordinarily, they expect a reversal rather than a continuation. However, when the streaks persist, their response is large and their expectation is overestimated (through overinference) (Freddy in Section 9.2 above).

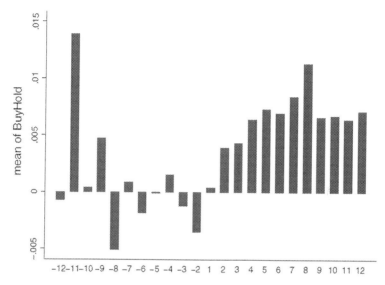

Figure 9.2 Mean Fama-French 3-Factor adjusted returns performance metric by sequence (streak) length (adapted from Forbes and Igboekwu, 2015).

Fig. 9.2 above shows a typical market response to various lengths of positive and negative streaks in earnings changes. Although there is a difference between the earnings changes metrics used in Loh and Warachka and Forbes and Igboekwu, their results are very similar.

Also, evidence suggests that streaks in earnings changes have implications for market microstructure processes such as order flow. Shanthikumar (2012) reports that growing strings of increasing earnings changes are associated with small to medium trades. The author shows that as earnings streakiness grows, the intensity of trading by small traders also increases. Consistent with the finding of Shanthikumar (2012), Frieder (2008), testing the "Investor Sentiment Model" of Barberis et al. (1998), reports that the net buying of small investors increases in stocks with growing earnings streakiness. Also, both of them believe that the gambler's fallacy is the underlying phenomenon driving the investors' behaviour. These findings are consistent with the return predictability evidence reported in both Loh and Warachka (2012) and Forbes and Igboekwu (2015).

Thus, it seems obvious that streaks in earnings and their signs could be potential cues in fast-and-frugal stock market valuation and the stock selection processes. In Gigerenzer's adaptive toolbox, one of the main challenges of fast-and-frugal decision-making is the ability of the decision-maker to identify credible cues that can be used in any of the fast-and-frugal models.

9.6 Will fast-and-frugal asset pricing models replace the standard asset pricing models?

As researchers, investors, and other market participants continue to search for that perfect model which is rational and which will fully explain asset returns, many are beginning to consider whether this is an entirely misplaced adventure and an effort in futility. This is least because, as psychology experiments show, human beings do not necessarily optimise or maximise their utility functions in the manner in which the rational choice model requires. There are obvious reasons why the standard rational choice models fail to fully capture the way economic agents and human beings, in general, behave when they face choice decisions under uncertainty. The entire array of assumptions upon which the standard models are based seems superficial – they are not representative of how humans behave within their environments and the constraints posed by their cognitive ability and budgets, as Simon (1956) succinctly put it when he observes:

> "an examination of the postulates of the economic models it appears probable that, however adaptive the behaviour of organisms in learning and choice situations, this adaptiveness falls far short of the ideal of 'maximising' postulated in economic theory. Evidently, organisms adapt well enough to 'satisfice'; they do not, in general, 'optimise.'"

The failure of the equilibrium asset pricing models and their factor variants to fully explain asset returns seems to lend credence to Simon's assertion above. The standard asset pricing models either ignore the limitations of human cognition in our everyday decision-making process or fail to account for how humans make decisions in real life.

There is an array of finance literature on the capital asset pricing model (CAPM) ((Sharpe, 1964), (Lintner, 1965a)), which is the foremost of the many asset pricing models around. As the precursor to other asset pricing models, the CAPM has been used as a building block by most of the later models. This implies that the CAPM's assumptions are passed on to these models along with its deficiencies. Although the CAPM seems to have worked fairly well in its early days, evidence from the 1980s either claims that the CAPM beta is 'dead' or incorrectly signed ((Clare et al., 1997), (Grinold, 1993)). This is not surprising, as the model specification of the CAPM claims that only an asset's beta matters in determining its expected returns. Scientifically, this argument seems flawed, because an asset or portfolio's beta is determined using historical data and we know that the past is never the best predictor of the future. It is even more difficult to determine the beta for assets with little or no historical data. For such cases, researchers and practitioners have to rely on proxies to determine an asset or portfolio's beta. Then there is the problem of the time-instability of both assets and portfolio betas. Changing the frequency of the return data, market index, length of the period of return data considered, and the absolute period of the data will most definitely change the value of any beta so determined. So, there is no such thing as a unique beta for any individual asset or portfolio. In addition to the above, the presence of abnormal returns from asset and portfolio returns is an indication that, besides betas, there are other potential returns explanatory variables which the CAPM does not capture (Fama and French, 1996).

So in an attempt to address what is seen as the CAPM's flaws, other equilibrium and factor models were postulated in the years that followed. Such models include the Arbitrage Pricing Theory (APT) (Ross, 1976), the Intertemporal Capital Asset Pricing Model (ICAPM) (Merton, 1973), and multi-factor models like the Fama-French 3-factor model (Fama and French, 1993), the Fama-French 5-factor model (Fama and French, 2015), and the Carhart 4-factor model (Cahart, 1997). It is interesting to note that these "improved" models still suffer from similar deficiencies as the CAPM. Some researchers question the exact theory behind the Fama-French and Carhart multifactor models. The "risk" factors in these models are portfolio characteristics rather than systematic risk factors which should not be priced in rational and efficient markets. Furthermore, if they are not systematic risk factors, going by the efficient market and CAPM assumptions, these factors cannot be compensated by the market.

Then there is the question of how many factors will be enough for the ideal asset pricing model. In 1993, Fama and French postulated their 3-factor model with the size (SMB), value (HML), and market premium (RM-Rf) as factors. In 2015, the authors postulated a 5-factor model showing two additional factors: the investment (CMA) and profitability (RMW) factors. The authors claim that the 5-factor model outperforms the 3-factor model. However, the results of their empirical research with US data from 1963 to 2013 show that with the introduction of the RMW and CMA factors into the 5-factor model, the HML becomes redundant. The authors argue that the CMA factor is strongly positive in regressions on the HML factor and this is because high book–to–market ratio companies tend not to invest heavily. Moreover, the authors argue that the reason why the RMW factor is strongly positive is that conditional upon control factors, value stocks behave as though they are highly profitable, even though they are usually not as profitable. There are two main issues with the story of the Fama-French 3- and 5-factor models. First, one would ask; why is it that the authors did not drop their HML factor in the 5-factor model and have a 4-factor model instead? Second, from the results of the 5-factor model, the intercepts are positive and statistically significant, so shall we expect further factors to be added to the 5-factor model in the coming years? This does lead to another question; how many factors will be enough in an asset pricing model? These questions have led recent researchers to argue that for factors to be accepted as risk factors, they must meet certain conditions. Pukthuanthong et al. (2018) propose a protocol for identifying risk factors. The authors argue that for factors to be classified as risk factors, they must be related to the covariance matrix of returns, be priced in the cross-section of returns, and yield a fair risk-return reward that is consistent for the risk so priced. In addition, they show evidence that the market factor, tradable macroeconomic factors, and a profitability factor pass the protocol test for risk factors. However, characteristic-based factors found in some of the asset pricing models do not pass the authors' protocol test even though some of them yield return premium in a cross-section of returns.

It is not difficult to see through the journey and story of the equilibrium asset pricing models and their factor counterparts that with all their elegant assumptions, the standard models do not seem to be working well in practice. Behavioural economists argue that without incorporating human behavioural characteristics into these models, the standard models at best will suffer from their incomplete specification. Behavioural economists such as Meir Statman advocate for integrated models which capture the utilitarian aspects of pricing risks as well as their value-expressive or 'satisficing' characteristics (Statman, 1999). Value-expressive characteristics capture sentiment, social, purpose, and belief aspects of human economic agents. Simon, Smith, Gigerenzer, and others argue that rational choice models do not reflect real-life decision-making processes. They propose alternative models that are based on two forms of rationality – bounded and ecological rationality (Simon, 1955), (Simon, 1956), (Gigerenzer and Goldstein, 1996).

9.7 Inference from streaks in earnings changes and their signs: a fast-and-frugal application

Through empirical evidence, we now know that as a result of the gambler's fallacy, investors underreact to the order in which past earnings information is received. One of the effects of this influence is that investors seem to follow firms' earnings streakiness closely and draw investment inferences from it. This behaviour seems to mimic the fast-and-frugal approach to decision-making. So, can we possibly apply the principles of fast-and-frugal approach to decision-making in the financial markets? Could the streaks in earnings changes be one of the candidates that should be included in the adaptive toolbox of fast-and-frugal decision-making in financial markets? To qualify as a candidate for any fast-and-frugal adaptive toolbox for the financial markets, such a variable must be empirically tested and found to work effectively in the environment where it is to be used. As (Todd, 2001) (in Gigerenzer and Selten's Bounded *Rationality: The Adaptive Toolbox*) puts it:

> *"The Adaptive Toolbox presents evidence to show that 'in the face of time and information costs, human decision making is adaptive through the use of fast-and-frugal heuristics'".*

Some popular PMM work such as (Gigerenzer, 1993) and Gigerenzer et al. (1991) are based on fast-and-frugal reasoning. The PMM theory presents several models that draw inferences from memory. This group of models is based on a fundamental psychological mechanism known as "one-reason decision-making" (Gigerenzer and Goldstein, 1996).

One-reason decision-making mechanism (Gigerenzer and Gaissaier, 2011) describes a process where a decision is made based on one single, good reason. This choice mechanism is non-compensatory; that is, unlike the rational choice model, it does not assume that objects such as securities, for example, are commensurable. Furthermore, it does not place emphasis on the weights of various cues entering a decision-making process as it relies on just one of them. The one cue so selected may differ from one decision-making environment to another. Thus, cues are dependent on the environment in which the choice is to be made. This is in contrast to the rational choice models, where inferences can easily be moved across various decision-making environments.

	a	b	c	d
Recognition	+	+	+	−
Cue 1	+	−	?	?
Cue 2	?	+	−	?
Cue 3	−	+	?	?
Cue 4	?	−	−	?
Cue 5	?	?	−	?

Figure 9.3 Illustration of bounded search through limited knowledge. Objects a, b, and c are recognised; object d is not. Cue values are positive (+) or (−); missing knowledge is shown by question marks. Cues are ordered according to their validities. To infer whether $a > b$, the Take the Best algorithm looks up only the cue values in the shaded space; to infer whether $b > c$, the search is bounded to the dotted space. The other cue values are not looked up (adapted from Gigerenzer and Goldstein, 1996).

Fig. 9.3 shows how PMMs work using an individual's limited knowledge of objects. To make inferences about the values of two objects "a" and "b" using the model involves searching what the authors call a "reference class" R. Both objects "a" and "b" are included in that set R. So the process involves searching the reference class R which is expected to consist of probability cues (C_i = 1,2,3,... n) and cue values a_i and b_i for the objects up to the ith value. These criteria might be applicable to the stock selection process in financial markets using earnings streakiness as probability cues.

So if we assume that objects "a" and "b" above represent two different companies' common shares listed on a certain stock exchange. The two shares represent part of a set of common shares listed in that exchange. Moreover, we can assume that streak in earnings changes could constitute the probability cues, in which case different streak lengths and their respective signs might constitute a single cue probability. So with the bounded search, the investor can create a matrix of objects (shares in our example above) using his knowledge of the cues to form portfolios of assets. The cue values come up as binary outcomes i.e. yes or no, positive or negative, high or low etc. Some of the objects may be unknown to the investor (cf. object d in Fig. 9.3).

According to Gigerenzer and Goldstein (1996), one of the PMMs with the one-reason decision-making mechanism is a satisficing model known as the "Take-the-Best" (and ignore the rest) model. Is it possible to apply this model in the financial markets as an investor's fast-and-frugal decision-making tool using streaks in earnings changes as cues? Investors can use the Take-the-Best model to select shares which they will use to construct their share portfolios.

9.8 Is earnings streakiness a value relevant decision cue?

Streakiness in earnings changes is a simple share performance cue. Information regarding earnings streakiness of any company can be obtained easily and quickly. Both the sign and the length of earnings streaks are associated with different levels of stock performance and could be used as cues. So, using the Take-the-Best model (Gigerenzer and Goldstein, 1996), we can demonstrate how streaks in earnings could be used in making fast-and-frugal investment decisions in the financial markets.

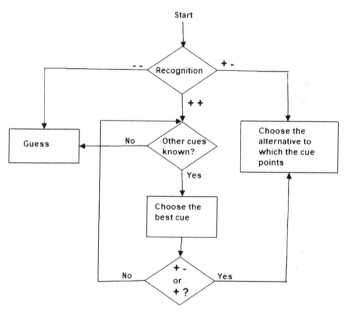

Figure 9.4 Flow diagram of the Take the Best Algorithm (adapted from Gigerenzer and Goldstein, 1996).

In a decision-making process, the Take-the-Best model makes a subjective ranking of cues based on their validities. An example is shown in Fig. 9.4, which is a flow diagram showing how the Take-the-Best model works in practice. Five different steps of action need to be carried out when applying the model.

1. The first step is the *Recognition Principle step*. This involves the simple recognition of objects, in our case, this means recognition of common shares conditioned on their streakiness as a predictor of an outcome variable, e.g., returns. If there are two objects to choose from, the recognition principle suggests that if only one object is recognised, then the recognised object should be chosen. Otherwise, if neither of the

two is recognised, then select one of them randomly. If both of them are recognised, move to Step 2.

2. *Search the Cue Values* rule: establish an ordering of the values of the cue with respect to the task at hand.
3. Use the *Discrimination rule* to select according to decision cues in Step 2.
4. *Cue-Substitution principle*, which provides a certain degree of freedom for assessing cues. And finally,
5. Use the *Maximising Rule* for choice, if all else fails. (interested readers are referred to the Gigerenzer and Goldstein (1996) paper for a full exposition of the concept).

In summary, it may be possible for investors to apply the Take-the-Best model to select stocks. For buy decisions, it seems plausible to use positive earnings streak as cues. Evidence (Loh and Warachka, 2012; Forbes and Igboekwu, 2015) suggests that streaks in earnings changes with positive signs are associated with positive abnormal stock returns. Both papers assert that larger abnormal returns are achieved almost monotonically as the streaks in earnings changes grow longer. Similarly, negatively signed earnings streaks are associated with negative abnormal returns. Forbes and Igboekwu (2015) show that unlike positive streaks in earnings changes, lengthening negative streaks do not predict falling returns monotonically. So, negative streaks could be used as cues to sell decisions. However, even though negative streaks in earnings predict falling stock market returns, the evidence is not clear-cut. A consistent no-change in earnings over a period of quarters might be a cue to a hold decision.

It would make an enlightening exercise to examine the replicability of the performance of Take-the-Best model in the stock market context, especially in the stock selection process. Carefully selected cues such as earning streak lengths and signs could be used in selecting stocks just like selecting objects in the Take-the-best model. There is no conclusive evidence to support this so more empirical studies are needed in this area.

9.9 Conclusion

The message of this chapter is that heuristics can be used to understand decision-making in financial markets better. First, the chapter compares the rational choice model with a behavioural finance model that is based on the law of small numbers. It shows the limitations of the standard models to fully capture how human beings make decisions in the real world.

These limitations arise from the lack of recognition for cognitive limitations of the human brain and the role of ecological adaptation in human decision-making processes. Second, the chapter shows evidence from the behavioural finance literature which further strengthens the argument that rational choice models are formed on impractical assumptions that make some of their outcomes less than accurate. One piece of such evidence is shown in the influence of the gambler's fallacy on investors when they interpret the ordering of changes in the earnings of companies over a given period of time. This evidence, for example, cannot be formally accounted for in the standard asset pricing models.

Furthermore, the chapter shows another perspective on how we can understand investors' decision-making based on the concepts of bounded rationality and ecological rationality. The bounded rationality concept holds that humans are rational but their cognitive skills are limited both in capacity and scope. The presence of these limitations challenge the assumptions of the rational choice models about human rationality. Some of the behaviours termed irrational by the rational choice models can be viewed as ecologically rational when formulated in alternative decision-making models. Alternative models such as those based on fast-and-frugal reasoning can have certain advantages over the standard models. Evidence from studies in cognitive psychology experiments suggests that the performance of these models are comparable (and sometimes superior) to those of the standard rational models. They can be used to describe the process underlying simple but successful inferences in decision-making processes. Based on the above, this chapter proposes that fast-and-frugal models that use earnings streakiness as cues can be useful in stock selection. Companies' earnings are readily accessible so their earnings streakiness can be established easily. Although there is yet no evidence for the effectiveness of this approach to stock selection, we argue that it is an adventure worth exploring.

CHAPTER 10

A fast-and-frugal finance

Fan: "You're Norma Desmond. You used to be big in pictures."
Norma: "I am big, the pictures got small."

https://www.youtube.com/watch?v=TMUJpec6Bdc

The retort by Norma Desmond (Gloria Swanson) to a visitor's suggestion that she had been eclipsed by the switch to "talkies" captures a key insight into what that transition meant. Silent film is not modern film with the sound turned off, it is a different, subtler, arguably richer, art form. Norma's bitterness in *Sunset Boulevard* does not stop her seeing something beautiful and true. This truth was recently explored in 2011 in the film "The Artist". The gestural repertoire of Louise Brooks, or Buster Keaton's sheer physical dexterity, reminds us of how much was lost when the wonder of sound was introduced to Cinema. Less, can more in financial modelling, as it has proved in Cinema.

Perhaps like Norma we might feel that economics has become small since the marginalist revolution pushed broader economic social discussion of problems out of the frame in favour of states, dates, and the discount rate linking the two. While a huge amount of insight, predictive power, was gained by the transformation of political economy into neo-classical economics. But much was also lost, or rendered marginal and perhaps somewhat embarrassing to mention. In this the neo-classical model and its embedded risk calculus has been overplayed and a corrective reaction was inevitable. Thus, as stated in the introduction, a "fast-and-frugal" approach is both a (heuristic) revolution and a restoration of an earlier, prevailing consensus. One striking example of this is its concern with improving regulatory practice, discussed in Chapter 4, which Adam Smith would felt most comfortable with, but, perhaps Merton Miller did not. For many of the Chicago School those who govern best govern least, making an interest in effective regulation almost a personal vice.

At the close of our study of this emerging area of finance we return to the three key goals identified by Gigerenzer et al. (2011). These are

A Fast and Frugal Finance
https://doi.org/10.1016/B978-0-12-812495-6.00018-5
229

the adaptive toolbox,
ecological rationality,
intuitive design.

Here we evaluate the progress and prospect of finance scholarship against these goals. As we have seen much progress has already been made, but often by those like Herbert Simon, Geoffrey Hodgson, etc., who were barely regarded as economists/finance academics at all by the ruling academic elite of Finance.

Fortunately, fast-and-frugal finance is a topic whose time has come, with major, already well-recognised academics, like Andrew Lo in the United States and Robert Hudson in the UK, embracing and developing its insights. While much remains to be done, significant progress has already been made and fast-and-frugal reasoners should deploy their talents with renewed enthusiasm.

If recognition of alternative approaches to finance has been a bit slow coming for some it is perhaps because the mainstream of scholarship in Finance has been quite successful. Who would want to be teaching and researching labour, transport, development, or any other subdiscipline of economics in the last forty years when you could be doing Finance?

Finance classes often have the biggest enrolments and demand the highest grades to enrol of any Business School subject. Many of us have ascended to good posts on academic achievements that may seem thin to colleagues in traditional academic subjects, such as history or Mathematics. In advancing an agenda for a fast-and-frugal finance we do not disparage, or minimise, what the mainstream has achieved or will continue to achieve. We can only be grateful for those achievements. Rather we simply invoke the precept of ecological rationality to argue that a changed environment necessitates a changed understanding, cognitive process, for understanding and managing financial markets. The beginning of this process is the construction of an adaptive toolbox for financial decision-makers.

10.1 Developing an adaptive toolbox for financial decision-making

In Chapter 2 we reviewed a number of the best known, tried, and tested, decision–making heuristics. Two that are worthy of mention in reflecting upon what went before are the tallying and $\frac{1}{N}$ heuristic. Tallying and the search for "just one reason" underlay the efficacy of the earnings "streakiness" variable in explaining the stock future trajectory of stock returns;

discussed in Chapter 9. The $\frac{1}{N}$ heuristic was also invoked to offer a fast-and-frugal alternative to profitable portfolio formation in Chapter 7. Both these applications developed heuristics already present in the ABC group's adaptive toolbox.

Changes in the environment within financial markets throw up new heuristic tools for a fast-and-frugal finance to deploy, explore. One source of exploration of such new tools is amongst the Chartist, technical analysis, school of thought who are currently largely dismissed as cranks, or rubes, ignorant of the basic tenets of how financial markets work. As we saw in Chapter 3 and 7 the error of such a small-minded dismissal of practitioner's wisdom is now being exposed and a renewed academic conscensus is emerging.

10.2 Evolutionary rationality

The dominance of finance by classical rationality and especially its expected utility calculus has been one of its major hallmarks. Under conditions of risk, such as we face at the roulette wheel, such an analytical framework has amazing power. But one rather wonders how often we encounter risky, as opposed to uncertain, situations. We might agree with Simon's view, expressed in Chapter 5, that we make decisions in an uncertain world. Of course, in modelling this way we ignore many instances of regular transactions in a well defined reference class, where standard risks metric can, and should, be applied. But perhaps this would be better than the current practice of simply assuming all financial decision-making is undertaken under conditions of risk. In time, we believe the application of a risk based calculus in finance will be more circumspect, and subject to challenge and therefore hopefully more effective.

Andrew Lo's book *Adaptive Markets* sets a very high standard for the application and development of ecological rationality in finance and we hope the present text shows a few more examples of such practice. Perhaps illustrations of progress will be more common in accounting than finance. This is because accounting practice has always been a craft and not a science, with good practice simply being adopted, ad hoc, by the Profession as its value was proved. We explored such evolutionary practice in our discussion of the rise of "intangible" value in Chapter 9. Here the "death of accounting", as its product loses its value relevance, is spurring the Profession to develop auditing practices more capable of giving a truly "true and fair view" of future shareholder value. Old valuation frameworks and accounting representations are being rendered useless by the transformation of real productive economy into a knowledge-based, intangible rich, and often digital economy.

10.3 Intuitive design of financial decision-making tools

It is the design and deployment of easy to use, robust, fast-and-frugal financial heuristics that is the key element of future work to roll out the implementation of a fast-and-frugal finance. Partly this is because we need a way of deciding what constitutes a good financial decision-making heuristic. Once again, this requires a "bigger" notion of what a financial analysis of a problem entails. This involves a deeper engagement with the actors in financial markets, the investors, traders, regulators, and customers whose interests are at stake. Such a project requires an engagement with financial practitioners which has become a rarity in recent years. Scholars such as John Graham, Donald McKenzie, and Michael Power have led the way in such practitioner-engaged research. We believe many more aspiring academics will soon be following in their footsteps. Only by doing so can the important task of the intuitive design of a fast-and-frugal adaptive toolbox for decision-making be progressed.

References

Abarbanell, Jeffery S., Bernard, Victor, 1992. Analysts' overreaction/underreaction to earnings information as an explanation for anomalous stock price behavior. Journal of Finance 47, 1181–1207.

Abbe, Emmanuel, Khandani, Amir, Lo, Andrew, 2012. Privacy preserving methods for sharing financial risk exposures. American Economic Review Papers and Proceedings 102, 65–70.

Adrian, Tobias, Brunnermeier, Markus, 2016. Covar, American Economic Review 106, 1705–1741.

Aikman, David, Galesic, Mirta, Gigerenzer, Gerd, Kapedia, Sujit, Katsikopolos, Konstantinos, Kothiyal, Amit, Murphy, Emma, Neumann, Tobias, 2014. Taking Uncertainty Seriously: Simplicity Versus Complexity in Financial Regulation. Financial Stability Board, vol. 28. Bank of England Threadneedle Street, London.

Akerlof, George, Shiller, Robert, 2009. Animal Spirits: How Global Psychology Drives the Economy, and Why It Matters for Global Capitalism. Princeton University Press, Princeton and Oxford.

Akert, Lucy, Deaves, Richard, 2010. Behavioural Finance: Psychology, Decision-Making and Markets. South-Western/Centage Learning, Mason, Ohio, USA.

Al-Horani, Ahmed, Pope, Peter, Stark, Andrew, 2003. Research and development activity and expected returns in the United Kingdom. European Finance Review 7, 27–46.

Alter, Adam, Oppenheimer, Daniel M., 2006. Predicting short-term stock fluctuations by using processing fluency. Proceedings of the National Academy of Science 103, 9369–9372.

Alter, Adam, Oppenheimer, Daniel M., 2008. Easy on the mind, easy on the wallet: the roles of familiarity and processing fluency in valuation judgements. Psychological Bulletin and Review 15, 985–990.

Altman, Morris, 2015a. Real-World Decision-Making. An Encyclopedia of Behavioral Economics. Greenwood, California, USA. Chap. Introduction, pp. xv–xxx.

Altman, Morris, 2015b. What a difference an assumption makes: effort discretion, economic theory and public policy. In: Altman, Morris (Ed.), Handbook of Contemporary Behavioral Economics: Foundations and Developments. Routledge, London, New York. Chap. 7.

Ang, Andrew, 2014. Asset Management: A Systematic Approach to Factor Investor. Oxford University Press, Madison Avenue, New York, USA.

Arrow, Kenneth, 2004. Is Bounded Rationality Unboundedly Rational? MIT Press.

Artinger, Florian, Gigerenzer, Gerd, 2016. The cheap twin: from the ecological rationality of heuristic pricing to the aggregate market. Academy of Management 2016, 1037–1042.

Artinger, Florian, Petersen, Malte, Gigerenzer, Gerd, 2014. Heuristics as adaptive decision strategies in management. Journal of Organizational Behaviour 36, S33–S52.

Ashton, John, Gerrard, Bill, Hudson, Robert, 2003. Economic impact of sporting success: evidence from the London stock exchange. Applied Economic Letters 10, 783–785.

Axelrod, Robert, 1984. The Evolution of Cooperation. Basic Books, Cambridge, Massachusetts, USA.

Ayton, Peter, Önkal, Dilek, McReynolds, Lisa, 2011. Effects of ignorance and information on judgements and decisions. Judgement and Decision Making 6, 381–391.

Azar, Ofer, 2014. The default heuristic in strategic decision-making: when is it optimal to choose the default without investing in information search? Journal of Business Research 67, 1744–1748.

Bai, Jennie, Phillipon, Thomas, Savov, Alexi, 2016. Have financial markets become more informative? Journal of Financial Economics 122, 625–654.

Ball, Ray, 2016. IFRS-10 years later. Accounting and Business Research 46, 545–571.

Barber, Brad, Odean, Terrance, 2001. Boys will be boys: gender, overconfidence and common stock investment. Quarterly Journal of Economics 116, 261–292.

Barberis, Nick, Huang, Ming, 2008. Stock markets as lotteries: the implications of probability weighting for security prices. American Economic Review 96.

Barberis, Nicholas, Huang, Ming, Santos, Timothy, 2001a. Prospect theory & asset prices. Quarterly Journal of Economics 53.

Barberis, Nick, Huang, Tanos, Santos, Ming, 2001b. Prospect theory and asset prices. Quarterly Journal of Economics 116, 1–53.

Barberis, Nicholas, Shleifer, Andrei, Vishny, Robert, 1998. A model of investor sentiment. Journal of Financial Economics 49 (3), 307–343.

Barker, Richard, 1998. The market for information evidence from finance directors, analysts and fund managers. Accounting & Business Research 29, 3–20.

Barker, Richard, 2000. FRS3 and analysts' use of earnings. Accounting and Business Research 30, 95–109.

Barov, Eli, 1992. Patterns in unexpected earnings as an explanation for post-announcement drift. Accounting Review 67, 610–622.

Benabou, Roland, Tirole, Jean, 2012. Law and norms. Econstor, 6290.

Benartzi, Shlomo, Thaler, Richard, 2001. Naive investor diversification strategies in defined contribution savings plans. American Economic Review 91, 79–98.

Berg, Nathan, 2014. Success from satisficing and imitation: entrepreneur's location choice and implications of heuristics for local economic development. Journal of Business Research 67, 1700–1709.

Berg, Nathan, Gigerenzer, Gerd, 2010. As-if behavioural economics: neoclassical economics in disguise? History of Economic Ideas 18, 133–136.

Bernard, Victor L., Thomas, Jacob K., 1989. Post-earnings-announcement drift: delayed price response or risk premium? Journal of Accounting Research, Supplement 27, 1–48.

Bernard, Victor L., Thomas, Jacob K., 1990. Evidence that stock prices do not fully reflect the implications of current earnings for future earnings. Journal of Accounting and Economics 13, 305–340.

Bernstein, Peter, 1996. Against the Gods: The Remarkable Story of Risk. John Wiley & Sons, New York, USA.

Billio, Monica, Getmansky, Mila, Lo, Andrew, Pelizzon, Loriana, 2012. Econometric measures of connectedness and systematic risk in the finance and insurance sectors. Journal of Financial Economics 104, 535–559.

Black, Fischer, 1986. Noise. Journal of Finance 41, 529–543.

Boatang, Jerôme, De Lara, Michael, 2016. The Biased Mind: How Evolution Shaped Our Psychology, Including Anecdotes and Tips for Making Sound Decisions. Springer International Publishing, Switzerland.

Borges, Bernhard, Goldstein, Daniel, Ortmann, Andreas, Gigerenzer, Gerd, 1999. Can Ignorance Beat the Stock Market? Oxford University Press. Chap. 3.

Boyd, Michael, 2001. On ignorance, intuition and investing: a bear market test of the recognition heuristic. Journal of Psychology and Financial Markets 2, 150–156.

Boyd, Robert, Richerson, Peter, 2005. The Origin and Evolution of Cultures. Evolution and Cognition. Oxford University Press, Oxford, England.

Brandstätter, E., Küberger, A., 2005. Outcome priority in risky choice. Department of Psychology, Johannes Kepler University Linz, Linz, Austria. Unpublished manuscript.

Brandstätter, Eduard, Gigerenzer, Gerd, Hertwig, Ralph, 2006. The priority heuristic: making choices without trade-offs. Psychological Review 113, 409–432.

Brighton, Henry, Gigerenzer, Gerd, 2015. The bias bias. Journal of Business Research. Forthcoming.

Brock, William, Lakonishok, Josef, Blake, LeBaron, 1992. Simple technical rules and the stochastic properties of stock price returns. Journal of Finance 47, 1731–1764.

Brown, Lawrence, Richardson, Gordon, Schwager, Steven, 1987a. An information interpretation of financial analyst superiority in forecasting earnings. Journal of Accounting Research 25, 49–67.

Brown, Lawrence, Zmijewski, Mark, 1987. The effect of labor strikes on security analysts' forecast superiority and the association between risk-adjusted stock–returns and expected earnings. Contemporary Accounting Research 4, 61–75.

Brown, Larry D., 1993. Earnings forecasting research: its implications for capital markets research. International Journal of Forecasting 9, 295–320.

Brown, Lawrence D., Hagerman, R.L., Griffin, P.A., Zmijewski, Mark E., 1987b. An evaluation of alternative proxies for the market's assessment of unexpected earnings. Journal of Accounting and Economics, 159–163.

Brown, Philip, Foster, George, Noreen, Eric, 1985. Security Analysts Multi-Year Forecasts Earnings Forecasts and the Capital Market. American Accounting Association, Sarasota, Fla.

Brown, Stephen, Goetzmann, William, Kumar, Alok, 1998. The Dow theory: William Peter Hamilton's track record. Journal of Finance 53, 1311–1333.

Brown, Stephen J., Goetzmann, William N., Ross, Stephen A., 1995. Survival. Journal of Finance 50, 853–873.

Brunnermeier, M., 2009. Deciphering the liquidity and credit crisis. Journal of Economic Perspectives 23, 77–100.

Brunswik, Egon, 1955. Representative design and probabilistic theory in a functional psychology in a functional psychology. Psychological Review 62, 193–217.

Cahart, M., 1997. On the persistence of mutual fund returns. Journal of Finance 52, 57–82.

Campbell, John Y., 2000. Asset pricing at the millennium. Journal of Finance 55, 1515.

Campbell, John Y., 1991. A variance decomposition of stock returns. Economic Journal 101, 157–179.

Campbell, John Y., Shiller, Robert J., 1988. Stock prices, earnings, and expected dividends. Journal of Finance 43, 661–676.

Carmichael, Fiona, 2005. A Guide to Game Theory. FT-Prentice Hall, Harlow, England.

Chase, William, Simon, Herebert, 1973. Perception in chess. Cognitive Psychology 4, 55–81.

Chen, Lei, Danbolt, Jo., Holland, John, 2014. Rethinking bank business models: the role of intangibles. Accounting, Auditing and Accountability 27, 563–589.

Clare, Andrew, Priestly, Richard, Thomas, Stephen, 1997. Is beta dead? The role of alternative estimation methods. Applied Economics Letters 4, 559–592.

Clark, John, 1918. Economics and modern psychology: I. Journal of Political Economy 26, 136–166.

Cochrane, John, 2011. Presidential address: discount rates. Journal of Finance 66, 1047–1108.

Coval, Joshua, Shumway, Tyler, 2005. Do behavioral bases affect stock prices? Journal of Finance 60, 1–34.

Cowles, Alfred, 1933. Can stock market forecasters forecast? Econometrica 1, 309–324.

Daniel, Kent, Hirshleifer, David, Subrahmanyam, Avanidhar, 1998. Investor psychology and security market under and overreactions. Journal of Finance 53, 1839–1885.

Daston, Lorraine, 1988. Classical Probability in the Enlightenment. History of Science-European History. Princeton University Press, New Jersey, USA.

Dawes, Robyn, 1979. The robust beauty of improper linear models in decision-making. American Psychologist 34, 571–582.

Dawes, Robyn, Corrigan, Bernard, 1974. Linear models in decision-making. Psychological Bulletin 81, 95–106.

Dawes, Robyn, Mulford, Matthew, 1996. The false consensus effect and overconfidence. Organisational Behavior and Human Decision Processes 65, 201–211.

De Long, J. Bradford, Shleifer, Andrei, Summers, Lawrence, Waldmann, Robert J., 1990. Noise trader risk in financial markets. Journal of Political Economy 98, 703–738.

De Long, J. Bradford, Shleifer, Andrei, Summers, Lawrence, Waldmann, Robert J., 1991. The survival of noise traders in financial markets. Journal of Business 64, 1–20.

de Mesquita, Bueno, 2009. The Predictioneer's Game. Random House, New York.

Deason, Stephen, Rajgopal, Shivararum, Waymire, Gregory, 2015. Who Gets Swindled in Ponzi Schemes? Discussion paper Social Science Research Network (SSRN).

DeBondt, Werner F.M., 1998. A portrait of the individual investor. European Economic Review 42, 831–844.

Demers, Elizabeth, Lev, Baruch, 2000. A rude awakening: Internet shakeout in 2000. In: Review of Accounting Studies, vol. 6. Stern Business School, University of New York, pp. 331–359.

Demirakos, Efthomos, Norman, Strong, Walker, Martin, 2004. What valuation models do analysts use? Accounting Horizons 18, 221–240.

DeMiguel, Victor, Garlappi, Lorenzo, Uppal, Raman, 2009. Optimal versus naive diversification: how inefficient is the 1/n portfolio strategy? Review of Financial Studies 22, 1922–1953.

Dyck, Alexander, Morse, Adair, Zingales, Luigi, 2014. How pervasive is corporate fraud? Social Science Research Network.

Easley, David, de Prado, Marcos, O'Hara, Maureen, 2011. The microstructure of the "flash crash": flow toxicity, liquidity crashes and probability of informed trading. Journal of Portfolio Management 37, 118–128.

Easton, Peter, Harris, Trevor, 1991. Earnings as an explanatory variable for returns. Journal of Accounting Research 29, 19–36.

Edwards, Ward, 1954. The theory of decision-making. Psychological Bulletin 51, 380–417.

Einhorn, Hillel, Hogarth, Robin, 1975. Unit weighting schemes for decision-making. Organisational Behavior and Human Performance 13, 171–192.

Elton, Edwin J., Gruber, Martin J., Gultekin, Mustafa N., 1984. Professional expectations: accuracy and diagnosis of errors. Journal of Financial and Quantitative Analysis 19, 351–363.

Engel, Christopher, Gigerenzer, Gerd, 2006. Law and heuristics: an interdisciplinary venture. In: Gigerenzer, Gerd, Engel, Christoph (Eds.), Heuristics and the Law. Dahlem University Press-MIT Press, Cambridge, Massachusetts, USA, pp. 3–16. Chap. 1.

Epstein, Richard, 1995. Simple Rules for a Complex World. Harvard University Press, Cambridge, Massachusetts, USA.

Erev, Ido, Wallsten, Thomas, Budescu, David, 1994. Simultaneous over and underconfidence: the role of error in judgement processes. Psychological Review 101, 519–527.

Fama, Eugene, Fisher, Lawrence, Jensen, Michael, Roll, Richard, 1969. The adjustment of stock prices to new information. International Economic Review 10, 1–21.

Fama, Eugene, French, Kenneth, 2016. Dissecting anomalies with a five-factor model. Review of Financial Studies 29, 69–103.

Fama, Eugene, Stern, Joel, 2016. A look back at modern finance: accomplishments and limitations: an interview with Eugene Fama. Journal of Applied Corporate Finance 28, 10–16.

Fama, Eugene F., 1970. Efficient capital markets: a review of theory and empirical work. Journal of Finance 25, 383–417.

Fama, Eugene F., 1990. Stock returns, expected returns, and real activity. Journal of Finance 45, 1089–1108.

Fama, Eugene F., 1991. Efficient capital markets II. Journal of Finance 46, 1575–1643.

Fama, Eugene F., 1998. Market efficiency, long-term returns and behavioral finance. Journal of Financial Economics. Forthcoming.

Fama, Eugene F., French, Kenneth, 2015. A five-factor asset pricing model. Journal of Financial Economics 116, 1–22.

Fama, Eugene F., French, Kenneth R., 1992. The cross-section of expected stock returns. Journal of Finance 47, 427–465.

Fama, Eugene F., French, Kenneth R., 1993. Common risk factors in the returns on stocks and bonds. Journal of Financial Economics 33, 3–56.

Fama, Eugene F., French, Kenneth R., 1996. Multifactor explanations of asset pricing anomalies. Journal of Finance 51, 55–84.

Fama, Eugene F., MacBeth, James, 1973. Risk, return and equilibrium: empirical tests. Journal of Political Economy 81, 607–636.

Fehr, Enst, Schmidt, K., 1999. A theory of fairness, competition and co-operation. Quarterly Journal of Economics 114, 817–868.

Fific, Mario, Gigerenzer, Gerd, 2014. Are two interviewers better than one? Journal of Business Research 67, 1771–1779.

Finklestein, Michael, Levin, Bruce, 2001. Statistics for Lawyers. Springer, New York, USA.

Fisher, Franklin, 1989. Games economists play: a non-cooperative view. Rand Journal of Economics 20, 113–124.

Forbes, William, 2009. Behavioural Finance. John Wiley & Sons, Chicester, West Sussex, England.

Forbes, William, Igboekwu, Aloysius, 2015. The explanatory power of representative agent earnings momentum models. Review of Quantitative and Finance 44, 473–492.

Foster, George, 1977. Quarterly accounting data: times–series properties and predictive ability results. Accounting Review 52, 1–21.

Foster, George, Olsen, Chris, Shevlin, Terry, 1984. Earnings releases, anomalies and the behaviour of security returns. Accounting Review 59, 574–603.

Frank, Robert, 2011. The Darwin Economy: Liberty, Competition and the Common Good. Princeton University Press, Princeton, New Jersey, USA.

Freidman, Daniel, Isaac, Mark, James, Shyam, Sunder, Duncan, 2014. Risky Curves: On the Empirical Failure of Expected Utility. Center of Analytical Finance University of California, Santa Cruz. Working Paper # 1.

Freidman, Milton, 1953. Essays in Positive Economics. University of Chicago Press.

Fried, Dov, Givoly, Dan, 1982. Financial analysts's forecasts of earnings: a better surrogate for market expectations. Journal of Accounting and Economics 4, 83–107.

Frieder, Laura, 2008. Investor and price response to patterns in earnings surprises. Journal of Financial Markets 11, 259–283.

Galesic, Mirta, Olsson, Rieskamp, Jörg, 2012. Social sampling explains apparent biases in judgements of social environments. Psychological Science 23, 1515–1523.

Garret, Ian, Antoniou, Antonios, 1993. To what extent did stock index futures contribute to the 1987 stock market crash? Economic Journal 103, 1444–1461.

Geman, Stuart, Bienenstock, Elie, Doursat, Rene, 1992. Neural networks and the biase-variance dilemma. Neural Computation 4, 1–58.

Gigerenzer, Gerd, 1991. How to make cognitive illusions disappear: beyond "heuristics and biases". European Review of Social Psychology 2, 85–116.

Gigerenzer, Gerd, 1993. Rationality: psychological and philosophical perspectives. In: The Bounded Rationality of Probabilistic Mental Models, vol. 11. Routledge, London and New York, pp. 284–313.

Gigerenzer, Gerd, 1996. On narrow norms and vague heuristics: a reply to Kahnehman and Tversky. Psychological Review 103, 592–596.

Gigerenzer, Gerd, 2000. Adaptive Thinking: Rationality in the Real World. Oxford University Press, Oxford, England.

Gigerenzer, Gerd, 2002. Calculated Risks: How to Know When Numbers Deceive You. Simon and Schuster, New York, USA.

Gigerenzer, Gerd, 2004. Striking a Blow for Sanity in Theories of Rationality. MIT Press.

Gigerenzer, G., 2006. Bounded and rational. In: Stainton, R.J. (Ed.), Contemporary Debates in Cognitive Science. In: Contemporary Debates in Philosophy, vol. 7. Blackwell, Oxford, UK, pp. 115–133.

Gigerenzer, Gerd, 2007. Gut Feelings: The Intelligence of the Unconscious. Penguin, New York, USA.

Gigerenzer, G., 2008. Why heuristics work. Perspectives on Psychological Science 3 (1), 20–29.

Gigerenzer, Gerd, 2014. Risk Savvy: How to Make Good Decisions. Penguin, New York, USA.

Gigerenzer, Gerd, 2015. Simply Rational: Decision–Making in the Real World. Evolution and Cognition. Oxford University Press, Oxford, England.

Gigerenzer, Gerd, Brighton, Henry, 2009. Homo heuristicus: why biased minds make better inferences. Topics in Cognitive Science 1, 107–142.

Gigerenzer, Gerd, Gaissaier, Wolfgang, 2011. Heuristic decision making. Annual Review of Psychology 62, 451–482.

Gigerenzer, Gerd, Goldstein, David, 1996. Reasoning the fast and frugal way: models of bounded rationality. Psychological Review 103, 650–669.

Gigerenzer, Gerd, Gray, Muir, 2011. Better Doctors, Better Patients, Better Decisions: Envisioning Health Care in 2020. MIT Press, Cambridge, Massachusetts, USA.

Gigerenzer, G., Todd, P.M., ABC Research Group, 1999. Simple Heuristics that Make Us Smart. Oxford University Press, New York.

Gigerenzer, Gerd, Hertwig, Ralf, Pachur, Thorsten, 2011. Introduction. In: Heuristics: The Foundations of Adaptive Behavior. Oxford University Press. ISBN 978-0-19974428-2, pp. xvii–xxiii.

Gigerenzer, Gerd, Hoffrage, Ulrich, Kleinbölting, Heinz, 1991. Probabilistic mental models: a Brunswickian theory of confidence. Psychological Review 98, 506–528.

Gigerenzer, Gerd, Murray, David, 1987. Cognition as Intuitive Statistics. Psychology Press.

Gigerenzer, Gerd, Selten, Rheinhard, 2001a. Rethinking rationality. In: Gigerenzer, Gerd, Selten, Rheinhard (Eds.), Bounded Rationality: the Adaptive Toolbox. MIT Press. Dahlem Workshops Reports. Chap. 1.

Gigerenzer, Gerd, Selten, Reinhard, 2001b. Rethinking rationality. In: Bounded Rationality: The Adaptive Toolbox. MIT Press.

Gigerenzer, Gerd, Selten, Rheinhard, 2002. Bounded Rationality: The Adaptive Toolbox. Dahlem Workshop Report. MIT Press, Cambridge, Massachusetts, USA.

Gigerenzer, Gerd, Todd, Peter, 1999. Simple Rules That Make Us Smart. Oxford University Press, Oxford, England.

Goldstein, Daniel, Gigerenzer, Gerd, 2002. Models of ecological rationality: the recognition heuristic. Psychological Review 109, 75–90.

Goldstein, Daniel, Gigerenzer, Gerd, 2009. Fast and frugal forecasting. International Journal of Forecasting 25, 760–772.

Graham, Benjimin, 1949. The Intelligent Investor: A Book of Practical Counsel, 4th edition (Whittlesey House originally and republished by McGraw-Hill, New York).

Graham, Benjimin, Dodd, David, 1934. Security Analysis (Whittlesey House originally and republished by McGraw-Hill, New York).

Graham, John, Harvey, Campbell, Puri, Manju, 2013. Managerial attitudes and corporate actions. Journal of Financial Economics 109, 103–121.

Graham, John, Harvey, Campbell, Puri, Manju, 2015. Capital allocation and delegation of decision–making authority within firms. Journal of Financial Economics 5, 449–470.

Graham, John, Harvey, Campbell, Rajgopal, Shiva, 2005. The economic implications of corporate reporting. Journal of Accounting and Economics 40, 3–73.

Green, Richard, Hollified, Burton, 1992. When will mean variance efficient portfolios be well diversified? Journal of Finance 47, 1785–1809.

Griffin, Dale, Tversky, Amos, 1992. The weighing of evidence and the determinants of overconfidence. Cognitive Psychology 24, 411–435.

Grinold, Richard, 1993. Is beta dead again. Financial Analysts Journal 49, 28–34.

Gromb, Denis, Vayanos, Dimitri, 2010. Limits to arbitrage. Annual Review of Financial Economics 2, 251–275.

Groner, Rudulf, Groner, Marina, Bischof, Walter, 2009. Methods of Heuristics. Routledge, New York and London.

Güth, Werner, 2008. (Non)behavioral economics: a programmatic assessment. Journal of Psychology (Zeitschrift für Psychologie) 216, 244–253.

Hacking, Ian, 2006. The Emergence of Probability: A Philosophical Study of Early Ideas About Probability Induction and Statistical Inference. Cambridge University Press, Cambridge, England.

Haldane, Andrew, 2012. The dog and the frisbee. In: Speech at Kansas City 36th Economic Policy Symposium. Bank of England Threadneedle Street, London.

Hall, Peter, Soskice, David, 2001. Varieties of Capitalism: The Institutional Foundations of Comparative Advantage. Oxford University Press, Oxford, England.

Hammerstein, Peter, 2012. Evolution and rationality: decisions, co-operation and strategic behaviour. In: Towards a Darwinian Theory of Decision-Making: Games and the Biological Roots of Behaviour, vol. 1. Cambridge University Press, Cambridge, England.

Hammerstein, Peter, Selten, Rheinhard, 1994. Game theory and evolutionary biology. In: Aumann, Robert, Hart, Sergiu (Eds.), Handbook of Game Theory With Economic Applications. In: Handbooks in Economics., vol. 2. Elsevier, pp. 931–992. Chap. 28.

Hand, John, 2001. The role of book income, web traffic and supply and demand in the pricing of US Internet stocks. European Finance Review 5, 295–317.

Harvey, Campbell R., Lui, Yan, Zhu, Heqing, 2016. ... and the cross-section of expected returns. Review of Financial Studies 29 (1), 5–68.

Hauser, John, 2014. Consideration-set heuristics. Journal of Business Research 67, 1688–1699.

Hayek, Freidrick, 1948. Economics and knowledge. In: Hayek, Freidrick (Ed.), Individualism and Economic Order. University of Chicago Press, Chicago, Illinois, pp. 33–56. Chap. 2.

Hayek, Freidrich, 1988. The Fatal Conceit: The Errors of Socialism. University of Chicago Press.

Hecht, Peter, Vuolteenaho, Tuomo, 2006. Explaining returns with cash-flow proxies. Review of Financial Studies 19, 159–194.

Hertwig, Ralph, Fisbacher, Urs, Bruhen, 2013a. Simple heuristics in a social game. In: Hertwig, Ralph, Hoffrage, Ulrich, ABC Group (Eds.), Simple Heuristics in a Social World, pp. 39–66 (Oxford Scholarship Online, Oxford, England). Chap. 2.

Hertwig, Ralph, Hoffrage, Ulrich, ABC Group, 2013b. Simple heuristics: the foundations of adaptive social behaviour. In: Hertwig, Ralf, Hoffrage, Ulrich (Eds.), Simple Heuristics in a Social World, pp. 3–36 (Oxford Scholarship Online: Oxford, England). Chap. 1.

Hey, John, 1982. Search for rules on search. Journal of Economic Behavior & Organisation 3, 65–81.

Hodgson, Geoffrey, 2001. How Economics Forgot History. Economics as Social Theory. Routledge, Taylor and Francis, London and New York.

Holland, John, 1998. Private disclosure and financial reporting. Accounting and Business Research 28, 249–267.

Hong, Harrison, Stein, Jeremy, 1999. A unified theory of underreaction, momentum trading and overreaction in asset markets. Journal of Finance 54, 2143–2184. Working Paper, MIT Sloan School of Management.

Hu, Zhan, Wang, X.T., 2014. Trust or not: heuristics for making trust–based choices in HR management. Journal of Business Research 67, 1573–1786.

Huberman, Gur, 2001. Familiarity breeds investment. Review of Financial Studies 14, 659–680.

Hudson, Robert, Keasey, Kevin, Littler, Kevin, Dempsey, Mike, 1999. Time diversification: an essay on the need to revisit finance theory. Critical Perspectives on Accounting 10, 501–519.

Imam, Shahed, Barker, Richard, Clubb, Colin, 2008. The use of valuation models by UK investment analysts. European Accounting Review 17, 503–535.

Imam, Shahed, Spence, Crawford, 2016. Context not predictions: a field study of financial analysts. Accounting, Auditing and Accountability 29, 226–247.

Ioannides, John, 2005. Why most published research findings are false. PLoS Medicine 2, 696–701.

Ioannidis, John, Stanley, Tom, Doucouliagos, Hristos, 2017. The power of bias in economic research. Economic Journal 127. F236–265.

Jagannathan, Ravi, Ma, Tongshu, 2003. Risk reduction in large portfolios: why imposing the wrong constraints helps. Journal of Finance 58, 1651–1683.

Johansson, G., Rumar, K., 1968. Visible distances and safe approach speeds for night. Driving, Ergonomics 11, 275–282.

Johnson, Eric, Goldstein, Daniel, 2003. Do defaults save lives? Science 302, 1338–1339.

Juslin, Peter, Winman, Anders, Hannson, Patrik, 2007. The naïve intuitive statistician: a naïve intuitive sampling model of intuitive confidence intervals. Psychological Review 114, 678–703.

Juslin, Peter, Winman, Anders, Olsson, Henrik, 2000. New empiricism and dogmatism in confidence research: a critical examination of the hard-easy effect. Psychological Review 107, 384–396.

Kahnehman, Daniel, 2003. Maps of bounded rationality: psychology of behavioral economics. American Economic Review 93, 1449–1475.

Kahnehman, Daniel, Knetsch, Jack, Thaler, Richard, 1991. Anomalies: the endowment effect, loss aversion, and status quo bias. Journal of Economic Perspectives 5, 193–206.

Kahneman, Daniel, 2011. Thinking Fast and Slow. Farrar, Strauss and Giroux, New York, USA.

Kahneman, Daniel, Tversky, Amos, 1979. Prospect theory: a analysis of decisions under risk. Econometrica 47, 313–327.

Karolyi, Andrew, 2011. The ultimate irrelevance proposition in finance. Financial Review 46, 485–512.

Katsikopolos, Konstantinos, Simsek, 'Ozgur, Buckmann, Marcus, Gigerenzer, Gerd, 2019. Classification in the Wild. MIT Press, Cambridge, Massachusetts, USA.

Keasey, Kevin, Hudson, Robert, 2007. Finance theory: a house without windows. Critical Perspectives on Accounting 18, 932–951.

Keynes, John M., 1936. The General Theory of Employment Interest and Money. Macmillan, London.

Khandani, Amir, Lo, Andrew W., 2011. What happened to the quants in August 2007? Evidence from factors and transactions data? Journal of Financial Markets 14.

Khandani, Amir, Lo, Andrew, 2007. What happened to the quants in August 2007? (digest summary). Journal of Investment Management 5, 29–78.

Knight, Frank, 1921. Risk, Uncertainty and Profit. Houghton, Miffin Company, Boston, Massachusetts.

Kothari, S.P., Lewellen, Jonathon, Warner, Jerold, 2006. Stock returns, aggregate earnings surprises, and behavioural finance. Journal of Financial Economics 79, 537–568.

Laeven, Luc, Valencia, Fabia, 2012. Resolution of Banking Crises: The Good, the Bad, and the Ugly. IMF Working Paper 146 International Monetary Fund Washington DC, USA.

Laibson, David, 1997. Golden eggs: and hyperbolic discounting. Quarterly Journal of Economics 112, 443–478.

Lall, Ranjit, 2009. Why Basel II failed and why any Basel III is doomed. Review of International Political Economy 19, 609–638.

Lall, Rajit, 2012. From failure to failure: the politics of international banking regulation. Review of International Political Economy 19, 609–638.

Laplace, Pierre Simon, 1951. A Philosophical Essay on Probabilities. Dover Publications, New York, USA.

Latané, Henry A., Jones, Charles P., 1977. Standardized unexpected earnings – a progress report. Journal of Finance 32 (5), 1457–1465.

Latané, Henry A., Jones, Charles P., 1979. Standardized unexpected earnings–1971-77. Journal of Finance 34 (3), 717–724.

Leibenstein, Harvey, 1983. Property rights and X-efficiency: comment. American Economic Review 73, 831–842.

Lev, Baruch, Gu, Feng, 2016. The End of Accounting and the Path Forward for Investors and Managers. Wiley, Hobeken, New Jersey.

Levins, Richard, Lewontin, Richard, 1985. The Dialectical Biologist. Harvard University Press, Cambridge, Massachusetts, USA.

Lewis, David, 2002. Convention: A Philosophical Study. Blackwell Publishers, Oxford, England.

Lewis, Michael, 2000. The New New Thing. Penguin, New York, USA.

Lewis, Michael, 2010. The Big Short: Inside the Doomsday Machine. WW Norton & Company, London, UK.

Li, William, Azar, Pablo, Larochelle, David, Hill, Paul, Lo, Andrew, 2015. Law as Code: A Software Engineering Approach to Analysing the United States Code. Digital commons University of Maryland Working Paper.

Lintner, John, 1965a. Security prices, risk and maximal gains from diversification. Journal of Finance 20, 587–616.

Lintner, John, 1965b. The valuation of risky assets and the selection of risky investments in stock portfolios and capital budgets. Review of Economics and Statistics 47, 13–37.

Liu, Weimin, Strong, Norman, Xu, Xinzhong, 2003. Post-earnings announcement drift in the UK. European Financial Management 9, 89–116.

Livnat, Joshua, Medenhall, Richard, 2006. Comparing the post-earnings announcement drift. Journal of Accounting Research 44, 177–205.

Lo, Andrew, 2004. The adaptive market hypothesis: market efficiency from an evolutionary perspective. Journal of Portfolio Management 30, 15–29.

Lo, Andrew, 2017. Adaptive Markets: Financial Evolution at the Speed of Thought. Princeton University Press, Princeton, New Jersey, USA.

Lo, Andrew, Hasanhodzic, Jasmina, 2010. The Heretics of Finance: Conversations With Leading Practitioners of Technical Analysis. Bloomberg Press, New York, USA.

Lo, Andrew, Mueller, Mark, 2010. WARNING: Physics Envy Maybe Dangerous to Your Wealth! Social Science Research Network MIT.

Loh, Roger, Warachka, Mitch, 2012. Streaks in earnings surprises and the cross-section of stock returns. Management Science 58, 1305–1321.

MacDonald, Larry, Robinson, Patrick, 2009. A Colossal Failure of Common Sense: The Inside Story of the Collapse of Lehman Brothers. Crown Business-Random House, New York, USA.

MacGillivray, Brian, 2014. Fast and frugal crisis management: an analysis of rule-based judgement and choice during water contamination events. Journal of Business Research 67, 1717–1724.

MacKenzie, Donald, 2008. An Engine not a Camera: How Financial Models Shape Markets. MIT Press, Cambridge, Massachusetts, USA.

Maniadis, Zacharius, Tufano, Fabio, 2017. The research reproducibility crisis and economics of science. Economic Journal 127, F200–F208.

Markowitz, Harry, 1959. Portfolio Selection: Efficient Diversification of Investments. Cowle Foundation Monograph. Yale University Press.

Markowitz, Harry M., 1952. Portfolio selection. Journal of Finance 7, 77–91.

Martignon, Laura, Vitouch, Oliver, Takezawa, Masanouri, Foster, Malcolm, 2011. Naive and yet enlightened: from natural frequencies to fast and frugal decision trees. In: Gigerenzer, Gerd, Hertwig, Ralph, Pachur, Thorsten (Eds.), Heuristics: The Foundations of Adaptive Behavior. Oxford University Press, Oxford, England, pp. 136–152. Chap. 6.

McBeath, M.K., Shafer, D.M., Kaiser, M.K., 1995. How baseball outfielders determine where to run to catch fly balls. Science 268, 569–573.

McCammon, Ian, Hägeli, Pascal, 2007. An evaluation of rule-based decision–making in avelance terrain. Cold Regions Science and Technology 47, 193–206.

Meritum, 2002. Guidelines for Managing and Reporting on Intangibles. Intellectual Capital Report. Tser Programme Meritum Tuscon, Arizona.

Merton, Robert C., 1973. An intertemporal capital asset pricing model. Econometrica 41, 867–887.

Michaely, Roni, Thaler, Richard H., Womack, Kent L., 1995. Price reactions to dividend initiations and omissions: overreaction or drift? Journal of Finance 50, 573–608.

Milgrom, Paul, Stokey, Nancy, 1979. Information, Trade and Common Knowledge. Working Paper of Northwestern University Graduate School of Management.

Minsky, Hyman, 1986. Stabilising the Unstable Economy.

Monti, M., Pelligra, V., Martignon, L., Berg, N., 2014. Retail investors and financial advisors: new evidence on trust and advice taking heuristics. Journal of Business Research 67 (8), 1749–1757.

Moore, Paul, Haworth, Mike, 2015. Crash, Bank, Wallop: The Inside Story of London's Big Bank and a Financial Revolution That Changed the World. New Wilberforce Media, St Ives. Cornwall.

Mousavi, S., 2017. Gerd Gigerenzer and Vernon Smith on ecological rationality and heuristics. In: Frantz, R., Chen, S., Dopfer, K., Mousavi, S. (Eds.), Routledge Handbook of Behavioral Economics. Routledge, pp. 88–100.

Mousavi, S., Gigerenzer, G., 2011. Revisiting the "error" in studies of cognitive error. In: Hofmann, D.A., Frese, M. (Eds.), Errors in Organizations. In: Society for Industrial and Organizational Psychology (SIOP) Frontiers Series Book. Psychology Press, Taylor and Francis, pp. 97–112.

Mousavi, Shabnam, Gigerenzer, Gerd, 2017. Heuristic tools for uncertainty. Homo Oeconomicus 34, 361–379.

Mousavi, S., Kheirandish, R., 2014. Behind and beyond a shared definition of ecological rationality: a functional view of heuristics. Journal of Business Research 67 (8), 1780–1785.

Mousavi, Shabnam, Kheirandish, Reza, 2017. Policy making with behavioral insight. Journal of Behavioral Economics for Policy 1, 35–39.

Mousavi, Shabnam, Meder, 2017. Heuristics: fast, frugal, and smart. In: Altman, Morris (Ed.), Handbook of Behavioral Economics and Smart Decision-Making: Rational Decision–Making Within the Bounds of Reason. Edward Elgar, Cheltenham, England. Chap. 6.

Mousavi, Shabnam, Shrefrin, Hersh, 2010. Prediction tools: financial market regulation, politics and psychology. Journal of Risk Management in Financial Institutions 3, 318–333.

Mousavi, S., Gigerenzer, G., Kheirandish, R., 2017a. Rethinking behavioral economics through fast-and-frugal heuristics. In: Frantz, R., Chen, S., Dopfer, K., Mousavi, S. (Eds.), Routledge Handbook of Behavioral Economics. Routledge, pp. 280–296.

Mousavi, S., Neth, H., Meder, B., Kheirandish, R., 2017b. Heuristics: fast, frugal, and smart. In: Altman, M. (Ed.), Handbook of Behavioral Economics and Smart Decision-Making: Rational Decision-Making within the Bounds of Reason. Edward Elgar, pp. 101–118.

Nagel, Rosemarie, Bayona, Anna, Kheirandish, Reza, Mousavi, Shabnam, Richard, Selten, 2017. The dualist. In: Franz, Roger, Chen, Shu-Heng, Dopfer, Kurt, Heukelon, Floris, Mousavi (Eds.), Handbook of Behavioral Economics Routledge International Handbooks. Routledge, New York, USA, pp. 66–87. Chap. 6.

Nelson, Richard, Winter, Sidney, 1982. An Evolutionary Theory of Economic Change. Harvard University Press, Cambridge, Massachusetts, USA.

Neth, Hansjörrg, Gigerenzer, Gerd, 2015. Heuristics: Tools for an Uncertain World. Emerging Tends in the Social and Behavioral Sciences. Wiley Online Library.

Neth, Hansjörg, Meder, Björn, Kothiyal, Amit, Gigerenzer, Gerd, 2014. Homo heuristicus in the financial world: from risk management to managing uncertainty. Journal of Risk Management in Financial Institutions 7, 134–144.

Newman-Toker, David, Kattah, Jorge, Talkad, Arun, Wang, David, Hseih, Yu-Hsiang, 2009. HINTS to diagnose a stroke in the acute vestibular syndrome: three-step bedside oculomotor examination more sensitive than MRI DWI. Stroke 40, 3504–3510.

Neyman, Jerzy (Ed.), 1955. Inadmissibility of the Usual Estimator for the Mean of a Multivariate Normal Distribution, vol. 1. Statistical Laboratory University of California. Third Berkeley Symposium on Mathematical Statistics and Probability. University of California Press.

Nikolaeva, Ralitza, 2014. Interorganisational imitation heuristics arising from cognitive frames. Journal of Business Research 67, 1758–1765.

Noreen, Eric, 1989. Computer Intensive Methods for Testing Hypotheses: An Introduction. John Wiley, USA.

North, Douglas, 1990. Institutions, Institutional Change and Economic Performance. Cambridge University Press.

Odean, Terrance, 1998. Volume, volatility, price and profit when all traders are above average. Journal of Finance 53, 1887–1934.

Ohlson, James, 1995. Earnings, book values and dividends in equity valuation. Contemporary Accounting Research 11, 661–687.

Ohlson, James, Juettner-Nauroth, B., 2000. Expected eps and eps Growth as a Determinant of Value. Working Paper of Stern Business School.

Ortmann, Andreas, Gigerenzer, Gerd, Borges, Bernhard, Goldstein, Daniel, 2008. The recognition heuristic: a fast and frugal way to investment choice? In: Handbook of Experimental Economics Results, vol. 1. Elsevier, Amsterdam, The Netherlands, pp. 993–1003. Chap. 107.

Ostrom, Elinor, 1990. Governing the Commons: The Evolution of Institutions of Collective Action. Political Economy of Institutions for Collective Action. Cambridge University Press.

Pachur, Thorsten, Hertwig, Ralph, Rieskamp, Jörg, 2013a. The mind as an intuitive pollster. In: Hertwig, Ralph, Hoffrage, Ulrich, ABC Group (Eds.), Simple Heuristics in a Complex World.

Pachur, Thorsten, Hertwig, Ralph, Rieskamp, Jörg, 2013b. The model as an intuitive pollster: frugal search in social spaces. In: Hertwig, Ralph, Hoffrage, Ulrich, ABC Group (Eds.), Simple Heuristics in a Social World, pp. 261–292 (Oxford Scholarship Online, Oxford, England). Chap. 9.

Pachur, Thorsten, Rieskamp, Joerg, Hertwig, Ralph, 2004. The social circle heuristic: fast and frugal decisions based on small samples.

Pelligra, Vittorio, 2010. Trust responsiveness: on the dynamics of fiduciary interaction. Journal of Socio-Economics 39, 653–660.

Penikas, Henry, 2015. History of banking regulation as developed by the Basel committee on banking supervision in 1974–2010 (brief overview). Financial Stability: Journal of the Bank of Spain 28, 9–48.

Persson, A., Ryals, L., 2014. Making customer relationship decisions: analytics v rules of thumb. Journal of Business Research 67 (8), 1725–1732.

Popper, Karl, 1978. Natural selection and the emergence of mind. Dialetica 32, 339–355.

Preda, Alex, 2007. Where do analysts come from? The case of financial chartism. The Sociological Review 55, 753–782.

Pukthuanthong, Kuntara, Roll, Richard, Subrahmanyam, Avanidhar, 2018. A Protocol for Factor Identification.

Rabin, Matthew, 1998. Psychology and economics. Journal of Economic Literature 36, 11–46.

Rabin, Matthew, 2002. Inference by believers in the law of small numbers. Quarterly Journal of Economics 117, 775–816.

Rabin, Matthew, 2013. An approach to incorporating psychology into economics. American Economic Review: Paper and Proceedings 103, 617–622.

Radner, Roy, 1968. Competitive equilibrium under uncertainty. Econometrica 36, 31–58.

Roberts, Russ, 2010. Gambling With Other People's Money: How Perverted Incentives Caused the Financial Crisis. Discussion paper Mercatus Center. George Mason University.

Ross, Stephen A., 1976. The arbitrage theory of capital asset pricing. Journal of Economic Theory 13, 341–360.

Rusetski, Alexander, 2014. Pricing by intuition: managerial choices with limited information. Journal of Business Research 67, 1733–1743.

Sadka, Gil, Sadka, Ronnie, 2009. Predictability and the earnings–return relation. Journal of Financial Economics 94, 87–106.

Samuelson, Paul, 1938a. The empirical implications of utility analysis. Econometrica 6, 344–356.

Samuelson, Paul, 1938b. A note on the theory of consumer's behaviour. Economica 5, 61–71.

Samuelson, Paul, 1948. Consumption theory in terms of revealed preference. Psychological Review 112, 610–628.

Savage, Leonard, 1954. The Foundations of Statistics. Dover Books on Mathematics, New York, USA.

Schooler, Lael, Hertswig, Ralf, 2005. How forgetting aids heuristic inference. Psychological Review 112, 610–628.

Selten, Reinhard, 1998. Adaptive aspiration theory. Journal of Mathematical Psychology 42, 191–214.

Selten, Rheinhard, 2001. What is bounded rationality? In: Gigerenzer, Gerd, Selten, Rheinhard (Eds.), Bounded Rationality: The Adaptive Toolbox. Dahlem University Press-MIT Press, Cambridge, Massachusetts, USA, pp. 13–35. Chap. 2.

Shanthikumar, Devin, 2012. Consecutive earnings surprises: small and large trader reactions. Accounting Review 87, 1709–1736.

Sharpe, William F., 1964. Capital asset prices: a theory of market equilibrium under conditions of risk. Journal of Finance 19, 425–442.

Shefrin, Hersh, 2010. Behaviouralizing finance. Foundations and Trends in Finance 4, 1–184.

Shefrin, Hersh, Nichols, Christina, 2014. Credit card behaviour, financial styles, and heuristics. Journal of Business Research 67, 1679–1687.

Shefrin, Hersh, Statman, Meir, 1985. The disposition to sell winners to early and ride losers too long: theory and evidence. Journal of Finance 40, 28–30.

Shiller, Robert J., Shiller, Virginia, 2011. Economists as worldly philosophers. American Economic Review Papers and Proceedings 101, 171–175.

Shleifer, Andrei, Summers, Lawrence, 1990. The noise trader approach to finance. Journal of Economic Perspectives 4, 19–33.

Shleifer, Andrei, Vishny, Robert, 1997. The limits to arbitrage. Journal of Finance 52, 35–55.

Shrefrin, Hersh, 2013. Assessing the contribution of Hyman Minsky's perspective to our understanding of economic instability. https://papers.ssrn.com/sol3/papers.cfm?abstract_id=2311045.

Shefrin, Hersh, 2016. Behavioral Risk Management: Managing the Psychology That Drives Decisions and Influences. Palgrave–MacMillan, Basingstoke, England.

Shefrin, Hersh, Statman, Meir, 2009. Striking regulatory irons while hot. Journal of Investment Management 7, 29–42.

Siebenmogen, Niklas, Weber, Martin, 2003. A behavioral model of asset allocation. Financial Markets and Portfolio Management 17, 15–40.

Simon, Herbert, 1955. A behavioral model of rational choice. Quarterly Journal of Economics 69, 99–118.

Simon, Herbert, 1956. Rational choice and the structure of the environment. Psychological Review 63, 129–138.

Simon, Herbert, 1959. Theories of decision-making in economics and behavioral science. American Economic Review 49, 253–283.

Simon, Herbert, 1990. Invariants of human behaviour. Annual Review of Psychology 41, 1–19.

Simon, Herbert, 1992. What is an "explanation" of behaviour? Psychological Science 3, 150–161.

Simon, Herbert A., Newell, Allen, 1971. Human problem solving: the state of the theory in 1970. American Psychologist 26 (2), 145.

Slovic, P., Griffin, D., Tversky, A., 1990. Compatibility effects in judgment and choice. In: Hogarth, R.M. (Ed.), Insights in Decision Making: A Tribute to Hillel J. Einhorn. The University of Chicago Press, Chicago, IL, pp. 5–27.

Smith, Vernon, 2003. Constructivist and ecological rationality in economics. American Economic Review 93, 465–508.

Smith, Vernon, 2008. Rationality in Economics: Constructivist and Ecological Forms. Cambridge University Press.

Statman, Meir, 1999. Behavioral finance: past battles and future engagements. Financial Analysts Journal 55, 18–27.

Statman, Meir, 2011. What Investors Really Want? Discover What Drives Investor Behaviour and Make Smarter Investment Decisions. McGraw-Hill, New York, USA.

Stewart, Neil, Reimers, Stian, Harris, Adam, 2015. On the origin of utility, weighting and discounting functions: how to change their shape. Management Science 61, 687–705.

Stigler, George, 1971. The theory of economic regulation. Bell Journal of Economics and Management 2, 3–21.

Stigler, Stephen, 2002. Statistics on the Table: the History of Statistical Concepts and Methods. Harvard University Press, Cambridge, Massachusetts, USA.

Stracca, Livio, 2004. Behavioral finance and asset prices: where do we stand? Journal of Economic Psychology 25, 373–405.

Svenson, Ola, 1981. Are we all less risky and more skillful than our fellow drivers? Acta Psychologica 47, 143–148.

Svenson, Ola, Fischoff, Baruch, MacGregor, Donald, 1985. Perceived driving safety and seatbelt usage. Accident Analysis and Prevention 17, 119–133.

Thaler, R., 1993. Advances in Behavioral Finance, vol. 1. The Russell Sage Foundation, New York, USA.

Thaler, Richard, 1994. Quasi Rational Economics. Russell Sage Foundation, New York, USA.

Thaler, Richard, 1999. The end of behavioral of finance. Financial Analysts Journal 55, 12–19.

Thaler, R., 2005. Advances in Behavioral Finance, vol. 2. Russell Sage Foundation-Princeton University Press, New York, USA.

Thaler, Richard, Sunstein, Cass, 2008. Nudge: Improving Decision About Health, Wealth and Happiness. Penguin, New York, USA.

Todd, Peter, 2001. Fast and frugal heuristics for environmentally bounded minds. In: Gigerenzer, Gerd, Selten, Rheinhard (Eds.), Bounded Rationality: The Adaptive Toolbox. MIT Press. Dahelm workshop reports 4.

Todd, Peter, Gigerenzer, Gerd, ABC Group, 2012. Ecological Rationality: Intelligence in the World. Oxford University Press, Oxford, England.

Tu, Jun, Zhou, Guofo, 2011. Markowitz meets Talmud: a combination of sophisticated and naive diversification strategies. Journal of Financial Economics 99, 204–215.

Tuckett, David, 2012. Financial markets are markets in stories: some possible advantages of using interviews to supplement existing economic data sources. Journal of Economics Dynamics and Control 36, 1077–1087.

Tuckett, David, Nikolic, Milena, 2017. The role of conviction and narrative in decision-making under radical uncertainty. Theory and Psychology 27, 501–523.

Turner, Adair, 2009. The Turner Review: A Regulatory Response to the UK. Discussion paper Financial Services Authority Canary Wharf, London.

Tversky, Amos, Kahneman, Daniel, 1974. Judement under uncertainty: heuristics and biases. Science 185, 1124–1131.

Tversky, Amos, Kahneman, Daniel, 1992. Advances in prospect theory: cumulative representation of utility theory. Journal of Risk and Uncertainty 5, 297–323.

Urquhart, Andrew, Gebka, Bartoz, Hudson, Robert, 2015. How exactly do markets adapt? Evidence from the moving average rile in three developed markets. Journal of International Financial Markets, Institutions and Money 38, 127–147.

Urquhart, A., Hudson, Robert, 2013. Efficient or adaptive markets? Evidence from major stock markets using very long run historic data. International Review of Financial Analysis 28, 130–142.

Urquhart, Andrew, McGoarty, Frank, 2016. Are stock markets really efficient? Evidence of the adaptive markets hypothesis. International Review of Financial Analysis 47, 39–49.

van der Sar, Nico, 2004. Behavioural finance: how matters stand. Journal of Economic Psychology 25, 425–444.

Viale, R., Moudsavi, B., Allemanni, S., Fillotto, U., 2018. The Behavioral Finance Revolution: a New Approach to Financial Policies and Regulations. BEFAIRLY. Edward Elgar Publishing, London, England.

Von Neumann, John, Morgenstern, Oskar, 1944. Theory of Games and Economic Behavior. Princeton University Press, Princeton, New Jersey, USA.

Warren, Elizabeth, 2017. The Fight Is Our Fight: the Battle to Save America's Middle Class. Metropolitan Books, New York, USA.

Wübben, Markus, Wangenheim, Florian, 2008. Instant customer base analysis: managerial heuristics often "get it right". Journal of Marketing 72, 82–93.

Zhu, Yingzi, Zhou, Guofu, 2009. Technical analysis: an asset allocating perspective on the use of moving averages. Journal of Financial Economics 92, 519–544.

Index

A

A priori probabilities, 111
Aadaptive market hypothesis, 52
ABC group, 99, 100
  adaptive toolbox, 231
Academic finance journals
  Journal of Finance, 137
  Journal of Financial Economics, 137
  Review of Financial Studies, 137
Adaptive
  behaviour, 39, 43
  dynamic models, 120, 122
  market hypothesis, 49, 73
  markets, 49, 67, 69
  models, 120
  toolbox, 13, 17, 18, 22, 23, 39, 110,
    169, 178, 220, 223, 230
  toolbox for portfolio management, 178
Aggressive investment profile, 147
Aggressively
  high investment, 152
  investing companies, 151
Algorithmic trading, 190
Alleged
  market failures, 58
  predictive value, 111
American Finance Association, 142
Analysts, 19, 108, 120, 179, 180, 184, 185,
    187, 192, 201, 215, 216
  "buy–side", 180
  "sell–side", 180
Arbitrage Pricing Theory (APT), 221
Assessing cues, 226
Asset, 81, 152, 160
  beta, 221
  MVP portfolio, 176
  portfolio weights, 163
  portfolios, 73, 173, 224
  price, 144, 148, 152, 155, 157
  price factor discovery, 155
  pricing, 18, 19, 49, 133, 134, 139, 148,
    153–155, 211, 222
    classic model, 155

equilibrium model, 49, 220, 222
Fama-French model, 143
fast-and-frugal model, 133, 154
ideal model, 221
Intertemporal Capital Asset Pricing
  Model (ICAPM), 221
risk-neutral model, 97
spurious, 142
standard models, 211–213, 220, 227
theory, 133
returns, 135, 136, 141, 148, 155, 162,
  164, 220
risk-adjusted returns, 176
turnover, 174
Asset price, 148
Asset–pricing models, 143, 155
linear, 153

B

Bank, 42, 43, 58, 71, 81, 84, 86, 92, 94,
    190–192
  analysts, 191
  failure, 90
  fortunes of, 10
  holidays, 92
  management, 192
  nationalisations, 92
  regulatory regime, 191
  restructuring costs, 92
  solvency, 92
  tax, 85
  valuation, 192
  value, 190
  vulnerability of, 79, 93
  wholesale funding level, 92
Bank of England, 85–87, 90, 94
Banking
  regulation, 90
  retail, 192
  sector, 92
Basel Accords, 79, 86, 95